Penguin Education

**New Horizons in Psychology 2**

Edited by P. C. Dodwell

# New Horizons in Psychology 2

Edited by P. C. Dodwell

Penguin Books

Penguin Books Ltd, Harmondsworth,
Middlesex, England
Penguin Books Inc., 7110 Ambassador Road,
Baltimore, Md 21207, USA
Penguin Books Australia Ltd,
Ringwood, Victoria, Australia

First published 1972


Made and printed in Great Britain by
Cox & Wyman Ltd, London, Reading and Fakenham
Set in Monotype Times

# Contents

# Editorial Foreword

Psychology books published by Penguin fall roughly into four classes. There are textbooks; collections of published papers (Penguin Modern Psychology Readings); and short monographs or 'unit texts' (Penguin Science of Behaviour). All of these are directed mainly at academics and professional psychologists, although many of them have appealed to a wider public. Finally, there are psychology Pelicans, intended primarily for laymen, though in the event many have turned out to be useful to students.

The first *New Horizons in Psychology* cut across this classification by reviewing aspects of academic psychology for the general public, while being well enough documented to be useful to students. Each chapter was written by a different specialist and there was little attempt at overall integration. This second volume adopts the same plan, and the choice of topics and authors is solely that of the editor, and reflects his own interests. In the case of Peter Dodwell these interests are wide. He is a polymath within his own subject as well as outside it, and is a prolific and distinguished experimenter and theorizer.

As Professor Dodwell points out in his Introduction, there will be an entirely new volume of *New Horizons in Psychology*, with a new editor, every three years. The successive volumes will not be revisions of previous ones but will be cumulative and complementary. It is hoped that they will engender a feeling for objectivity when dealing with complex material, and a sense of intellectual excitement.

B. M. Foss

# Introduction

The idea for a regular Penguin review of contemporary scientific psychology arose from the success of *New Horizons in Psychology*,* a book which first appeared in 1966. In *New Horizons* some twenty psychologists wrote about areas of psychology of particular current interest or in which important advances had occurred in recent years. While the emphasis was on things new, in most cases the different chapters contained enough historical introductory material to make them valuable avenues of first approach to many of the specialized research areas of psychology. *New Horizons in Psychology 1* should remain a valuable book for many years, yet cannot remain up to date without extensive and frequent revision. Rather than attempt this, it was decided to extend the idea into a review series which would fulfil much the same purpose as the first *New Horizons*, yet not supplant it by having much overlap in coverage. *New Horizons in Psychology 2* is the first such extension.

It is intended to bring out a review volume in the series once every three years, to coincide with the triennial International Congress of Psychology. These reviews will attempt to assess the main lines of recent advance in a number of areas of psychology. Generally speaking different areas will be covered in consecutive volumes, unless unusual activity or extraordinary progress warrants further review of a field within three years. Obviously the reviews cannot be exhaustive, and are in no sense meant to compete with the *Annual Review of Psychology*† as source or reference texts. Our purpose is to provide highly selective accounts of developments within particular areas, as seen by individuals actively engaged in research in them. As with our forerunner, *New Horizons in Psychology 1*, we shall attempt to concentrate on new ideas and findings, but not at the expense of perspective on the long-term developments in a field and their significance for psychology as a whole. We hope that the level achieved in the reviews will be appropriate to students who have completed a first course in psychology, and are ready for more specialized introductions to particular fields. The aim has been to give, in capsule form, a good idea of what is thought to be important in a particular

* Brian Foss (ed.), *New Horizons in Psychology*, Penguin, 1966, now re-issued as Brian Foss (ed.), *New Horizons in Psychology 1*, Penguin, 1972.

† *Annual Reviews* Inc., Palo Alto, California.

field, how this is reflected in recent developments, and where it is likely to lead in the near future. Further material for study is suggested by the references at the end of each chapter, and in most cases an additional list of especially recommended readings is appended.

The book is aimed (as will be its successors) at the post-introductory student, but of course one hopes that its appeal will be to a much wider audience than that. Contributors have been encouraged to write in as non-technical a manner as is consistent with adequate presentation of their topics, and most of the chapters in this book should be readily comprehensible to scientists in other disciplines and to the interested layman.

Not only has there been severe selection of topics within the fields covered; inevitably there has been selection of the general areas to be presented in this review. In deciding on what contributions to invite I was guided by two main considerations. In the first place, of course, I was concerned to present reviews of fields which are of general interest in psychology, as well as being actively researched at the present time. Secondly, I was guided to some extent by the contents of *New Horizons in Psychology 1*. Although the present book departs from the concept of the first *New Horizons* to some extent, it is addressed to the same sort of audience and with similar aims in mind. Therefore several topics have been omitted here because they were adequately covered in the earlier volume. This is true for example of the physiological psychology of sensory and motivational systems, which otherwise would be surprising and perhaps indefensible omissions.

To turn more specifically to the contents of the present book, it should be said first of all that I take full responsibility for the topics selected for coverage. Although advice was offered from various quarters, for which I am grateful, it did not in fact alter appreciably the final list. I have divided the twelve chapters – somewhat loosely – into four sections, but hope that readers will not take the division as reflecting any strict compartmentalization of material. Indeed, it seems to me that one of the signal features of psychology today is that methods developed in one area are applied fruitfully in quite different fields of inquiry. A prime example is the use of physiological measures in the study of social and cognitive phenomena. Conversely, one finds that physiological and motivational inquiries are increasingly taking into account cognitive factors which, even a few years ago, would have been considered irrelevant.

The topics presented have, with few exceptions, to do with human experimental psychology. This certainly does not reflect a judgement that studies of animal behaviour are not important; rather it means that very much of the genuinely new in the way of ideas and research methods is to be found in the study of human beings as thinking, intelligent organisms. This it seems to me is evidence of a new maturity in psychology, a willingness to look at what is unique in our subject-matter and to find appropriate ways of studying it, rather than to ape the older-established sciences or to shy away from the complications which the study of language, thought and other cognitive activities entail.

I have written short introductory paragraphs to each of the four sections, in order to give the reader some general picture of what each one represents, and to introduce the major themes of the review. The grouping is as follows: the first section can be characterized as studies of the behaviour of normal adult organisms, and might be thought of as representing the 'hard core' of experimental psychology. My hope is that these chapters demonstrate clearly that the core is not hard in the sense of desiccation or fossilization in an antiquated mould. Indeed it seems to me that the new wine of fresh ideas and methods has – to change the image – burst old bottles of established orthodoxy in quite exciting ways. The second group turns to the study of sources of motivation and interest, and (in one case) study of the breakdown of normal behaviour, i.e., to psychopathology. In the third section are just a pair of papers, but on two of the major current issues in the study of development: these are the contributions which Jean Piaget's theories and research make to psychology, and the study of young children's language. Finally there is a group of three papers on social behaviour. Here again the willingness to break new ground, which both integrates findings and methods from the older traditions of psychology, and also addresses problems of uniquely human concern, is evident.

# Part One
# Experimental Psychology

To many psychologists the field of learning represents the *sanctum sanctorum*, the inner temple of principles and ideas which most nearly define the characteristics which we believe allow us to claim the title 'Scientists of Behaviour'. The modern origins of this field have been closely identified with eminent American scholars of fifty years ago, especially J. B. Watson and E. L. Thorndike. It seems especially appropriate, therefore, that we have the good fortune to be able to open this volume with an assessment of the field by another American, also an eminent scholar in it, W. K. Estes. He has been closely associated with one of the major recent developments in theories of learning, namely the shift from emphasis on theories about control of behaviour through reward and punishment to a more 'cognitive' view, to asking what information organisms pick up from their environments and how this information serves to guide their various activities. As Professor Estes shows, this change of view has had a profound influence on the directions in which learning theory has developed in recent decades, and on the experimental analyses that are attempted.

In chapter 2 Dr Baddeley shows that there have been related changes in the study of human memory. Rather than its appearing as a passive process in which events are 'impressed' upon a receptive medium, to be recalled in a somewhat mechanical way, we now find that memory is best conceived of as an active process of information assimilation and metamorphosis, the various stages of which are amenable to investigation by experimental techniques. The concepts of information processing, stemming largely from the field of systems engineering and computer science, have likewise had a steady impact on the study of vision, particularly as this relates to the acquisition of symbolic information, as in reading.

Our third chapter, on visual information-processing, demonstrates nicely the interdependence of studies of vision and short-term memory (indeed, one might be hard put to it to distinguish sharply between the two). Dr Coltheart also shows how language and linguistic habits affect the ability to handle symbolic material. Again the notions of information transfer and process control are much in evidence.

Certainly one of the most exciting and important developments in psychology in the last few decades has been the emergence of mathematical psychology. While many psychologists have tended to regard this as an esoteric discipline, only open to the initiate in mathematics, and treating only of a very narrow range of specialized topics, I believe that this is far from the truth. Professor Greeno, in the fourth chapter of the book, demonstrates both how wide the applications are, and how accessible to the non-mathematician willing to work to understand a level of conceptual analysis which is not really more difficult or abstruse than those with which we are already familiar, say in statistical analysis or information theory.

These first four chapters, then, represent a review of some of the major fields – which are also major growing-points – of experimental psychology. In demonstrating how new ideas, new methodologies and new types of analysis have emerged, they point the way to probable developments in the immediate future.

# 1 Learning
William K. Estes

Selecting the most significant contributions to a science over any brief period is feasible only at relatively long range, for the significant contributions are those that stand the test of time. From our present vantage point, it seems that it would have been an easy and pleasant task to prepare an overview of recent developments in the psychology of learning for a volume on, say, 'Psychology 1932'. Both the general theoretical orientations and the specific concepts that were to dominate research on learning from that time to the present had appeared during the preceding half dozen years. Köhler's *Mentality of Apes*, appearing in 1925, amassed evidence for the importance of cognitive processes in animal learning, but his approach did not fall on so receptive ground as Pavlov's *Conditioned Reflexes*, which was translated into English in 1927.

The conceptions of latent learning and inference in animals which emerged in the work of Tolman and his collaborators during this period were fertile instigators of research, and Tolman's codification of a mixture of Gestalt and behavioural ideas into an elaborate system (Tolman, 1932) was to exert a lasting influence. However, the longer established associationist tradition, reinforced by concepts of conditioning, gathered momentum more rapidly. Contemporaneous with major reformulations of association theory by Carr (1931), Robinson (1932) and Thorndike (1932) were the seminal papers by Hull, interpreting higher mental processes as habit mechanisms (1930, 1931), by Guthrie on conditioning by contiguity (1930), and by Skinner on the concept of the reflex and the distinction between respondent and operant behaviour (1931).

Among the experimental studies that were to have far-reaching implications, at least the following would surely have been cited: Bartlett (1932) on remembering, initiating the luxuriant literature concerning organization in recall; Jenkins and Dallenbach (1924) on the retardation of forgetting by sleep, pointing the way to the interference theory of memory; Tolman and Honzik (1930) on maze learning without reward, an early landmark in the lengthy controversy over 'latent learning'; Wolfle (1932) on temporal relationships in conditioning, which foreshadowed the quantitative and parametric treatment of eyelid conditioning in American laboratories during subsequent decades.

A résumé of learning for a 'Psychology 1952' was provided, in effect, by Melton in the first *Annual Review of Psychology* (1950). He noted that over the preceding twenty years theoretically oriented research on learning had come increasingly under the influence of the opposed systems of Tolman and Hull. Following the early indications from Tolman's laboratory that a rat can learn something about a pathway through a maze even on trials during which it is neither hungry nor rewarded, research on latent learning had risen to a fever pitch, then had begun to decline, leaving a rather puzzling array of findings, some favourable to a reinforcement interpretation, some to a cognitive viewpoint. Melton felt that on balance the findings provided apparent exceptions to a reinforcement theory of learning, but none the less he concluded that reinforcement theory was too well established to be abandoned (if at all) on the basis of any one experimental attack.

Other popular motifs of the early 1950s included continuity versus non-continuity in discrimination learning, and place versus response learning in the maze, in each case with a course of events and inconclusive denouement paralleling those of the latent-learning controversy. In each instance the specific line of research eventually ran into diminishing returns, but in none did the ideas responsible for the controversies remain long dormant. The crux of the continuity/non-continuity issue was to reappear in later decades in the question of all-or-none versus incremental learning, that of latent learning in the question of informational versus motivational aspects of reinforcement, and that of place versus response learning in the stimulus-selection versus response-selection theories of discrimination learning.

With regard to transfer of training and retention, major developments of that period included Harlow's formulation of learning set (1949), the emergence of the stimulus generalization concept in studies growing out of Hull's theory and its fruitful application to verbal learning by Gibson (1940), the use of electroconvulsive shock as a means of modifying the presumed course of consolidation of recently learned material (Duncan, 1949), and the two-factor theory of proactive and retroactive inhibition (Melton and Von Lackum, 1941), which held almost unchallenged sway over research on retention in human learning for more than another decade.

The end of the period covered by Melton's review saw fertile applications of information theory to the psychology of learning by G. A. Miller and an increasing role of mathematical models in learning theory (Bush and Mosteller, 1951; Estes, 1950).

Coming down to the contemporary scene, which is our concern in the remainder of this review, we will meet declining interest in the classical systems *per se*, but with persisting influence of the ideas around which they were organized. Rather than the resolution of the differences between cognitive and stimulus-response approaches that many hoped for, I believe we will see a divergence, the former being reinforced by information-processing concepts and leading to computer-simulation models of cognitive processes (Hunt, 1962; Newell and Simon, 1963), the latter, overawed by the spectacular successes of electrophysiological methods, leaning towards the interpretation of learning phenomena in terms of neurophysiological mechanisms. Cutting across these trends, we will find new emphases on attentional factors in learning, on the development and organization of learning strategies, and on processes of memory storage and retrieval.

**The substrate of learning**

The heritage of the *tabula rasa* and the mental chemistry of the British associationist philosophers was clearly apparent in the learning theories which flourished in the period 1930 to 1960. It was generally assumed that the organism begins any learning experiment with a repertory of available responses and a stock of innately determined, 'unconditioned', stimulus-response relations. By conditioning and learning processes any effective stimulus could be associated with any available response. It was recognized that speed of learning varies somewhat for different types of stimuli and responses, but these differences were treated as second-order phenomena for theoretical purposes and largely subsumed under the effects of stimulus intensity.

Instances of learning or failure to learn which do not fit this schema have doubtless been observed by all experimenters, but they only began to fall on fertile ground after the infiltration into learning theory of some of the ideas expounded by ethologists and behavioural biologists in the 1950s. Breland and Breland (1966) first brought together a substantial collection of extreme instances of refractoriness to conditioning under conditions which, from the standpoint of classical theories, should have been effective.

These and related observations helped prepare the way for the recently emerging conception that learning should be regarded, not as a matter of writing on a *tabula rasa*, but rather of building upon relatively elaborate, largely innately determined, species-specific behavioural organizations. In this vein, Glickman and Schiff (1967) have proposed a biological interpretation of reinforcement which assumes that rewards serve to facilitate activity in neural systems that ensure species-typical responses, in particular consummatory behaviours, to appropriate stimuli. In a cybernetic model for reward and punishment, arising from quite different basic conceptions, the writer (1969a, 1969b) has assumed that rewarding events activate feedback mechanisms which deliver facilitatory stimulus input to families of stimulus-response units. These systems are initially innately organized, but they may 'assimilate' stimuli which precede rewarding events in the organism's experience.

In a detailed review of literature bearing upon the generality of basic laws of learning over different types of behaviours, Seligman (1970) produced quotations from a number of major learning theorists to document the ubiquity of the assumption that all stimuli and responses are equally associable according to common laws of learning. Among the sources of evidence Seligman brought forward to challenge this assumption are numerous data attesting to the extreme difficulty of establishing avoidance conditioning in a number of standard laboratory situations with animals which under other circumstances can be observed readily to learn to avoid painful stimuli, often in a single trial. In a similar vein, Bolles (1970) argued that successful avoidance training must be based upon the species-specific repertoire of defence reactions of the particular organism. Thus it may be nearly impossible to train a pigeon to avoid a shock by pecking a key, whereas the animal would readily learn to avoid shock by flying away from the location in which shock occurred.

It seems plausible to me that the principal difference in these latter two instances may have to do with directness, that is the number of associative linkages which must be established in order to mediate the required behavioural adjustment. In the innate organization of the animal's behaviour, activation of a drive mechanism by a painful stimulus delivers facilitatory input to a family of defence and flight reactions, not to the family of reactions involving pecking and swallowing. If, none the less, an experimenter requires a member of the latter family as an avoidance response, a rather elaborate chain of new associations must be established, whereas in the former instance it is necessary only to associate a new signal stimulus with an already organized behavioural (flight) routine.

Another striking case in point is the series of studies of J. Garcia and his associates on the conditioning of aversive behaviour to stimuli which precede radiation illness. The initial observation in the series was simply that stimulation from saccharine-flavoured water could become an effective conditioned stimulus for an avoidance response after a single pairing with illness produced by X-radiation, even with intervals of an hour or more between the two events. Follow-up experiments showed that a critical feature of this result was the relationship between the gustatory character of the conditioned stimulus and the visceral responses involved in the illness, since visual or auditory stimuli could be made to take on the same function only with great difficulty, if at all (Garcia and Koelling, 1966). Contrariwise, an avoidance response to electric shock to the feet could readily be established with visual or auditory conditioned stimuli but not, under the same temporal relationships, with saccharine-flavoured water as the conditioned stimulus.

None the less, one should be cautious about overgeneralizing from the impressive accumulation of evidence which attests to the importance of building upon an organism's original species-specific organization of behaviours in order to produce efficient learning. To give one particularly pungent bit of documentation, during the same period when the observations just cited were accumulating, a series of researches by Miller, DiCara and their associates challenged another assumption which had been widely held over a long period by investigators of learning, namely that only skeletal behaviours, and not visceral responses, undergo operant or instrumental learning as a function of rewards and punishments. These investigators not only completely overturned the idea of a necessary association between classical conditioning and visceral responses on the one hand and instrumental learning and skeletal behaviours on the other, but showed that they could produce effective learning under conditions about as remote from those ordinarily obtaining in animals' natural environments as could be imagined. They have shown for example that a rat can learn either to obtain rewarding intracranial electrical stimulation or to avoid punishing shocks by changing its heart rate, contracting its intestines, or even changing its rate of uric-acid formation (see DiCara and Miller, 1968; Miller, 1969).

**Theories of reinforcement**

The importance of the reinforcement concept remains unquestioned, but the long-familiar response-strengthening conception of the effects of reinforcement appears to be giving way to a cybernetic type of model. In classical association theories, and in the learning theories of Thorndike, Hull and Skinner, the effect of reward was assumed to be an immediate, direct and automatic strengthening of associations involving the rewarded response and the stimuli which evoked it. Two aspects of this interpretation of reinforcement have seemed about equally noteworthy to those who have followed developments from vantage points outside the immediate research area. They are, on the one hand, the resilience of the law of effect concept in the face of experimental attacks, and, on the other, the difficulty of resolving the disparity between the rather rigid and mechanistic picture of the organism involved in the theory, and the conspicuous variability and flexibility characterizing the ways in which organisms adjust to changing circumstances as a result of differential rewards and punishments.

A major change in prevailing viewpoints concerning the nature of reinforcement over the past decade or so is typified by the writings of Mowrer. Originally one of those most concerned with pressing to the limit the potentialities of the law of effect as a universal explanation of learning, Mowrer subsequently championed a two-factor interpretation in which conditioning by contiguity and response-strengthening by reinforcement were assigned the role of parallel basic laws, each applying to a different principal category of learning. At this stage Mowrer shared the view of a number of investigators, for example, Schlosberg and Skinner, that classical conditioning by contiguity sufficed as a basic mechanism for the conditioning of visceral and glandular responses where the law of effect was the primary mechanism for overt skeletal behaviour.

Most recently, Mowrer (1960) has gone much further away from the original law of effect conception, rejecting entirely the idea of learning as strengthening and weakening of habit strength. In this newest formulation he assumes that rewards and punishments give rise to emotional reactions, 'hope' and 'fear', which become associated in the organism's memory with response-produced stimuli from actions which have led to rewards and punishments. Upon reinstatement of a situation in which reinforcement has occurred, the animal is conceived to scan its repertory of available responses, inhibiting those which give rise to negative emotions and selecting those which give rise to positive emotions.

Miller (1963), influenced especially by the rapidly developing body of information concerning rewarding and punishing centres which can be activated by direct electrical stimulation of the midbrain, has similarly evinced dissatisfaction with his own earlier attempts to defend a monistic conception of reinforcement. At the same time he criticizes Mowrer's present theory on the grounds that it is implausible that the organism must continually scan its entire repertory of behaviours in order to select those which have previously led to reward in any situation. Miller suggests instead that a general facilitating or 'go' mechanism is set into operation when hypothalamic reward centres are activated by the effects of reward. The 'go' mechanism intensifies ongoing responses or the neural traces of recently occurring responses, and thus causes them to be more strongly conditioned than other responses which do not lead to reward and thus do not receive the same facilitation.

Whereas Mowrer's reformulation, like the earlier forms of law of effect theory, is based on the notion of response selection, a somewhat different type of theory currently under development by the writer (Estes, 1969a, 1969b, 1969c) might be termed a stimulus-selection theory. In this theory it is assumed that an organism in a choice situation scans, not its repertory of available responses, but rather the stimuli confronting him. The consequence is that representations of events associated with these stimuli on previous occasions are brought into the organism's active memory and serve as a basis for the feedback mechanism which guides responding. The feedback mechanism has somewhat the character of Miller's 'go' mechanism. However, I find it preferable to assume that input from the feedback mechanism operates, not by intensifying the response which has just led to reward, but rather by summating with incoming stimulation from further stimulus-response units in the sequence which led from the initiating stimulus to the rewarding consequence on a previous occasion, and thus increasing the likelihood that the sequence will run to completion.

The organism is assumed to learn relationships between changes in stimulus properties and changes in level of activity of positive and negative feedback mechanisms in such a manner that subsequently quantitative gradations in stimulus input produced by variations in behaviour are reflected in corresponding gradations in anticipated reward or punishment. Thus, following experiences with reward or punishment in a given situation, the organism's behaviour will thereafter be systematically guided by reinforcing feedback towards a source of reward or away from a source of painful stimulation.

In human learning one sees a similar trend away from the conception of reinforcement as a stamping in of associations by their after-effects, which dominated the research of several generations of investigators (see Postman, 1962, for a thorough review of the classical Thorndikean literature). But in the human case the changing theoretical climate has had much more notable effects in altering the nature of research. My own revised theory has led to strenuous continuing attempts to separate experimentally the informational and motivational aspects of reinforcement in human learning experiments. Contemporaneously, Atkinson and Wickens (1971) and Buchwald (1969) have developed a cognitive interpretation of reinforcement which shares many properties with mine. The learning which occurs in selective learning experiments is assumed in these views to be a matter of the individual's acquiring and storing in memory information concerning relationships between stimuli, choices (responses) and rewarding outcomes. Nuttin (see Nuttin and Greenwald, 1968) has gone further in working out the mechanism whereby the changing state of information with regard to rewards and punishments modifies behaviour on future occasions. In this respect he has introduced the important concept of 'open' and 'closed' task situations. The salient feature of an open task is that reward or punishment conveys information to the individual concerning the likelihood that the same stimulus-reinforcement relationships will recur on later occasions. When conditions are such that reinforcement provides this information, then the behaviour leading to the reinforcement is assumed to become incorporated into a 'persisting task-tension system', whereas in the absence of this information the behaviour leading to reinforcement does not become organized into the current pattern of activity.

### Basic conditions of association

If reinforcement is a performance process, then can we assume that learning requires only the contiguous occurrence of the stimulus and response elements to be associated? It will be difficult to find an investigator at the present time who would give an unconditional affirmative to this question. Even those who are satisfied with a slightly modernized version of Pavlovian conditioning theory require that the organism give some evidence of attention to a conditioned stimulus (CS), as for example by evincing an orienting reflex. In a sweeping revision of his own earlier version of conditioning theory, Konorski (whose 1967 volume deserves careful perusal by every serious student of conditioning) proposes firstly that a stage of perceptual learning must precede associative learning in order to establish the units to be associated, and secondly that on any trial of a conditioning experiment the neural structures underlying reactions to the conditioned and unconditioned stimuli (US) must be aroused by the action of drive systems. In brief, the organism must previously have come to discriminate the conditioned and unconditioned stimuli as distinct units, and on an effective conditioning trial must actively attend to both.

But even attention and arousal may not be sufficient. A number of recent studies suggest that in addition it is necessary that the outcome of a conditioning trial provide new information to the organism in the sense of reducing some active uncertainty as to what state of affairs will follow the occurrence of the conditioned stimulus (Egger and Miller, 1962; Kamin, 1969, Wagner, 1969).

Kamin took his start from the Pavlovian conception of overshadowing, referring to the observation that if a strong and a weak stimulus (for example a loud sound and a dim light) together precede the onset of an unconditioned stimulus, only the more intense component will subsequently be found to have taken on the character of a conditioned stimulus. Then he raised the question as to whether all members of a stimulus compound may be expected to undergo learning to a comparable extent even if they are similar in intensity. Utilizing the conditioned emotional response (CER) procedure of Estes and Skinner (1941), Kamin presented various originally neutral stimuli of approximately equal intensities prior to administration of electric shock, then tested the stimuli for their capacity to depress food-motivated behaviour (the depression in the situation being taken as evidence for a conditioned emotional state). In what came to be termed the 'blocking' experiment, the CER was first established to a simple stimulus, $S_1$, then $S_1$ was presented with another originally neutral stimulus, $S_2$, prior to the shock, and finally the animal was tested with $S_2$ alone. The result was that $S_2$ showed no tendency whatever to depress the food-motivated behaviour, leading to the conclusion that the prior conditioning of $S_1$ had 'blocked' the conditioning of $S_2$ when it was added to the CS compound.

An obvious and intuitively attractive interpretation of this finding is that, owing to the prior conditioning of $S_1$, the animal failed to attend to $S_2$ on the compound conditioning trials. This interpretation had to be devaluated, however, when Kamin subsequently found that if he altered the unconditioned shock stimulus, for example by increasing its intensity or by adding a second shock immediately following, on those trials on which $S_2$ was added to the CS compound, $S_2$ did elicit the CER on subsequent tests. This observation, and some related ones, led Kamin to the view that in order for effective conditioning to occur, the animal had to be in a sense 'surprised' by some aspect of the unconditioned stimulus. In the original blocking experiment, the compound $S_1+S_2$ was followed by precisely the same shock that had previously followed $S_1$ alone. In a later experiment, by contrast, addition of $S_2$ to the compound was correlated with a change in the shock stimulus, so $S_2$ had some additional predictive value, that is, it conveyed information to the organism which $S_1$ alone did not.

Although I am impressed with the importance of the informational variable, I think some continued caution in accepting intuitively appealing explanations is called for. It is possible, for example, that the information value of an added stimulus determines the degree to which it will gain control over performance rather than determining its probability of entering into associative learning. This interpretation, which would be the most natural one within my own revised theory, gains some independent support from Kamin's observation in a later experiment that although $S_2$ does not evoke the CER following its occurrence in the 'blocking' paradigm, it does gain the capacity to evoke the CER much more rapidly when subsequently paired alone with shock than does the same stimulus for control animals who have not had the previous pairings of $S_1+S_2$ with shock. Thus, as has occurred rather frequently in other contexts, the 'savings' method may here be revealing evidence of associative learning which was not manifest in an immediate performance measure.

Trabasso and Bower (1968) have presented an instructive discussion of the relationships between Kamin's experiments and others having to do with overshadowing and learning with respect to redundant relevant cues both in animal discrimination learning and human conceptual learning. In the latter case they demonstrate, for example, that if subjects have previously been trained to categorize stimuli according to one dimension, they may fail to learn to respond appropriately to cues of another dimension which is later introduced and made redundant with the first. These authors argue that the blocking effect is a graded phenomenon, appearing in different degrees in different experiments according as conditions lead the individual to focus attention more or less sharply and rigidly upon the cues first learned in a particular situation. However, the type of control procedure which Kamin introduced into his conditioning experiment and which led to weakening of the attentional interpretation has not yet found its way into the other experimental situations in which phenomena akin to blocking have been observed.

In any event we are by no means at the end of the story. Even contiguous occurrence of previously established stimulus and response units, with the organism attending actively to the stimuli and receiving new information on the stimulus-response conjunction, does not complete the set of necessary and sufficient conditions for obtaining effective conditioning. Rescorla (1968), again working with the CER procedure, has shown that in addition we must take into account the relationship of contingency between the CS and the presence or absence of the US. In a particularly instructive experiment, Rescorla trained rats to press a bar for food reinforcement, then in a different apparatus gave paired presentations of a CS and shock with, in different groups of animals, the probability of shock occurring during any two-minute interval in which the CS, a tone, was sounding being set equal to 0, 0·1, 0·2 or 0·4 and the probability of a shock during a two-minute interval in the absence of the CS being varied similarly. On subsequent tests of the ability of a tone to evoke the CER, Rescorla showed that when the probability of a shock in the absence of the CS is zero, comparable high levels of conditioning are manifest for groups receiving the shock in the presence of the CS with probabilities of 0·1, 0·2 or 0·4. However, if the probability of a shock in the absence of the CS is equal to 0·4, no CER is manifest even if the probability of shock in the presence of the CS is equal to 0·4. The generalization covering all of Rescorla's groups with various combinations of contingencies is that if the probabilities of shock in presence and absence of CS are equal, no CER is apparent on later tests regardless of the number of CS–shock pairings, whereas the CER is readily obtained whenever the probability of shock in the presence of the CS is greater than the probability in the absence of the CS during the CER conditioning trials. Like Kamin, Rescorla concludes that he has demonstrated another item which must be added to the list of necessary conditions for associative learning to occur in conditioning experiments.

Although I am as impressed as anyone with the important role Rescorla has demonstrated for differential contingencies, again I am not convinced that the effects of this variable can be localized in the process of associative learning rather than in the control of performance by learned associations. An alternative interpretation (Estes, 1969a), is that when the probabilities of shock in the presence and absence of CS are equal, the animal at the end of training has not failed to learn anything, rather it has learned that the conditional probability of shock is the same under both conditions. When the test is given under these circumstances, the tone produces no change in the animal's current anticipation of shock, therefore no change in activity of drive-feedback mechanisms and consequently no change in performance.

**Probability learning**

Not only the developments concerning animals' sensitivity to contingencies in classical conditioning, but research on choices among alternatives associated with differing magnitudes of reward (Estes, 1966) and a recent line of research concerning the development of learning sets (Medin, 1972), suggest that in a large variety of situations organisms learn probabilistic relations between events with considerable fidelity, and then modify their behaviour in accord with changes in these probabilities.

The process of learning to predict uncertain events was studied intensively during the early 1950s. A pioneering study by Brunswik (1939) set the stage for numerous studies of the behaviour of rats in a T-maze when the two choices are rewarded with differing probabilities. The general finding with rats was that under a correction procedure, in which the animal is forced to enter each of the two goal boxes with frequencies proportional to the probabilities of reward, the animal tends over a series of trials to adjust its probability of choice of a given side to equal the probability of reward on that side; however, under a non-correction procedure, animals tend to maximize their successes by learning always to go to the side with the higher probability of reward.

Probability learning in human subjects has been studied largely in a situation originated by Humphreys (1939) in which a reinforcing signal, for example illumination of a light, occurs with some fixed probability on each trial of a series, and the subject's task on each trial is to predict whether or not this event will occur. For those human subjects run in this situation without payoffs or penalties for success or failure and without *a priori* knowledge as to the actually random character of the sequence of events they are predicting (indeed without any information other than that gained from their own observations of the sequence), the usual result has been that over a series of a few hundred trials probability of predicting an event tends on the average to match its true probability.

The initial wave of research concerned with the rather striking phenomena of probability matching and the circumstances under which it appears or fails to appear naturally began in a few years to run into diminishing returns. More recently, motivated no doubt by a growing realization of the variety of behavioural situations in which probability learning is a component process, a second wave of activity has appeared, involving perhaps a smaller volume of research but rather more in the way of new ideas and new procedures (Estes, 1964, 1972). One new and interesting line of research seeks to analyse the processes involved in probability learning and to relate them to current work on short- and long-term memory. To this end, memory probes are inserted into the sequence of probability learning trials in order to determine relatively directly the individual's state of information concerning the sequence of events he has been experiencing at various stages of learning (Millward and Reber, 1968).

Another methodological innovation is the use of separate observations and test trials in order to separate the role of the information the learner obtains on each trial of a sequence from his experiences of success or failure in attempting to predict events in advance (Arima, 1965; Reber and Millward, 1968). Initial results with this procedure have given considerable support to theories which assume that, in the standard probability-learning experiment with human subjects, learning is a function of the information the individual receives from a sequence of events rather than of the rewarding or non-rewarding outcomes of his attempts at prediction.

Given some understanding of the conditions of probability learning, we may still want a more detailed understanding of the fine grain of the process. One reasonable surmise, growing naturally out of conditioning concepts, is that the individual's tendency to predict a particular event receives an increment on trials when the event occurs and a decrement on trials when it fails to occur, so that his probability of predicting it moves by small and irregular steps from its original value to a final one in the neighbourhood of the true probability. This conception is essentially that of the linear model, which was proposed by the writer and others in the early 1950s and which proved successful in predicting some features of probability-learning data, notably the probability-matching phenomenon.

An alternative conception is that the individual attends to various features of the outcomes of a few recent trials which he can hold in his immediate memory, notices what event follows a particular sub-sequence, and stores this relationship in his memory in an all-or-none fashion. Thus, if an individual were learning to predict the fall of a biased coin and noticed at a particular point in the series that the sub-sequence heads–tails–heads was followed by tails, he might remember this and the next time the sub-sequence heads–tails–heads occurred predict the same outcome. This last description is in the spirit of the 'engram' model produced by Restle (1961) and the pattern model of stimulus sampling theory (Atkinson and Estes, 1963).

Recent attempts to provide differential experimental tests of these two types of models have been generating results which almost uniformly support the all-or-none rather than the incremental conception. Within the all-or-none family, some data seem to be a bit more favourable to the conception that runs of events are coded and stored in memory as units in somewhat the manner proposed by Restle (Myers, 1970), but others provide rather direct and cogent support for some variation of the pattern model. The analyses by Feldman and Hanna (1966) of individual response protocols for probability-learning series in which particular sub-patterns of events recurred frequently demonstrated clearly that subjects can learn to respond to patterns of events as units; and the incisive experiment of Yellott (1969), directed specifically to the problem of differentiating the linear and pattern models, unequivocally favoured the latter. Further, Yellott showed that even the simple form of the pattern model can provide a rather detailed quantitative account of probability-learning data under some circumstances.

These results, though encouraging, provide no grounds for complacency. Incidental observations of subjects' behaviour and of their verbal reports in the experiments cited, and also the type of quantitative evidence beginning to emerge from experiments in which subjects are asked not only to make predictions but to estimate probabilities of events in probability-learning experiments, suggest that we have scarcely begun to tease out the roles of memory and decision processes in generating the sometimes simple (perhaps deceptively simple) observed behaviour of subjects who generate predictions of uncertain events, in or out of the laboratory.

### Discrimination learning

The interpretation of discrimination learning which guided the vast preponderance of research for some twenty-five years following the classic statements by Skinner (1938) and Spence (1937) was characterized by an elegance and parsimony which we do not see in current theories and are unlikely to see again in the future. Discrimination learning was conceived to be simply a combination of component processes of conditioning and extinction which could be studied separately in simpler situations. Once a response had been conditioned to any stimulus, generalization would be expected to any other stimulus similar to the first on such dimensions as loudness, brightness or pitch, to the extent that the two shared common elements or attributes. However, discrimination between the two could be developed if over a series of trials response to the first was reinforced and to the second non-reinforced, thus causing response tendencies to the positive and negative stimuli to draw apart. Following discrimination training, the generalization gradient around a positive stimulus would be steepened since the animal's response tendency to elements common to the positive and negative stimuli would have undergone extinction.

Some contemporary investigators closely aligned with the operant-conditioning school, or with the classical version of Hull's system, still appear to find the single-process, reinforcement–extinction theory satisfactory. Most however find that to make sense of many phenomena emerging from the currently flourishing literature on discrimination learning they require a more complex and multi-layered theory which separates more sharply the perceptual, associative and performance aspects of discrimination learning.

It will be possible here to sample only a few of the kinds of findings which are motivating the newer theoretical developments. The idea that discrimination is simply a matter of strengthening an organism's tendency to make a particular indicator response in the presence of one stimulus and weakening it in the presence of others becomes difficult to maintain in the face of such studies as that of Bower and Grusec (1964). These investigators, following up earlier studies of the writer and others in non-discriminative situations, showed that an animal can make considerable progress towards mastering a discrimination as a result of preliminary training in which it is exposed to correlated occurrences of discriminative stimuli and presence or absence of rewarding stimuli, but with no opportunity to make the response which will later be used as an indicator of discrimination learning. Similarly the idea that stimulus generalization is a rather mechanical matter of transfer via common elements cannot begin to cope with phenomena of conditional discrimination and generalization.

Consider, for example, an experiment reported by Heinemann and Chase (1970). These experimenters trained pigeons to peck one of a pair of response keys when a high tone was sounding and the other when a low tone was sounding, provided both keys were illuminated with a particular colour of light, say red. Concurrently the birds learned always to peck one key regardless of the frequency of the tone when both keys were illuminated with another colour, say green. Following this training, stimulus generalization gradients with respect to frequency of the tone were obtained separately in the presence of the two stimulus colours. In the presence of the 'positive' colour, red in the example, generalization gradients were of the usual form, with a peak in the vicinity of the positive training frequency and decreasing for test tones of lower or higher frequency. But by contrast, in the presence of the 'negative' colour, green in the example, the generalization gradients were flat, and one would have concluded from these alone that the tone had acquired no control whatever over the animal's behaviour. Relaxing the usual inhibitions on anthropomorphism, one might be tempted to say that the birds had learned to pay attention to the tone, and thus to notice variations in its frequency in the presence of one light and to ignore it in the presence of the other.

These and other findings which are difficult to accommodate within traditional theories have led to two active lines of contemporary theory construction. The one of these which seeks to conserve the conceptual framework of stimulus-response theory by incorporating a concept of selective attention is represented by the closely related theories of Lovejoy (1968) and Zeaman and House (1963). In this theory an organism learning, say, a form–colour discrimination (for example, learning always to choose a triangle and avoid a circle regardless of whether these forms are coloured red or green and regardless of their spatial positions) is conceived to undergo two parallel learning processes. One of these is learning which dimension, form, colour or position in the example to attend to, and the other to learn what particular value or cue on the relevant dimension should be associated with an overt choice response.

Major support for this type of theory has been forthcoming from an extensive literature upon discrimination reversals and upon intra- and extra-dimensional shifts following the learning of a discrimination (for a review see Estes, 1970). In terms of the example, it would characteristically be found that a child would learn a form–colour discrimination with red positive and green negative much more rapidly following experience with a discrimination in which yellow was positive and blue negative than following a discrimination in which triangles were positive and circles negative. The reason, in terms of the theory, for the difference is that in the first case the child would have learned during his experience with the first discrimination problem to attend to the stimulus dimension which would again be relevant in the second, whereas in the second instance, in which the relevant dimension changes, the child would have to learn both which dimension was appropriate and which value on the dimension was associated with a correct choice response.

**Coding and information processing**

The model presented by Trabasso and Bower (1968) occupies an intermediate position between theories elaborated within the stimulus-response framework and others couched in terms of cognitive and information-processing operations. A weak point in the former group of theories has been the virtually undefined character of the central concept of stimulus dimension. A suggestion towards filling in this critical gap was offered by Lawrence (1963) in his important paper on stimulus coding.

In order to deal with the organism's ability to discriminate stimuli which have elements or properties in common, Lawrence suggested that the organism generates a unique code for each stimulus and then makes his choice responses on the basis of the stimuli as coded. In the case of adult human subjects these codes might be simply verbal labels, whereas in young children or animals they would be assumed to be covert responses which, though non-verbal, would serve a similar function. A stimulus dimension is simply a set of codes. Within Lawrence's approach the organism, during the early stages of discrimination learning, would be said, not to be learning to attend to a stimulus dimension, but rather to be generating a dimension by making appropriate coding responses to the various stimuli presented. This idea of coding, or conceptions very closely related to it, have been applied by Kendler and Kendler (1968) to discrimination learning in children, by Greeno (1970) to paired-associate learning, by Martin (1968) to interference phenomena in retention of verbal material, and by Johnson (1970) to short-term memory span.

Impatient with the apparently endlessly escalating difficulties of reducing complex human behaviour to stimulus-response terms, and perhaps impressed also with the analogies between human intellectual functioning and that of digital computers, a number of contemporary investigators propose to abjure entirely the notion of interpreting human learning and thought in terms of stimuli, responses and associations, and to seek instead theories built entirely on the basis of concepts of information processing (see, for example, Miller, Galanter and Pribram, 1960; Newell and Simon, 1963). Perhaps the most systematic effort of this sort to date is the work of

Hunt on an information-processing model for concept learning (Hunt, 1962; Hunt, Marin and Stone, 1966).

For my own part, I am inclined to take issue with proponents of this school of thought only when they turn polemical and argue that information-processing concepts provide the only proper basis for describing learning and cognitive processes. Multiple levels of analysis and description within psychology seem to me a desirable and indeed necessary development. Personally I find concepts of information storage and retrieval suggestive and useful in formulating hypotheses about human learning and memory for experimental attack. And I can readily visualize the development of a viable and useful body of theory at this level, autonomous relative to stimulus-response theory just as the latter is with respect to neurophysiology. But I think of this autonomy as something to be put up with in practice rather than something to be sought after in principle. It is often useful and usually easy to generate new sets of concepts at higher levels of analysis. It is always essential in the long run, and usually much more taxing, to bring these results of the various more or less autonomous sub-disciplines of a scientific field within a common theoretical framework.

## Summary

The selection of recent studies reviewed here, though diverse in content and approaches, have in common a direct concern with ideas and issues which have been central to the evolution of learning theory over several decades. One of the more novel lines of research tends to confirm the belief of previous generations of investigators that the basic conditions of association involve more than sheer contiguity of experiences; but now the something more appears to be, not belongingness, nor need reduction, but arousal or information value. Another provides substantial evidence that the learning of probabilities is a much more basic and pervasive process than hitherto realized.

An influx of new findings and methods from ethology and electrophysiology has substantially modified long-prevailing views on the substrate of learning and the nature of reinforcement – and in the process has tended to bring learning theory closer to biology. But concurrently, the influence of informational and computer models has instigated major attempts to reformulate stimulus-response principles of learning in terms of coding and information processing. The activating effects of these interactions with other disciplines have certainly been salutary. But for those who still foresee the possibility of continued progress towards a general theory of learning, the central question now is whether the divergent forces already have gained too much momentum to permit effective efforts towards theoretical integration and synthesis.

## Further reading

BOWER, G. H. (ed.), *The Psychology of Learning and Motivation*, vol. 4, Academic Press, 1970.

CAMPBELL, B. A., and CHURCH, R. M. (eds.), *Punishment and Aversive Behavior*, Appleton-Century-Crofts, 1969.

ESTES, W. K., *Learning Theory and Mental Development*, Academic Press, 1970.

KONORSKI, J., *Integrative Activity of the Brain*, Chicago University Press, 1967.

MACKINTOSH, N. J., and HONIG, W. K. (eds.), *Fundamental Issues in Associative Learning: Proceedings of a Symposium held at Dalhousie University, Halifax, June 1968*, Dalhousie University Press, 1969.

TAPP, J. (ed.), *Reinforcement and Behavior*, Academic Press, 1969.

TRABASSO, T., and BOWER, G. H., *Attention in Learning Theory and Research*, Wiley, 1968.

## References

ARIMA, J. K. (1965), 'Human probability learning with forced-training trials and certain and uncertain outcome choice trials', *Journal of Experimental Psychology*, vol. 70, pp. 43–50.

ATKINSON, R. C., and ESTES, W. K. (1963), 'Stimulus sampling theory', in R. D. Luce, R. R. Bush and E. Galanter (eds.), *Handbook of Mathematical Psychology*, vol. 2, Wiley, pp. 121–268.

ATKINSON, R. C., and WICKENS, T. D. (1971), 'Human memory and the concept of reinforcement', in R. Glaser (ed.), *The Nature of Reinforcement*, Academic Press.

BARTLETT, F. C. (1932), *Remembering*, Cambridge University Press.

BOLLES, R. (1970), 'Effects of escape training on avoidance learning', in F. R. Brush (ed.), *Aversive Conditioning and Learning*, Academic Press.

BOWER, G. H., and GRUSEC, T. (1964), 'Effect of prior Pavlovian discrimination training upon learning an operant discrimination', *Journal of Experimental Analysis of Behavior*, vol. 7, pp. 401–4.

BRELAND, K., and BRELAND, M. (1966), *Animal Behavior*, Macmillan Co.

BRUNSWIK, E. (1939), 'Probability as a determiner of rat behavior', *Journal of Experimental Psychology*, vol. 25, pp. 175–97.

BUCHWALD, A. M. (1969), 'Effects of "right" and "wrong" on subsequent behavior: a new interpretation', *Psychological Review*, vol. 76, pp. 132–43.

BUSH, R. R., and MOSTELLER, F. (1951), 'A mathematical model for simple learning', *Psychological Review*, vol. 58, pp. 313–23.

CARR, H. A. (1931), 'The laws of association', *Psychological Review*, vol. 38, pp. 212–28.

DICARA, L., and MILLER, N. E. (1968), 'Instrumental learning of systolic blood-pressure responses by curarized rats: dissociation of cardiac and vascular changes', *Psychosomatic Medicine*, vol. 30, pp. 489–94.

DUNCAN, C. P. (1949), 'The retroactive effect of electroshock on learning', *Journal of Comparative and Physiological Psychology*, vol. 42, pp. 32–44.

EGGER, M. D., and MILLER, N. E. (1962), 'Secondary reinforcement in rats as a function of information value and reliability of the stimulus', *Journal of Experimental Psychology*, vol. 64, pp. 97–104.

ESTES, W. K. (1950), 'Toward a statistical theory of learning', *Psychological Review*, vol. 57, pp. 94–107.

ESTES, W. K. (1964), 'Probability learning', in A. W. Melton (ed.), *Categories of Human Learning*, Academic Press, pp. 90–128.

ESTES, W. K. (1966), 'Transfer of verbal discriminations based on differential reward magnitude', *Journal of Experimental Psychology*, vol. 72, pp. 276–83.

ESTES, W. K. (1969a), 'New perspectives on some old issues in association theory', in N. J. Mackintosh and W. K. Honig (eds.), *Fundamental Issues in Associative Learning: Proceedings of a Symposium held at Dalhousie University, Halifax, June 1968*, Dalhousie University Press, pp. 162–89.

ESTES, W. K. (1969b), 'Reinforcement in human learning', in J. Tapp (ed.), *Reinforcement and Behavior*, Academic Press, pp. 63–94.

ESTES, W. K. (1969c), 'Outline of a theory of punishment', in B. A. Campbell and R. M. Church (eds.), *Punishment and Aversive Behavior*, Appleton-Century-Crofts, pp. 57–82.

ESTES, W. K. (1970), *Learning Theory and Mental Development*, Academic Press.

ESTES, W. K. (1972), 'Research and theory on probability learning', *Journal of the American Statistical Association*, vol. 67, pp. 81–102.

ESTES, W. K., and SKINNER, B. F. (1941), 'Some quantitative properties of anxiety', *Journal of Experimental Psychology*, vol. 29, pp. 390–400.

FELDMAN, J., and HANNA, J. F. (1966), 'The structure of responses to a sequence of binary events', *Journal of Mathematical Psychology*, vol. 3, pp. 371–87.

GARCIA, J., and KOELLING, R. A. (1966), 'Relation of cue to consequence in avoidance learning', *Psychonomic Science*, vol. 4, pp. 123–4.

GIBSON, E. J. (1940), 'A systematic application of the concepts of generalization and differentiation to verbal learning', *Psychological Review*, vol. 47, pp. 196–229.

GLICKMAN, S. E., and SCHIFF, B. B. (1967), 'A biological theory of reinforcement', *Psychological Review*, vol. 74, pp. 81–109.

GREENO, J. G. (1970), 'How associations are memorized', in D. Norman (ed.), *Models of Human Memory*, Academic Press, pp. 257–84.

GUTHRIE, E. R. (1930), 'Conditioning as a principle of learning', *Psychological Review*, vol. 37, pp. 412–28.

HARLOW, H. F. (1949), 'The formation of learning sets', *Psychological Review*, vol. 56, pp. 51–65.

HEINEMANN, E. G., and CHASE, S. (1970), 'Conditional stimulus control', *Journal of Experimental Psychology*, vol. 84, pp. 187–97.

HULL, C. L. (1930), 'Knowledge and purpose as habit mechanisms', *Psychological Review*, vol. 37, pp. 511–25.

HULL, C. L. (1931), 'Goal attraction and directing ideas conceived as habit phenomena', *Psychological Review*, vol. 38, pp. 487–506.

HUMPHREYS, L. G. (1939), 'Acquisition and extinction of verbal expectations in a situation analogous to conditioning', *Journal of Experimental Psychology*, vol. 25, pp. 294–301.

HUNT, E. B. (1962), *Concept Learning: An Information Processing Problem*, Wiley.

HUNT, E. B., MARIN, J., and STONE, P. J. (1966), *Experiments in Induction*, Academic Press.

JENKINS, J. G., and DALLENBACH, K. M. (1924), 'Oblivescence during sleep and waking', *American Journal of Psychology*, vol. 35, pp. 605–12.

JOHNSON, N. F. (1970), 'The role of chunking and organization in the process of recall', in G. H. Bower (ed.), *The Psychology of Learning and Motivation*, vol. 4, Academic Press, pp. 171–247.

KAMIN, L. J. (1969), 'Selective association and conditioning', in N. J. Mackintosh and W. K. Honig (eds.), *Fundamental Issues in Associative Learning: Proceedings of a Symposium held at Dalhousie University, Halifax, June 1968*, Dalhousie University Press, pp. 42–64.

KENDLER, H. K., and KENDLER, T. S. (1968), 'Mediation and conceptual behavior', in K. W. Spence and J. T. Spence (eds.), *The Psychology of Learning and Motivation*, vol. 2, Academic Press, pp. 197–244.

KÖHLER, W. (1925), *The Mentality of Apes*, trans. E. Winter, Harcourt, Brace.

KONORSKI, J. (1967), *Integrative Activity of the Brain*, University of Chicago Press.

LAWRENCE, D. H. (1963), 'The nature of a stimulus: some relationships between learning and perception', in S. Koch (ed.), *Psychology: A Study of a Science*, vol. 5, McGraw-Hill, pp. 179–213.

LOVEJOY, E. (1968), *Attention in Discrimination Learning*, Holden-Day.

MARTIN, E. (1968), 'Stimulus meaningfulness and paired-associate transfer: an encoding variability hypothesis', *Psychological Review*, vol. 75, pp. 421–41.

MEDIN, D. L. (1972), 'The role of reinforcement in discrimination learning set in monkeys', *Psychological Bulletin*, in press.

MELTON, A. W. (1950), 'Learning', *Annual Review of Psychology*, vol. 1, pp. 9–30.

MELTON, A. W., and VON LACKUM, W. J. (1941), 'Retroactive and proactive inhibition in retention: evidence for a two-factor theory in retroactive inhibition', *American Journal of Psychology*, vol. 54, pp. 157–73.

MILLER, G. A., GALANTER, E., and PRIBRAM, K. H. (1960), *Plans and the Structure of Behavior*, Holt, Rinehart & Winston.

MILLER, N. E. (1963), 'Some reflections on the law of effect produce a new alternative to drive reduction', in M. R. Jones (ed.), *Nebraska Symposium on Motivation*, Nebraska University Press, pp. 65–112.

MILLER, N. E. (1969), 'Learning of visceral and glandular responses', *Science*, vol. 163, pp. 434–45.

MILLWARD, R. B., and REBER, A. S. (1968), 'Event-recall in probability learning', *Journal of Verbal Learning and Verbal Behavior*, vol. 7, pp. 980–89.
MOWRER, O. W. (1960), *Learning Theory and Behavior*, Wiley.
MYERS, J. L. (1970), 'Sequential choice behavior', in G. H. Bower (ed.), *The Psychology of Learning and Motivation*, vol. 4, Academic Press, pp. 109–70.
NEWELL, A., and SIMON, H. A. (1963), 'Computers in psychology', in R. D. Luce, R. R. Bush and E. Galanter (eds.), *Handbook of Mathematical Psychology*, vol. 1, Wiley, pp. 361–428.
NUTTIN, J., and GREENWALD, A. G. (1968), *Reward and Punishment in Human Learning*, Academic Press.
PAVLOV, I. P. (1927), *Conditioned Reflexes*, trans. G. V. Anrep, Oxford University Press.
POSTMAN, L. (1962), 'Reward and punishment in human learning', in L. Postman (ed.), *Psychology in the Making*, Knopf, pp. 331–401.
REBER, A. S., and MILLWARD, R. B. (1968), 'Event observations in probability learning', *Journal of Experimental Psychology*, vol. 77, pp. 317–27.
RESCORLA, R. A. (1968), 'Probability of shock in the presence and absence of CS in fear conditioning', *Journal of Comparative and Physiological Psychology*, vol. 66, pp. 1–5.
RESTLE, F. (1961), *Psychology of Judgment and Choice: A Theoretical Essay*, Wiley.
ROBINSON, E. S. (1932), *Association Theory Today*, Appleton-Century-Crofts.
SELIGMAN, M. E. (1970), 'On the generality of the laws of learning', *Psychological Review*, vol. 77, no. 5, pp. 406–18.
SKINNER, B. F. (1931), 'The concept of the reflex in the description of behavior', *Journal of General Psychology*, vol. 5, pp. 427–58.
SKINNER, B. F. (1938), *The Behavior of Organisms*, Appleton-Century-Crofts.
SPENCE, K. W. (1937), 'The differential response in animals to stimuli varying within a single dimension', *Psychological Review*, vol. 44, pp. 430–44.
THORNDIKE, E. L. (1932), *The Fundamentals of Learning*, Teacher's College, Columbia University.
TOLMAN, E. C. (1932), *Purposive Behavior in Animals and Men*, Appleton-Century-Crofts; reprinted, University of California Press, 1949.
TOLMAN, E. C., and HONZIK, C. H. (1930), 'Introduction and removal of reward and maze performance in rats', *University of California Publications in Psychology*, vol. 4, pp. 257–75.
TRABASSO, T., and BOWER, G. H. (1968), *Attention in Learning Theory and Research*, Wiley.
WAGNER, A. R. (1969), 'Stimulus validity and stimulus selection in associative learning', in N. J. Mackintosh and W. K. Honig (eds.), *Fundamental Issues in Associative Learning: Proceedings of a Symposium held at Dalhousie University, Halifax, June 1968*, Dalhousie University Press, pp. 90–122.

WOLFLE, H. M. (1932), 'Conditioning as a function of the interval between the conditioned and the original stimulus', *Journal of General Psychology*, vol. 7, pp. 80–103.
YELLOTT, J. I., Jr (1969), 'Probability learning with non-contingent success', *Journal of Mathematical Psychology*, vol. 6, pp. 541–75.
ZEAMAN, D., and HOUSE, B. J. (1963), 'The role of attention in retardate discrimination learning', in N. R. Ellis (ed.), *Handbook of Mental Deficiency*, McGraw-Hill, pp. 159–223.

# 2 Human Memory*

## A. D. Baddeley

Fundamental changes have been occurring in the study of human memory in recent years. The stimulus-response (S–R) associative interference theory of forgetting which has dominated the field for the last thirty years is in a state of crisis, having difficulty in establishing its relevance to forgetting in everyday life, and more recently encountering phenomena in the laboratory which appear to be inconsistent with its basic assumptions. At the same time there has been a tremendous growth in the application to the study of memory of information-processing concepts, heavily influenced by the techniques and terminology of computer science. This has produced a considerable broadening of the scope of memory studies together with a wealth of new techniques and phenomena.

The present chapter aims to provide an overall view of this extremely active and rapidly changing field by examining three basic questions, namely: Is there more than one kind of memory? Why do we forget? How do we remember?

### Is there more than one kind of memory?

One of the major controversies of the 1960s concerned the question of whether separate memory systems underlie short-term memory (STM) such as might be used to hold a telephone number in memory long enough to dial it, and long-term memory (LTM), as would be employed in remembering one's own familiar telephone number. Such a distinction was assumed by Hebb (1949) and was given considerable emphasis in Broadbent's *Perception and Communication* (1958), which was one of the first and most important examples of the information-processing approach to memory. Broadbent's conception of the memory system involved three stages. The first of these was a sensory buffer store which was capable of holding a considerable amount of information for a very short period of time; the

* This chapter was written while the author was visiting the Center for Human Information Processing, University of California, San Diego, supported by grant MH 15828 from the National Institute of Mental Health. I am grateful to members of the Center and particularly to George Mandler for many stimulating discussions, and to Karalyn Patterson for helpful comments on this chapter.

present chapter will not deal with this peripheral sensory store since it is discussed in the chapter by Coltheart (pp. 62–85). Information was assumed to be transferred from the sensory buffer to a limited-capacity STM system. The short-term trace was assumed to decay rapidly, but could be maintained by recirculating the information by means of a rehearsal loop. The third part of the memory system was the long-term store. Forgetting in LTM was assumed to be attributable to interference from other information (see p. 42) rather than to trace decay as in STM.

Traditional interference theory made no distinction between LTM and STM, and an influential paper by Melton (1963) attacked the dichotomous view of memory, arguing that the existing evidence was compatible with the concept of a single unitary system, in which forgetting followed the principles of interference theory (see pp. 41–5). He supported this claim by citing a range of similarities between the results of STM experiments and the known phenomena of LTM, and argued that in the absence of evidence to the contrary, it was more parsimonious to assume a single memory system.

In discussing the resultant controversy it is useful to distinguish between the different experimental *procedures* typically used in the study of LTM and STM, on the one hand, and the separate memory *systems* assumed to underlie the distinction on the other. We shall therefore employ separate terms, using STM to refer to an experimental procedure typically involving a single presentation of a small amount of material which is tested within seconds, and primary memory (PM) to refer to the labile memory system that is assumed to be operative in such situations. We shall use LTM to refer to a procedure typified by the repeated presentation of a relatively large amount of material which may be tested after a considerable delay, and we shall use the term secondary memory (SM) to refer to the memory system assumed to underlie such delayed recall.

Melton's paper stimulated a good deal of work on the question of how many kinds of memory exist. In general it was subsequently argued that the similarities between LTM and STM noted by Melton occurred because most STM techniques reflect not only the labile PM system but also the more durable SM or long-term system. It is the presence of this SM component that is assumed to produce the similarities between LTM and STM. Evidence which seemed difficult to fit into a unitary memory system began to accumulate from several sources. These included:

1. *Two-component tasks.* A wide range of memory tasks appear to have two quite separate components which are readily indentifiable with PM and SM. One of the clearest examples comes from the free-recall task, in which a subject is presented with a sequence of words which he must subsequently recall in any order he wishes. As curve A on Figure 1a shows, the probability that a word will be recalled depends on when it was presented. More specifically, there is a marked tendency for the last few words presented to

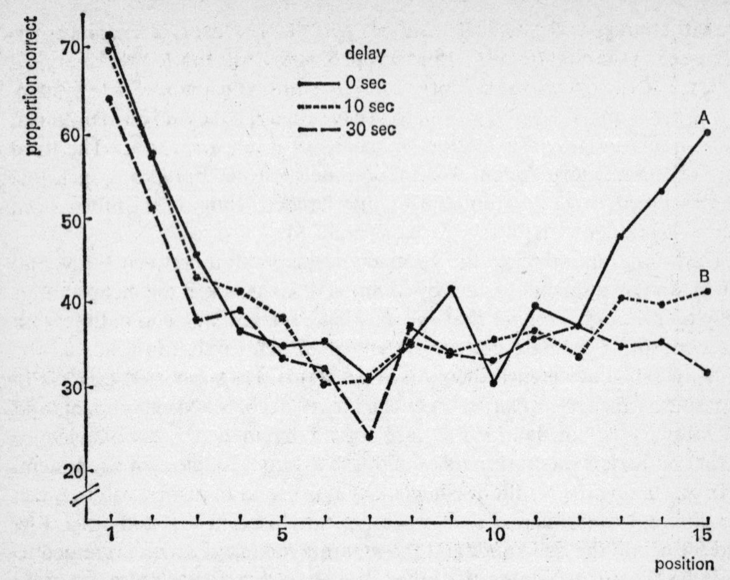


Figure 1(a)

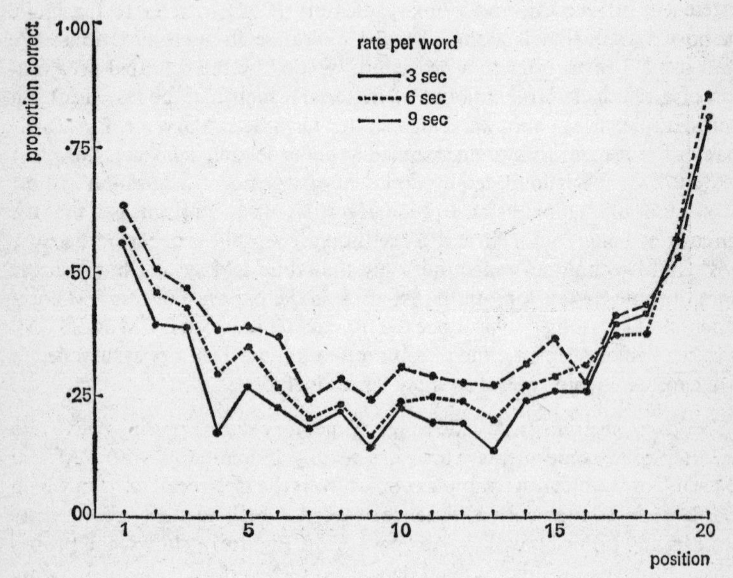


Figure 1(b)

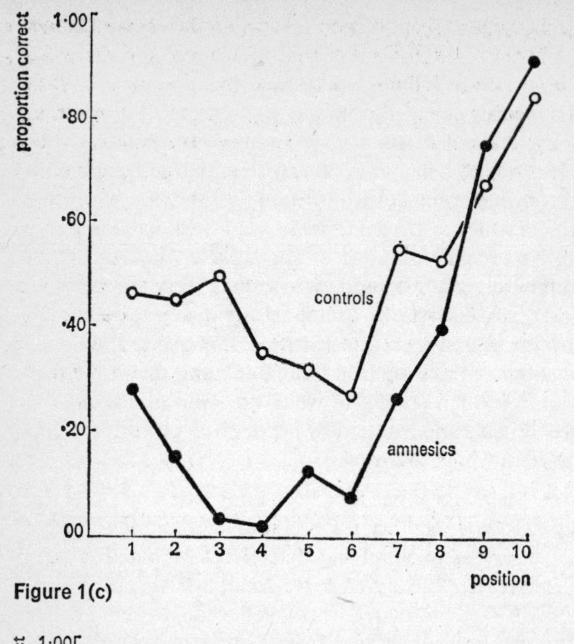


Figure 1(c)

Figure 1(d)

Figure 1 The evidence for separate long- and short-term components in free recall. (a) The disappearance of the recency effect when recall is delayed. (b) Increasing time available for learning from 3 to 9 sec/word improves retention of earlier items but has no effect on the recency effect (both (a) and (b) are taken from Glanzer and Cunitz, 1966). (c) Amnesic patients with defective long-term memory show a normal recency effect (from Baddeley and Warrington, 1970). (d) Shows the free-recall performance of a subject with defective short-term memory: note that his recency effect is limited to a single short-term item (from Shallice and Warrington, 1970)

be recalled particularly well, a phenomenon known as the *recency effect*. However, Glanzer and Cunitz (1966) showed that when recall is delayed for a few seconds, during which rehearsal is prevented by an additional task such as counting, the recency effect disappears, while memory for earlier items is comparatively unaffected (see Figure 1a curve B). Although the recency effect is so sensitive to delay, it is otherwise remarkably stable. In this respect it differs from performance on the rest of the list which is affected by virtually any variable which is known to influence LTM, including rate of presentation, word frequency, the age of the subject, the amount of attention he pays to the learning task, and many others (Raymond, 1969).

A range of other tasks have been shown to comprise two such components; these include short-term paired-associate learning (Peterson, 1966), the Brown–Peterson short-term forgetting task (see p. 46), and the probe task devised by Waugh and Norman (1965), in which the subject attempts to remember a sequence of items and is tested by being given one of the items and asked to give the item which followed it.

2. *Evidence from amnesic patients*. It has long been known that neurological patients with grossly defective memory for everyday events might have a normal immediate memory span, implying defective SM together with normal PM. When such patients are given a free-recall task they are found to have grossly defective SM, as measured by delayed recall, together with a normal recency effect on immediate recall, indicating unimpaired PM (see Figure 1c). Recently, Shallice and Warrington (1970) have presented evidence that the opposite may also occur, namely normal SM with defective PM. Their patient showed unimpaired retention of events in everyday life, his long-term learning ability was normal, and yet he was unable to repeat back sequences of more than two digits, and in free recall showed a recency effect of only one item (see Figure 1d). The clearly dichotomous way in which memory breaks down in such cases is difficult to explain in terms of a single unitary system.

3. *Capacity limitations*. In contrast with the enormous capacity of SM to store information, PM appears to have a very limited storage capacity, whether measured in terms of span of immediate memory (Miller, 1956), or size of the recency effect in a probe or free-recall task (Craik, 1971). On the other hand, in a free-recall experiment in which the subject's information-processing capacity was reduced by the requirement to sort cards during the presentation of the list of words, it was found that the informational demands of the sorting task impaired input into SM but not into PM (Baddeley, Scott, Drynan and Smith, 1969). It appears then that the informational limitations on PM occur in its *storage* capacity, whereas SM is limited at the *input* stage.

4. *Differential coding*. Conrad (1964) showed, in a task involving STM for

sequences of six consonants, that errors tend to be similar in sound to the correct item (e.g. B instead of D, M instead of N) despite the fact that the letters were presented visually. This indicates that subjects were remembering the letters phonemically (i.e. in terms of either their sound, or the way in which they are spoken).

Using sequences of unrelated words, it was subsequently shown that although STM was adversely affected by the phonemic similarity within the list (e.g. Mad Cat Map Mat Cap), it was relatively unaffected by similarity of meaning (e.g. Huge Big Great Wide Large) (Baddeley, 1966a). For LTM, however, the opposite was true. The rate of learning a ten-word sequence when the STM component was eliminated showed no effect of phonemic similarity, but a marked semantic similarity decrement (Baddeley, 1966b). Kintsch and Buschke (1969) studied the same question using a probe task, which has the advantage of allowing the separation of the primary and secondary memory components. Kintsch and Buschke found that phonemic similarity influenced only the PM component, while semantic similarity affected only SM. Finally, Sachs (1967) in a study of recognition memory for prose found that whereas the phonemic or grammatical features of a sentence were forgotten almost immediately, semantic features were well retained even after a sizeable delay, suggesting that the relationship between semantic coding and LTM may have considerable generality.

### How many kinds of memory?

While it is possible to fit individual aspects of the evidence discussed into a unitary memory system, it is not easy to see how such a system could simultaneously account for all the evidence described, and consequently the single-system view is no longer widely held. Indeed it is now beginning to appear that a dichotomy is also an oversimplification, although it may prove fruitful to distinguish between a long-term semantic memory on the one hand, and a hierarchy of specific sensory memory stores on the other (see Baddeley and Patterson, 1971, for a more detailed discussion).

### Why do we forget?

*Forgetting in long-term memory*

Forgetting has traditionally been attributed to one of two processes, trace decay or interference. Decay theories interpret forgetting as the result of the spontaneous fading or weakening with time of a neural memory trace. Interference theories on the other hand argue that forgetting is caused by subsequent events which make the memory trace weaker or less accessible.

Associative interference theory regards the association between a stimulus and a response as the basic unit of learning. Forgetting occurs when the original association is followed by an interfering association: it is particularly marked when the same stimulus is associated with a different response.

Table 1 illustrates this classical interference paradigm in which the subject first learns a list comprising pairs of items, denoted the A–B list (where A represents the stimuli and B the responses), and subsequently learns an A–C list. If he is then asked to recall the A–B list he will remember less than a control subject, who after A–B learned either nothing, or a completely unrelated list, X–C. Interference from subsequent learning is termed retroactive interference (RI). Its effect tends to *diminish* with increasing delay between the interfering task and subsequent recall. If instead of testing the first association we test the second (A–C or X–C), we again find poorer recall when two different responses have been learned to the same stimulus. In this case however the forgetting is attributable to the effect of a *prior* association; it is termed proactive interference (PI) and tends to *increase* with the delay between learning and retention.

Modern interference theory assumes that A–B learning establishes an A–B association, A–C learning produces both a competing A–C association, and at the same time an unlearning or weakening of the A–B association. Immediately after A–C learning, retention of the weakened A–B response is impaired (hence, RI). With the passage of time, however, the A–B response is assumed to recover some of its strength (a phenomenon claimed to be analogous to spontaneous recovery in classical Pavlovian conditioning). As the A–B response recovers it becomes increasingly able to compete with A–C, which hence tends to be forgotten (PI).

*The extra-experimental interference hypothesis*

It is certainly the case that learning two incompatible responses to the same stimulus presents problems. The English-speaking visitor to Italy may 'know' that 'C' means 'caldo = hot', but is still liable inadvertently to turn on the hot tap when he wants cold water. However, situations in which we must learn incompatible responses to the same stimulus are fortunately comparatively rare, and would seem to provide a rather narrow foundation for a general theory of forgetting. Why, for example, should a subject who has learned a single list of items ever forget it, particularly if they are items such as nonsense syllables (e.g. Yig) which he is unlikely to have encountered in any other situation? Yet forgetting of such items clearly does occur.

Underwood and Postman (1960) proposed that the additional source of interference was the subject's language habits. In learning Yig, they argued, the subject must unlearn more probable letter combinations; hence learning to associate Y and I in Yig causes the unlearning of the more frequent combination Y–O. This prior association will tend to recover over time, thus producing forgetting of the Y–I association. The less probable the letter sequences making up the syllables, the greater will be the discrepancy with normal language habits and the greater the subsequent interference. A similar effect was assumed to occur for word sequences, but in this case the

Table 1 **Design of interference experiments**

*Proactive Interference (PI) Experimental Design*

| *Condition* | *Learn first* | *Learn second* | *Delay* | *Recall* |
| --- | --- | --- | --- | --- |
| PI | List of A–B pairs<br>e.g. Drunken–Vicar | List of A–C pairs<br>e.g. Drunken–Nudist | Delay | List of A–C pairs<br>e.g. Drunken–? (Nudist) |
| Control 1 | Rest | List of A–C pairs<br>e.g. Drunken–Nudist | Delay | List of A–C pairs<br>e.g. Drunken–? (Nudist) |
| Control 2 | List of X–B pairs<br>e.g. Savage–Vicar | List of A–C pairs<br>e.g. Drunken–Nudist | Delay | List of A–C pairs<br>e.g. Drunken–? (Nudist) |

*Retroactive Interference (RI) Experimental Design*

| *Condition* | *Learn first* | *Learn second* | *Delay* | *Recall* |
| --- | --- | --- | --- | --- |
| RI | List of A–B pairs<br>e.g. Drunken–Vicar | List of A–C pairs<br>e.g. Drunken–Nudist | Delay | List of A–B pairs<br>e.g. Drunken–? (Vicar) |
| Control 1 | List of A–B pairs<br>e.g. Drunken–Vicar | Rest | Delay | List of A–B pairs<br>e.g. Drunken–? (Vicar) |
| Control 2 | List of A–B pairs<br>e.g. Drunken–Vicar | List of X–C pairs<br>e.g. Savage–Nudist | Delay | List of A–B pairs<br>e.g. Drunken–? (Vicar) |

effect was assumed to be between words, and to be greatest for high-frequency words. These are assumed to have more and stronger prior associations which will subsequently recover and cause forgetting (Underwood and Postman, 1960).

However, attempts to demonstrate faster forgetting of either low-frequency letter sequences or high-frequency words have proved uniformly unsuccessful (see Keppel, 1968, for a review). Rate of forgetting appears to be remarkably insensitive to the nature of the material to be recalled. Both Underwood and Postman have offered tentative explanations of the failure of the extra-experimental interference hypothesis (see Postman, 1969), but neither interpretation does anything to bridge the gap between the artificially extreme negative-transfer studies on which interference theory is based, and forgetting in everyday life.

*Recent developments in interference theory*

There has in recent years been a growing body of evidence that associative interference theory is inadequate even within its traditional limits. For example, it has been usual to assume that learning to associate a pair of items involves two stages: learning to produce the response, and learning to associate the response with the stimulus. Interference was assumed to occur at this later associative stage, since there would appear to be no difference in the response learning stage between an A–B, A–C interference condition and the much better retained A–B, X–C control condition, since both involve learning B and C as responses.

A major difficulty for such a view is presented by the recent discovery that RI effects are drastically reduced when the subject is provided with the responses and required to match them to the appropriate stimuli. Since this procedure is assumed to eliminate the response-learning stage without influencing the associative stage, the theory should predict particularly clear interference effects (see Postman, 1969, for an account of the problems of modifying interference theory to take account of this evidence).

A second major difficulty is raised by what Martin (1971) has termed the *independent retrieval phenomenon.* Associative interference theory assumes that forgetting occurs because of mutual interference between the A–B and the A–C associations. Hence, when recall of both is required, there should be a negative correlation between the probability of recalling the two associations; the stronger the competing A–C association, the less likely the recall of A–B, and vice versa. In 1966 Da Polito discovered that this was not so; probability of recalling A–C was quite independent of A–B recall. This has proved to be the case across a wide range of experimental conditions (Greeno, 1969), and as such presents a major phenomenon which is quite incompatible with orthodox associative interference theory.

Interference theory appears at present then to be in a somewhat critical condition. Is it likely to survive? There is no doubt that interference does occur when we try to learn two incompatible responses in similar situations, and whether or not this is representative of all learning and forgetting, it certainly presents a genuine and interesting problem. However, it seems much less likely that the traditional S–R associationist theory based on automatic connections between discrete atomic stimulus and response units will survive. Recent attempts to modify interference theory, although using S–R associationist terms, tend to employ concepts which are closer to the spirit of Gestalt psychology than to that of traditional associationism. Thus Postman (1969) relies heavily on a response selection mechanism that is very close to the Gestalt concept of 'set'. A similar process is assumed by Martin (1971), who also proposes that when a stimulus and response are associated they form a single integrated unit (i.e. a Gestalt). For example, a stimulus A is different, when it is paired with B, from the same stimulus when paired with C (i.e. the whole is greater than the sum of its parts). It would, however, be unfair to give the impression that interference theory is simply saying today what Gestalt theory said forty years ago. The technical sophistication on which, for example, Martin (1971) bases his conclusions is vastly greater than any available to Gestalt psychology, with the result that he can propose specific testable hypotheses where Gestalt psychology offered only speculation. The main point is that interference theory is becoming increasingly more flexible and less doctrinaire in both its concepts and experimental techniques, and although it no longer appears to offer a credible explanation of all forgetting, it is far from moribund.

*Forgetting in short-term memory*

Simultaneous with the controversy as to whether memory constitutes a unitary system was the associated discussion of what produces forgetting in STM. The two issues were initially very closely related, since Broadbent's (1958) claim that trace decay was responsible for forgetting in STM but not in LTM was one of his principal arguments for a dichotomy, and conversely Melton's (1963) arguments in favour of a unitary system relied heavily on his claim that STM was subject to the same laws of interference as LTM. In recent years the two issues have separated, so that rejection of the unitary-system view by no means implies an acceptance of trace decay as the main source of short-term forgetting. Nevertheless the two issues remain closely related, since if, as is now widely accepted, most STM tasks comprise both PM and SM components, one can only draw valid conclusions about PM when the effects of the SM component are controlled. In LTM, this is much less of a problem, since most traditional experimental techniques tend to wipe out the PM component by controlling the order in which items are tested. Since it is only rarely the case that the last item presented is the first tested, the role of PM is usually minimal.

*The Brown–Peterson technique*

Unfortunately most of the work on forgetting in STM has used the Brown–Peterson technique in which a short sequence (e.g. three consonants) is presented, and recall is tested after a delay of 0–30 seconds, during which rehearsal is prevented by a counting task. Forgetting is dramatic and typically reaches asymptote within 15–20 seconds. The very first sequence tested, however, does not show this marked forgetting, a fact which has led to an interpretation of forgetting in terms of proactive interference (Keppel and Underwood, 1962), although a more detailed analysis of the phenomenon suggests that a classical interference-theory interpretation is not satisfactory (e.g. Conrad, 1967; Peterson and Gentile, 1965; Turvey, Brick and Osborne, 1970). Furthermore, when competition from prior sequences is avoided by testing each subject only once, forgetting reaches a maximum within the first 5 seconds, after which performance is relatively stable (Baddeley and Scott, 1971). This suggests that the Brown–Peterson task may reflect only a small PM component which affects performance only over the first 5 seconds. It seems likely that the dramatic forgetting shown in the typical multi-trial situation reflects mainly the competition between SM traces.

*The serial probe technique*

This task has the advantage of allowing a clear separation of PM and SM effects, and it was used by Waugh and Norman (1965) specifically to investigate the nature of forgetting in PM. Subjects were presented with sequences of 16 digits at the rate of 1 or 4 digits per second. One of the 16 digits was then repeated (the probe), and the subject's task was to respond with the digit which had followed the probe. Their results are shown in Figure 2, which shows the probability of recalling an item as a function of number of items following it for the two rates of presentation. A simple trace-decay theory would predict much better retention of the rapidly presented digits, since less time will have elapsed between presentation and test. Elapsed time is however clearly less important than number of subsequent items in determining recall probability, and Waugh and Norman interpret their result in terms of a displacement model in which new items tend to displace old items in a limited-capacity PM store. However, their result does not exclude the possibility of trace decay. Shallice (1967) has pointed out that the rapidly presented digits show less marked forgetting than those presented slowly, as trace-decay theory would predict (i.e. the 4 digit per second slope in Figure 2 is less steep than the 1 per second slope). Furthermore the slower rate of presentation seems likely to lead to a higher degree of initial learning, which in turn might be expected to reduce the rate of forgetting. However, it does seem to be the case that PM has a limited capacity, and

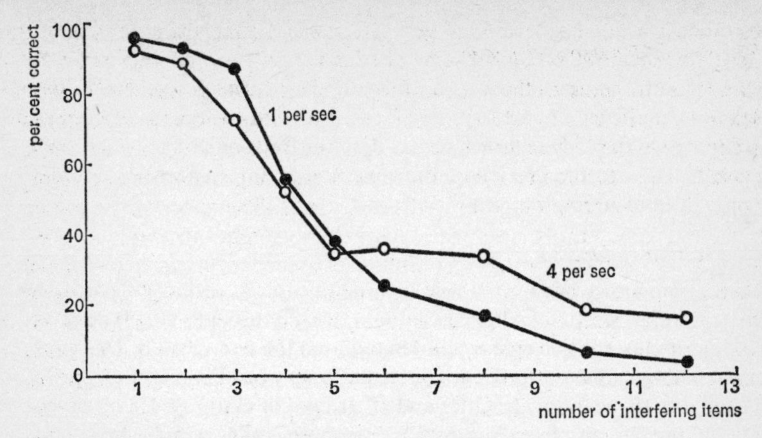


**Figure 2 Short-term memory for digits as a function of rate and number of interpolated digits: based on the serial probe technique (from Waugh and Norman 1965)**

that when its capacity is exceeded, the main cause of forgetting is probably the displacement of earlier items by later ones.

*The PM component in free recall*

Somewhat surprisingly there has been little detailed study of the factors determining the loss of the recency effect in free recall, with the exception of an extensive study by Glanzer, Gianutsos and Dubin (1969). They tested a range of hypotheses including trace decay, interference due both to the similarity of the task interpolated between presentation and to its information-processing demands, and finally a simple displacement hypothesis. Displacement proved to be the major factor, with five items being enough to eliminate the recency effect. There was however a small effect of temporal delay, suggesting the possibility of a decay component.

*Conclusion*

There is relatively little good data on what causes forgetting in PM. It is clear however that the displacement of old items by new ones is a major factor, as one might expect in a system that has limited storage capacity. There is also *some* evidence for trace decay, although the effects shown so far tend to be small and easily obscured by other factors.

**How do we remember?**

The S–R associationist approach underlying interference theory regards learning as the formation of a bond or association between a stimulus and response. Given the appropriate stimulus, the response will be evoked, unless other learning has interfered with the association, causing forgetting. In such a system the process of remembering is assumed, and interest tends to focus on forgetting rather than on recall. This is much less true of the organizational view of memory, which declined with the eclipse of Gestalt psychology in the 1940s, but which has developed strongly in the latter half of the 1960s with the growth of the cognitive or information-processing approach to memory.

*Organization and memory*

The first modern work on the role of organization in memory developed within the classical associationist tradition, with Bousfield's (1953) demonstration of clustering in free recall. He required the free recall of lists containing sub-groups of words; for instance, a 40-word list might comprise 10 animals, 10 weapons, 10 cities and 10 articles of clothing. He observed that although items from the 4 categories were randomized when presented, subjects tended to recall them in clusters of items from the same category. Thus, given the recall of one animal, the next item to be recalled was likely to be another animal. In a similar vein, Jenkins and Russell (1952) showed that pairs of words that are highly associated (e.g. bread–butter, table–chair) tend to be recalled as a pair, even though they are separated during the learning presentation. Both of these results imply some degree of organization by the subject, but since they both take advantage of pre-existing associations, these results are quite consistent with a passive associationist view of learning.

A series of subsequent experiments by Tulving, however, suggests that the subject is playing a much more active role. Tulving (1962) studied the free-recall learning of lists of randomly selected words. He observed that subjects consistently tended to recall groups of words in the same order, despite the fact that the order of presentation was changed on each trial. He attributed this consistency to the subject's imposing his own organization on the list, and devised an index of degree of overlap in recall-order from one trial to the next. This index, which Tulving called subjective organization (SO), tended to increase with successive trials and was correlated with amount recalled. In a subsequent study, Tulving (1966) presented further evidence that organization rather than rote repetition was necessary for learning. His first experiment involved the free-recall learning of a list of 22 nouns. Half the subjects had previously read through the list 6 times, while control subjects had 6 readings of a completely unrelated list. There was no difference in the rate at which the two groups learned the critical list, indicating that mere repetition does not lead to learning, at least with common words. A second experiment showed that the prior formation of inappropriate subjective clusters may impede learning. Tulving required his subjects to learn a list of 18 unrelated words. All subjects had previously learned a list of 9 words; for half the subjects they were 9 of the subsequent list, whereas control subjects learned 9 irrelevant words. Performance on learning the 18-word list is shown in Figure 3. It is clear that despite an initial advantage,

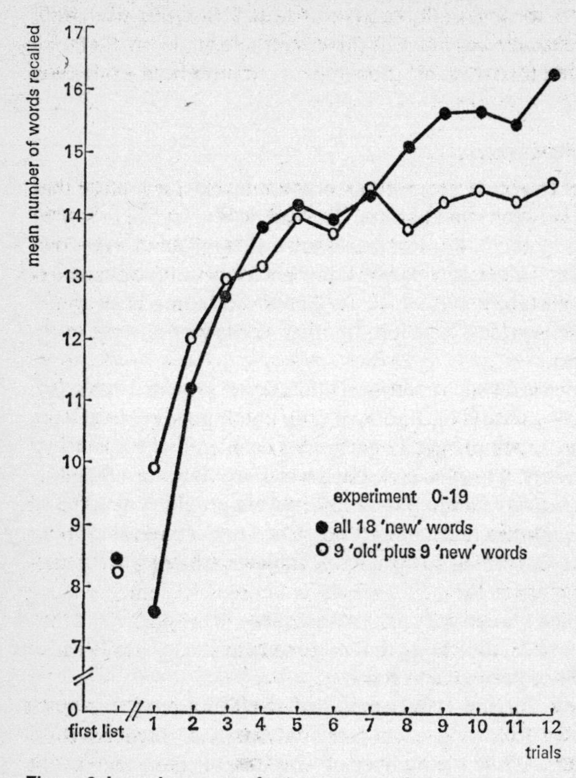


Figure 3 Learning curves for two groups of subjects on a whole list of 18 words. One group (open circles) had learned half of the whole list before learning the whole list; the other group (filled circles) had learned an irrelevant list (from Tulving, 1966)

subjects who have already learned half the list are subsequently handicapped, presumably because the subjective units that were most appropriate for learning the initial 9-word list were not optimal for learning the later list.

A third approach to the role of organization in memory is that taken by Mandler, who has shown that instructions to organize lead to learning, even though the subject is not attempting to remember the material. For example, in one experiment, Mandler (1967) gave his subjects a pack of 52 cards, on each of which was printed a word. Half the subjects were instructed to sort the cards into from 2 to 7 categories, as they deemed appropriate. The other half were simply told to place the cards one after the other in 7 columns. Half of each group was told to try to remember the words, while the other half was not. After 5 sorting trials, recall was tested. Subjects who were told only to organize recalled as much as those instructed to learn. So far as this study is concerned then, organization appears to have been equivalent to learning.

### *How does organization aid recall?*

*The role of retrieval.* In recent years it has become increasingly clear that we must distinguish between what has been learned, and what can in fact be recalled at any given moment. For instance, we are all familiar with the frustrating inability to recall a name, which we know perfectly well, could recognize with complete certainty and which we know will 'come back to us' eventually, often when we least expect it. In other words we know the name but can not retrieve it.

Experimental evidence for such a retrieval limitation is provided by a study by Tulving and Pearlstone (1966). In one of their conditions, subjects were read a list of 48 words, comprising 12 categories each containing 4 words (e.g. 4 animals, 4 flowers, 4 metals, etc). Each word-group was preceded by its category name. During recall half the subjects were provided with the 12 category names as recall cues, and half were not. Cued subjects recalled about 30 words compared to a score of 20 for uncued subjects, who recalled just as many words per category as the cued subjects, but completely omitted some of the categories. When the category names were subsequently provided they increased their score to 28, indicating that there were at least 8 words which they knew, but had not been able to retrieve.

In a further study Tulving (1967) modified the traditional free-recall learning technique by following each presentation of a word by three successive recall trials. While the number of words recalled on each of the three trials remained fairly constant, the specific items recalled changed from trial to trial, with only about 50 per cent of the items recalled occurring on all three trials. It seems clear that on any trial the subject was recalling only part of what he knew; it seems likely that his recall score was in some way limited by his retrieval capacity rather than by the number of words he had learned. It may be that organization is one way of combating this problem.

Mandler (1967) has suggested on the basis of his study of categorization and memory that the retrieval system has difficulty in handling more than 5 items at a time, possibly due to the limitations of STM (c.f. Miller, 1956). This being so, recall will be optimal when the material can be organized hierarchically in such a way that the number of alternatives at no point exceeds 5. A study by Bower, Clark, Lesgold and Winzenz (1969) is consistent with such a view. They required their subjects to learn a list of 112 words organized into 4 hierarchies, one of which is shown in Table 2. In the experimental group the subjects were presented with the words displayed

Table 2 **The minerals conceptual hierarchy used by Bower *et al*. (1969)**

| Minerals | | | | |
|---|---|---|---|---|
| | Metals | | Stones | |
| Rare | Common | Alloys | Precious | Masonry |
| Platinum | Aluminium | Bronze | Sapphire | Limestone |
| Silver | Copper | Steel | Emerald | Granite |
| Gold | Lead | Brass | Diamond | Marble |
| | Iron | | Ruby | Slate |

hierarchically, while for the control group the ordering of the words was random. After a single presentation the hierarchical group recalled 73 of the 112 words, compared with a score of 21 for the random group. It is interesting in connection with Mandler's hypothesis to note that none of the categories or sub-categories exceeded 5 alternatives.

One form of organization which has been studied extensively in recent years is that based on visual imagery. Paivio (1969) has shown rated 'concreteness' (the ease with which a word evokes a sensory image) is probably the most powerful predictor of the ease with which the word will be learned. There has also been a growth of interest in mnemonic systems, many of which are based on visual imagery. Much of the initial experimentation was simply concerned to see if the mnemonics really worked (they usually did), and only recently has a systematic attempt been made to explore such systems and relate them to existing knowledge (e.g. Bower, 1970).

In general, it seems likely that one of the main limitations on human memory is set by the difficulty of locating and retrieving information that has in fact been stored. Organization probably reduces this problem by allowing a systematic search strategy. It seems unlikely, however, that its effects are limited to the retrieval stage. While the effects of organization may occasionally disappear when retrieval is facilitated by using a recognition task, this is by no means always the case, and it seems likely, as Mandler (1972) has argued, that organization influences both the storage and retrieval of information.

### *Reaction time and memory*

All the work we have discussed so far has studied memory using a percentage correct, or error score. This means that memory is always studied at the point of breakdown, since only if errors are made do we have any information. However, most of the remembering we do in everyday life is probably error-free, whether it is remembering our address or indeed retrieving words from our linguistic vocabulary as we talk. Any approach to memory which ignores such error-free recall is at best incomplete, and may indeed be misleading.

How can one study error-free memory? In an ingenious series of experiments Sternberg (1966) has recently shown that reaction time (RT) measures can be used to test highly specific models of error-free memory. His first experiment was concerned with short-term recognition memory for digits. Subjects saw a sequence of from 1 to 6 digits, followed after a 2-second pause by a probe digit. The subject's task was to decide whether or not the probe digit had been in the presented sequence, and pull a 'yes' or 'no' lever accordingly. The results of this study are shown in Figure 4.

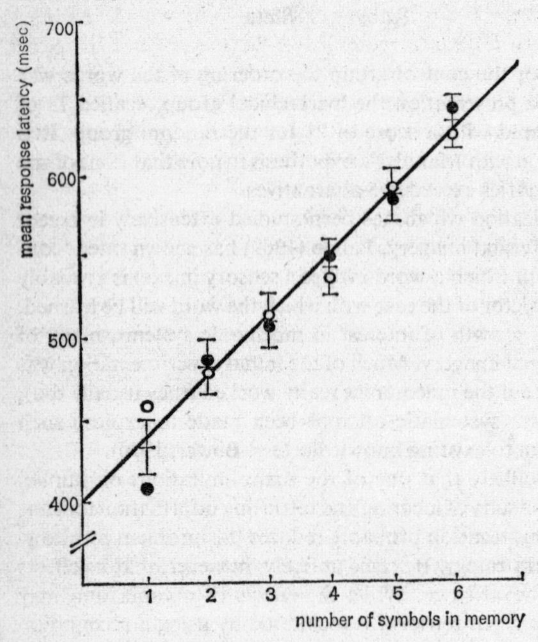


Figure 4 Relation between response latency and the number of symbols in memory for positive (filled circles) and negative responses (open circles) (based on Sternberg, 1966)

Note the linear relationship between number of digits being retained and RT, and that 'yes' and 'no' responses give the same slope. Sternberg interprets his results in terms of what he calls the high-speed exhaustive-scanning hypothesis. This assumes that the list of items in memory is scanned serially, with the probe being compared with each item in the list one after the other. The most obvious decision rule would be for the comparison to stop as soon as a match is detected between the probe and a remembered item. The subject would rarely have to scan the whole set before detecting a match, and on average would have to scan only half the items. In the case where no match occurred, however, he would always have to scan all the items. Hence one would expect the increase in RT with size of memory set to be roughly twice as steep for 'no' responses as for 'yes' responses. Since the two slopes are equal, this version of the model is clearly incorrect. Sternberg suggests that all items are in fact scanned in both 'yes' and 'no' conditions, and he suggests that this would be reasonable if the time taken to scan an item is much less than that taken to decide whether or not a match has occurred. Since the observed rate of scanning is very rapid indeed (38 msec per item), this is not an implausible suggestion. According to Sternberg then, what happens is as follows: the sequence of digits is entered into a short-term store. When the probe digit is presented, a high-speed scanning mechanism compares the probe with each of the digits in STM in turn. If a match occurs it is registered in the comparator. When the scan is complete, the comparator is tested to see if a hit did or did not occur, and the appropriate 'yes' or 'no' response is made.

Sternberg goes on to show that an almost identical relationship holds between size of remembered set and RT in an LTM situation in which the set of digits to be recognized remains the same throughout the session (e.g. a subject might be told to respond 'yes' to digits 2, 6, 7 and 9, and 'no' to all others, for the duration of that session). Sternberg's model has been applied successfully across a wide range of materials, and a number of ingenious modifications of the original paradigm have been studied (see Sternberg, 1969, for an excellent review). However, a number of phenomena have recently been reported which do not fit easily into the model. The exhaustive-scanning hypothesis assumes that information about individual items within the sequence is not preserved; the comparator merely records whether or not one or more of the items matched the probe. There is, however, growing evidence that information about individual items *is* retained. Thus a number of experimenters have found serial position effects, with later items evoking faster responses, particularly when the delay between presentation and test is reduced (Clifton and Birenbaum, 1970). Baddeley and Ecob (1970) observed that repeated digits (e.g. 7 in 7973) evoked faster RTs than non-repeats from equivalent sequences, a result which would not be predicted on an exhaustive-scanning hypothesis; and Krueger (1970) has shown with the LTM procedure that if certain digits are tested more often than others, they tend to evoke faster RTs. It is, furthermore, not easy to see what function a high-speed exhaustive-scan could have outside the rather specialized situation devised by Sternberg, in which the subject is making yes/no judgements about a small group of items he is holding in memory. Such a mechanism is clearly not, for instance, used in deciding whether or not a sequence of letters is an English word, since an exhaustive search of one's vocabulary at the 38-msec-per-item rate repeatedly observed by Sternberg would take somewhere in the region of half an hour, not 700 msec as is in fact the case (Meyer and Ellis, 1970).

The importance of Sternberg's work, however, is independent of whether high-speed exhaustive scanning in fact occurs. It lies in his demonstration that RT measures can be used to devise and test hypotheses about error-free memory, thereby extending enormously the potential range of experimental work on human memory. The work of Posner on visual memory is another good example of the value of RT measures in the study of memory (see the chapter by Coltheart for a more detailed review). One of the most promising applications of RT techniques, however, is in the rapidly developing field of semantic memory.

*Semantic memory*

As we concluded from the first section of the chapter, there appears to be a very close relationship between semantic coding and LTM, and there is currently a great deal of interest in attempting to understand semantic memory. The various groups working on semantic memory all tend to a greater or lesser degree to be influenced by computer science and linguistics, and most use RTs as their main source of experimental data. Most of the attempts to model semantic memory are at an early stage of development, and we shall therefore limit ourselves to one model, that of Quillian (1969), which has already generated a good deal of experimental work (see Collins and Quillian, 1972).

This work stems from a computer model, the Teachable Language Comprehender (Quillian, 1969), which is a program for understanding written text by relating it to memory structures in a semantic network. The initial purpose of the model was to process text, not to simulate human behaviour, although the subsequent experiments were concerned with the extent to which the model could in fact be applied to human memory. The type of semantic network occurring in the model is illustrated by Figure 5, which comprises three levels of a hierarchy. At each level, words are connected by pointers to both a more general level (e.g. bird to animal), and to a more specific level (e.g. bird to canary). With each such word are stored its properties (e.g. with canary is stored 'can sing' and 'is yellow'). However, properties that are true of all birds (or nearly all) are stored together with the concept 'bird'. This uses much less storage space than would be needed if such properties were stored separately with each of the many instances of the concept 'bird'. In the case of exceptions, such as ostrich, the information that it cannot fly is stored with the instance.

The model 'comprehends' a sentence by finding a grammatically per-

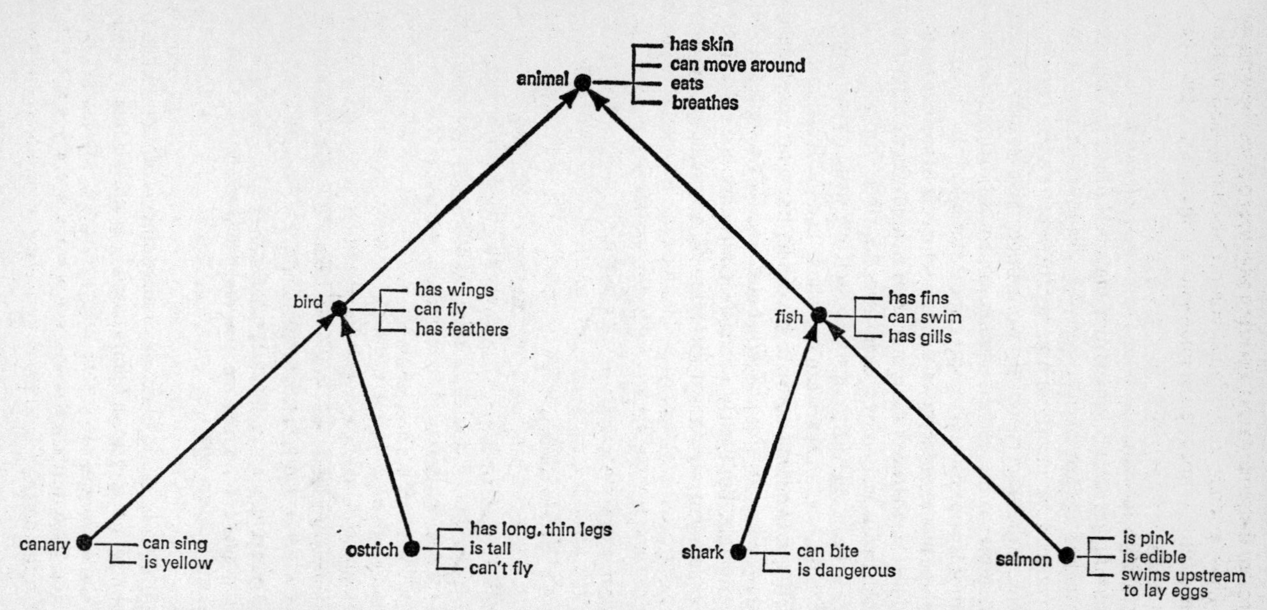


Figure 5 Illustration of the hypothetical memory structure for a three-level hierarchy in Quillian's semantic memory model (from Collins and Quillian, 1972)

missible path through the semantic network in a way that relates the words in the sentence. Thus 'a canary has skin' is 'comprehended' by finding the path: a canary is a bird, a bird is an animal, and an animal has skin (see Figure 5).

In attempting to apply the model to human memory, Collins and Quillian (1972) assume that it takes time to move from one level of the hierarchy to another, and since the steps are taken successively, they predict that comprehension time will increase linearly with number of steps. It is also assumed to take time to retrieve the properties of any word, but in this case the various properties are assumed to be scanned simultaneously, so that number of properties per word is not assumed to be a critical variable.

In order to test the model, subjects were shown sentences of various types and required to judge them true or false, and press an appropriate button as quickly as possible. In one such study the sentences described properties that could be assumed to be stored with the instance itself (e.g. a canary can sing), or at one level above (e.g. a canary can fly: where 'can fly' is assumed to be stored with *bird*), or two levels above (e.g. a canary has skin: where 'has skin' is assumed to be stored with *animal*). False sentences were selected so as to be reasonable, but clearly wrong (e.g. a canary has gills). The results of this experiment are shown in Figure 6. As predicted by the

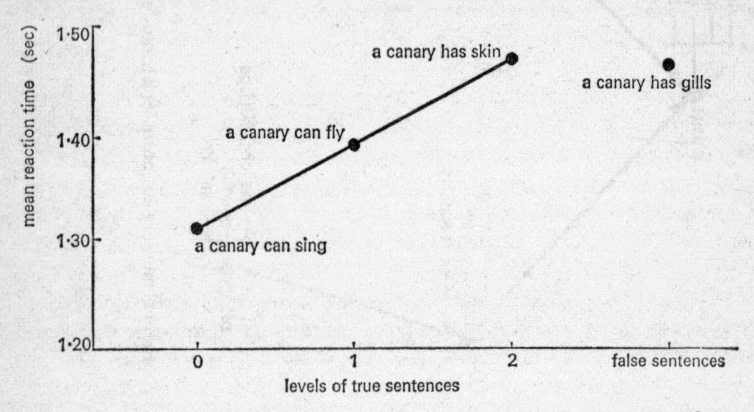


Figure 6 Average time to process a sentence as a function of the number of hierarchical levels involved in Quillian's model of semantic memory (based on Collins and Quillian, 1972)

model, decision time increases linearly with number of steps in the hierarchy that must be traversed. Unfortunately it proves much more difficult to explain how subjects decide that a sentence is false, and the initial assumptions have to undergo considerable modification in order to cover this (see Collins and Quillian, 1972).

**Summary**

In his stimulating book *The Structure of Scientific Revolutions* (1962), Kuhn describes what he terms 'paradigm changes', situations in which a science rejects the established view of the world in favour of a new and different basic viewpoint. Something approaching this appears to have happened in the study of human memory. The S–R view of memory, which for decades dominated American psychology, saw human memory basically in terms of the 1930s view of Pavlovian conditioning. Such assumptions are no longer held, even by those who continue to use an S–R associationist language. The electronic computer, or more specifically the computer program, has replaced conditioning as the basic paradigm. It is enormously more flexible than the conditioning analogue, and herein lies both its strength and its weakness. It has allowed the study of memory to break out of the rigid and stultifying confines of traditional verbal learning, but its very flexibility means that we can generate far more theoretical models than we are at present capable of testing. The value of the information-processing approach to memory must ultimately depend on its capacity for revealing new phenomena and producing experimentally testable theories.

**Further reading**

Given the diversity of recent views on memory, plunging directly into the literature is liable to prove somewhat confusing. A better strategy is probably to begin with a single viewpoint and then move on to review papers. The most widely held current model of human memory is probably that proposed in the first section of Atkinson and Shiffrin (1968), together with the subsequent application of this model to LTM (Shiffrin and Atkinson, 1969).

The recent issue of the *British Medical Bulletin* devoted to cognitive psychology contains several relevant reviews, including papers on primary memory (Craik, 1971), amnesia (Warrington, 1971) and the relationship between LTM and STM (Baddeley and Patterson, 1971). A recent paper by Martin (1971) provides an excellent discussion of both the origins of interference theory and some of its current problems. It should be read in conjunction with the penetrating review paper by Postman (1969).

Work on organization and memory is covered in Kintsch's book *Learning, Memory and Conceptual Processes* (1970). For anyone already familiar with the basic phenomena, Postman's (1972) scholarly discussion of organization and memory from an associationist viewpoint is recommended.

In the area of RT and memory by far the best account is Sternberg's (1969) paper summarizing his own work. Landauer and Freedman (1968) present the first attempt to apply Sternberg's techniques to retrieval from semantic memory, and as such provide an alternative to the Collins and Quillian (1972) approach. For other interpretations of Collins and Quillian's results see Schaeffer and Wallace (1970) and Wilkins (1971). Even more ambitious than Quillian's model is that described by Rumelhart, Lindsay and Norman (1972), which draws on recent developments in semantics (e.g. the case grammar of Fillmore, 1968) and in artificial intelligence (e.g. Winograd's (1971) program for communicating with a computer in normal English), and attempts to simulate such complex features of human semantic memory as remembering prose, scenes and actions.

## References

ATKINSON, R. C., and SHIFFRIN, R. M. (1968), 'Human memory: a proposed system and its control processes', in K. W. Spence and J. T. Spence (eds.), *The Psychology of Learning and Motivation*, vol. 2, Academic Press, pp. 89–105.

BADDELEY, A. D. (1966a), 'Short-term memory for word sequences as a function of acoustic, semantic and formal similarity', *Quarterly Journal of Experimental Psychology*, vol. 18, pp. 362–6.

BADDELEY, A. D. (1966b), 'The influence of acoustic and semantic similarity on long-term memory for word sequences', *Quarterly Journal of Experimental Psychology*, vol. 18, pp. 302–9.

BADDELEY, A. D., and ECOB, J. R. (1970), 'Reaction time and short-term memory: a trace-strength alternative to the high-speed exhaustive-scanning hypothesis', University of California, San Diego, *Center for Human Information Processing Report No. 13*.

BADDELEY, A. D., and PATTERSON, K. (1971), 'The relationship between long-term and short-term memory', *British Medical Bulletin*, vol. 27, pp. 237–42.

BADDELEY, A. D., and SCOTT, D. (1971), 'Short-term forgetting in the absence of proactive interference', *Quarterly Journal of Experimental Psychology*, vol. 23, pp. 275–83.

BADDELEY, A. D., SCOTT, D., DRYNAN, R., and SMITH, J. C. (1969), 'Short-term memory and the limited capacity hypothesis', *British Journal of Psychology*, vol. 60, pp. 51–5.

BADDELEY, A. D., and WARRINGTON, E. K. (1970), 'Amnesia and the distinction between long- and short-term memory', *Journal of Verbal Learning and Verbal Behavior*, vol. 9, pp. 176–89.

BOUSFIELD, W. A. (1953), 'The occurrence of clustering in the recall of randomly arranged associates', *Journal of General Psychology*, vol. 49, pp. 229–40.

BOWER, G. H. (1970), 'Analysis of a mnemonic device', *American Scientist*, vol. 58, pp. 496–510.

BOWER, G. H., CLARK, M. C., LESGOLD, A. M., and WINZENZ, D. (1969), 'Hierarchical retrieval schemes in recall of categorized word lists', *Journal of Verbal Learning and Verbal Behavior*, vol. 8, pp. 323–43.

BROADBENT, D. E. (1958), *Perception and Communication*, Pergamon.

CLIFTON, C., and BIRENBAUM, S. (1970), 'The effects of serial position and delay of probe in a memory-scan task', *Journal of Experimental Psychology*, vol. 86, pp. 69–76.

COLLINS, A. M., and QUILLIAN, M. R. (1972), 'Experiments on semantic memory and language comprehension', in L. W. Gregg (ed.), *Cognition in Learning and Memory*, Wiley.

CONRAD, R. (1964), 'Acoustic confusions in immediate memory', *British Journal of Psychology*, vol. 55, pp. 75–84.

CONRAD, R. (1967), 'Interference or decay over short retention intervals?', *Journal of Verbal Learning and Verbal Behavior*, vol. 6, pp. 49–54.

CRAIK, F. I. M. (1971), 'Primary memory', *British Medical Bulletin*, vol. 27, pp. 232–6.

DA POLITO, F. J. (1966), 'Proactive effects with independent retrieval of competing responses', unpublished doctoral dissertation, Indiana University.

FILLMORE, C. J. (1968), 'The case for case', in E. Bach and R. T. Harms (eds.), *Universals in Linguistic Theory*, Holt, Rinehart & Winston.

GLANZER, M., and CUNITZ, A. R. (1966), 'Two storage mechanisms in free recall', *Journal of Verbal Learning and Verbal Behavior*, vol. 5, pp. 351–60.

GLANZER, M., GIANUTSOS, R., and DUBIN, S. (1969), 'The removal of items from short-term storage', *Journal of Verbal Learning and Verbal Behavior*, vol. 8, pp. 435–7.

GREENO, J. G. (1969), 'A cognitive interpretation of negative transfer and forgetting of paired-associates', *Human Performance Center Memorandum Report No. 9*, University of Michigan.

HEBB, D. O. (1949), *The Organization of Behavior*, Wiley.

JENKINS, J. J., and RUSSELL, W. A. (1952), 'Associative clustering during recall', *Journal of Abnormal and Social Psychology*, vol. 47, pp. 818–21.

KEPPEL, G. (1968), 'Retroactive and proactive inhibition', in T. R. Dixon and D. L. Horton (eds.), *Verbal Behavior and General Behavior Theory*, Prentice-Hall.

KEPPEL, G., and UNDERWOOD, B. J. (1962), 'Proactive inhibition in short-term retention of single items', *Journal of Verbal Learning and Verbal Behavior*, vol. 1, pp. 153–61.

KINTSCH, W. (1970), *Learning, Memory and Conceptual Processes*, Wiley.

KINTSCH, W., and BUSCHKE, H. (1969), 'Homophones and synonyms in short-term memory', *Journal of Experimental Psychology*, vol. 80, pp. 403–7.

KRUEGER, L. E. (1970), 'Effect of stimulus probability on two-choice reaction time', *Journal of Experimental Psychology*, vol. 84, pp. 377–9.

KUHN, T. S. (1962), *The Structure of Scientific Revolutions*, University of Chicago Press.

LANDAUER, T. K., and FREEDMAN, J. L. (1968), 'Information retrieval from long-term memory', *Journal of Verbal Learning and Verbal Behavior*, vol. 7, pp. 291–5.

MANDLER, G. (1967), 'Organization and memory', in K. W. Spence and J. T. Spence (eds.), *The Psychology of Learning and Motivation*, vol. 1, Academic Press.

MANDLER, G. (1972), 'Organization and recognition', in E. Tulving and W. Donaldson (eds.), *Organization and Memory*, Academic Press.

MARTIN, E. (1971), 'Verbal learning theory and independent retrieval phenomena', *Psychological Review*, vol. 78, pp. 314–32.

MELTON, A. W. (1963), 'Implications of short-term memory for a general theory of memory', *Journal of Verbal Learning and Verbal Behavior*, vol. 2, pp. 1–21.

MEYER, D. E., and ELLIS, G. B. (1970), 'Parallel processes in word recognition', paper presented at the tenth annual meeting of the Psychonomic Society, San Antonio, Texas.

MILLER, G. A. (1956), 'The magical number seven plus or minus two: some limits on our capacity for processing information', *Psychological Review*, vol. 63, pp. 81–97.

PAIVIO, A. (1969), 'Mental imagery in associative learning and memory', *Psychological Review*, vol. 76, pp. 241–63.

PETERSON, L. R. (1966), 'Short-term verbal memory and learning', *Psychological Review*, vol. 73, pp. 193–207.

PETERSON, L. R., and GENTILE, A. (1965), 'Proactive interference as a function of time between tests', *Journal of Experimental Psychology*, vol. 70, pp. 473–8.

POSTMAN, L. (1969), 'Mechanisms of interference in forgetting', in G. A. Talland and N. C. Waugh (eds.), *The Pathology of Memory*, Academic Press.

POSTMAN, L. (1972), 'A pragmatic view of organization theory', in E. Tulving and W. Donaldson (eds.), *Organization and Memory*, Academic Press.

QUILLIAN, M. R. (1969), 'The teachable language comprehender: a simulation program and theory of language', *Communications of the Association for Computing Machinery*, vol. 12, pp. 459–76.

RAYMOND, B. (1969), 'Short-term storage and long-term storage in free recall', *Journal of Verbal Learning and Verbal Behavior*, vol. 8, pp. 567–74.

RUMELHART, D. E., LINDSAY, P. H., and NORMAN, D. A. (1972), 'A process model for long-term memory', in E. Tulving and W. Donaldson (eds.), *Organization and Memory*, Academic Press.

SACHS, J. S. (1967), 'Recognition memory for syntactic and semantic aspects of connected discourse', *Perception and Psychophysics*, vol. 2, pp. 437–42.

SCHAEFFER, B., and WALLACE, R. (1970), 'The comparison of word meanings', *Journal of Experimental Psychology*, vol. 86, pp. 144–52.

SHALLICE, T. (1967), paper presented at the NATO Advanced Study Institute on Short-Term Memory, Cambridge.

SHALLICE, T., and WARRINGTON, E. K. (1970), 'Independent functioning of verbal memory stores: a neuropsychological study', *Quarterly Journal of Experimental Psychology*, vol. 22, pp. 261–73.

SHIFFRIN, R. M., and ATKINSON, R. C. (1969), 'Storage and retrieval in long-term memory', *Psychological Review*, vol. 76, pp. 179–93.

STERNBERG, S. (1966), 'High-speed scanning in human memory', *Science*, vol. 153, pp. 652–4.

STERNBERG, S. (1969), 'Memory scanning: mental processes revealed by reaction-time experiments', *American Scientist*, vol. 57, pp. 421–57.

TULVING, E. (1962), 'Subjective organization in free recall of unrelated words', *Psychological Review*, vol. 69, pp 344–54.

TULVING, E. (1966), 'Subjective organization and effects of repetition in multi-trial free-recall learning', *Journal of Verbal Learning and Verbal Behavior*, vol. 5, pp. 193–7.

TULVING, E. (1967), 'The effects of presentation and recall of material in free-recall learning', *Journal of Verbal Learning and Verbal Behavior*, vol. 6, pp. 175–84.

TULVING, E., and PEARLSTONE, Z. (1966), 'Availability versus accessibility of information in memory for words', *Journal of Verbal Learning and Verbal Behavior*, vol. 5, pp. 381–91.

TURVEY, M. T., BRICK, P., and OSBORNE, J. (1970), 'Proactive interference in short-term memory as a function of prior-item retention interval', *Quarterly Journal of Experimental Psychology*, vol. 22, pp. 142–7.

UNDERWOOD, B. J., and POSTMAN, L. (1960), 'Extra-experimental sources of interference in forgetting', *Psychological Review*, vol. 67, pp. 73–95.

WARRINGTON, E. K. (1971), 'Neuropsychological studies of memory', *British Medical Bulletin*, vol. 27, pp. 243–7.

WAUGH, N. C., and NORMAN, D. A. (1965), 'Primary memory', *Psychological Review*, vol. 72, pp. 89–104.

WILKINS, A. J. (1971), 'Categorization time and category size', *Journal of Verbal Learning and Verbal Behavior*, vol. 10, pp. 382–5.

WINOGRAD, T. (1971), 'Procedures as a representation for data in a computer program for understanding natural language', *Artificial Intelligence Laboratory Technical Report MAC TR-84*, Massachusetts Institute of Technology.

# 3 Visual Information-Processing
Max Coltheart

### Introduction

The physicist Edward Teller was once asked what he most liked doing. His reply was: 'Making clear to others what they find obscure, and obscuring what they find clear.' This chapter is concerned with something which most people would find clear, namely, the explanation of how a person performs the simple task of looking at a brief display of letters or numbers and writing down what he has just seen. Obviously, one might say, the person simply sees the items in the display, and then remembers them one by one as he is writing them down. As soon as we try to learn more about what is meant by 'sees' and 'remembers' here, however, the kinds of obscurities to which Teller was referring emerge from this apparently simple situation. What seems clear in psychology can be just as obscure as what seems clear in physics.

There are several reasons for wishing to know more about how people perform this simple task. Perhaps the most obvious reason is that there is a close resemblance between this task and what we do when we read. As we read the eye jumps from place to place on the page. At each place it remains stationary for a few tenths of a second, and it is during this stationary period (or 'fixation') that information is taken in from the printed page. Thus, if we flash a display of letters or numbers for a few tenths of a second, we are presenting information to the eye in the same way as it is presented during reading; so experiments involving such brief visual displays are likely to provide basic information about the elements of the process of reading. Quite apart from this, a deep enough understanding of how people remember briefly presented visual displays will be required as an integral part of a general understanding of human memory.

What psychologists seek to learn in particular from these experiments is how the temporal gap between the stimulus (the brief visual display) and the response (the writing down of the contents of the display) is bridged. It seems to be the case that the operation of several distinct cognitive systems is required if this gap is to be bridged. The task of the psychologist is to tease apart the different cognitive processes involved so as to discover more about their properties.

When this kind of experiment was first carried out, about a century ago, a basic result was immediately obtained: if a subject is presented with a visual display of letters or numbers for a brief period (up to half a second or so) and is asked to report what items were in the display, he can usually report at most four or five of these items. This finding was originally explained by saying that the subject cannot 'apprehend' (i.e. perceive) more than four or five items in a single act of apprehension.

This kind of explanation was accepted for many years, but it was eventually refuted by Sperling (1960), who showed that subjects can in fact perceive virtually all the items in displays of as many as eighteen items. Consequently some other explanation was needed for the fact that subjects can only report four or five items from such displays. No satisfactory explanation has yet emerged, as we shall see. However, in attempting to find such an explanation, Sperling made a number of discoveries which are vital to an understanding of this situation. In particular, he discovered that a visual representation of a brief visual display is still available to a subject after the display has been turned off. This post-exposural visual representation consists of an accurate but rapidly fading visual memory of the display. This form of memory was subsequently named 'iconic memory' by Neisser (1967).

**Iconic memory**

*Sperling's research*

Sperling (1960) introduced a critical modification of the usual visual-display experiment. His subjects were presented with displays consisting of three rows of four letters, but were not asked to report all the letters; instead, they were asked to report only one row. Which row they should report was indicated by a tone presented immediately after the offset of the display; a high tone asked for the top row, a medium tone for the middle row, and a low tone for the bottom row. Subjects could never tell until after the display had terminated which row they would have to report. Nevertheless, they could report virtually all the items in the indicated row. This showed conclusively that they must have perceived virtually all of the twelve items in the display.

Sperling next investigated what would happen if the tone were presented, not immediately after the display, but at various delays after display offset. The number of items reported from the row decreased as the tone delay increased, up to a delay of half a second. At that point, subjects reported no more items from the cued row than they would have if they simply reported four or five items from anywhere in the display, regardless of row. Performances was not further impaired by delaying the tone more than half a second.

Sperling suggested that these results occurred because, after the offset of

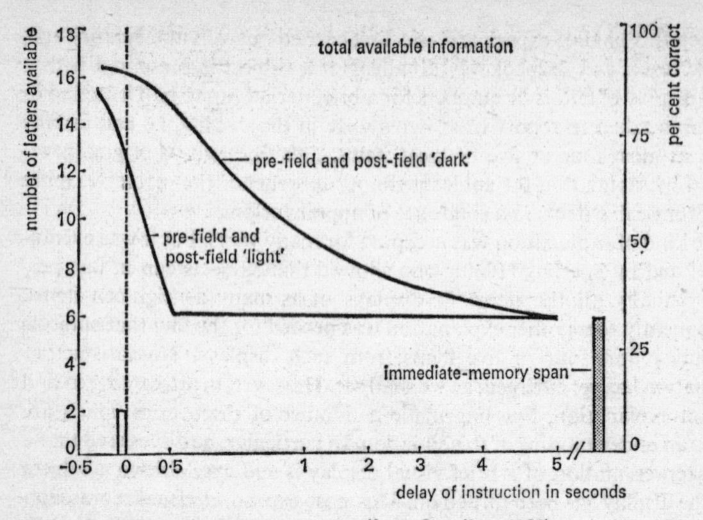


**Figure 1** The decay of iconic memory (from Sperling, 1963)

the visual display, the contents of the display are represented in a visual-memory store ('iconic memory') which decays rather rapidly. If items are to be retained they must, before they decay away, be processed so as to be stored in some different and more stable form. Subjects can choose which items in the display they will process; for example, they can choose to process the items in a particular row. The longer they wait after display offset before beginning to process items stored in iconic memory, the more these items will have decayed before processing begins. Thus performance will deteriorate as cue delay increases.

It is clear that the spatial location of items must be represented in iconic memory; otherwise subjects could not selectively process items in iconic memory according to their particular spatial location. Subsequent experiments have shown that this selective processing can also be done on the basis of colour, size or shape (Clark, 1969; Turvey and Kravetz, 1970; von Wright, 1968, 1970). However, if a display consisting of a mixture of letters and digits is presented, and a post-exposure tone asks for items of one kind (for example, a high tone asks for report of the letters whereas a low tone asks for report of the digits), the number of letters reported when the high tone is sounded is no greater than the number of letters reported when the subject is simply asked to report as many items from the display as he can, regardless of whether they are letters or digits (Sperling, 1960; von Wright, 1968, 1970). Thus the subject cannot selectively process items in iconic memory according to whether they are letters or digits. This is because he cannot tell whether an item is a letter or a digit *until* it is processed, and so whether an item is a letter or a digit cannot determine whether it will be processed or not. On the other hand, simple physical characteristics such as the spatial position, size, shape or colour of an item can be discriminated without the item having been identified, and so whether an item will be identified can be controlled by the physical characteristics it possesses.

In this situation, a question which remains unanswered is this: what does the subject do while waiting for the cue to arrive? Sperling seemed to assume that he did nothing, and this is supported by an observation by von Wright (1968), who accidentally omitted the post-cue in this kind of experiment. On trials when this happened, subjects could not report any items from the visual display. Presumably they were waiting until the cue occurred before processing the display, and when no cue occurred the display decayed away without any items having been processed.

On the other hand, Sperling's subjects could not have been behaving like this; otherwise, when the cue delay was greater than the duration of iconic memory, they would not have reported anything. Instead, they were always able to report about four items; what declined as cue delay increased was the proportion of these items which belonged to the cued row, until with delays greater than half a second there were no more items from the cued row in the report than would be expected if the items in the report were chosen at random from the display.

It cannot be the case that subjects were waiting for the cue and then, when it had not arrived within some particular delay, processing as much as they could at random from iconic memory before it decayed too far. The number of items reported from the display (ignoring whether they were from the cued row or not) would in this case be smaller than the number reported when the subject is simply asked to report as much as possible from anywhere in the display, since in this case he has an undecayed memory to work on, and this should make him perform better than if he were to wait some time and then process as much of the decayed trace of the display as possible.

What may be happening is that the subject begins to process all the material as soon as possible, but when the cue occurs he switches to the cued material and selectively processes it. This is not consistent with von Wright's observation, but it is consistent with the results of an experiment by Mewhort (1967), who presented his subjects with pairs of eight-letter rows and used a post-exposure tone to tell them which row (upper or lower) to report. The amount of material reported from the cued row was greater when the *uncued* row was rather like English (e.g. VERNALIT), and therefore easy to process, than when it was unlike English (e.g. YRULPZOC), and so hard to process. This demonstrates elegantly that subjects must have been processing the uncued row; otherwise its nature could not have affected their performance.

This topic deserves further study; it seems clear, at least, that the simplest interpretation of these post-cue experiments (that the subject selectively processes the cued material and entirely ignores the rest) is wrong. What, then, is the function of the cue?

These basic experiments on selection in iconic memory elucidate two features of this form of memory. First of all, it decays rapidly; just after the offset of a visual display, the contents of the display are accurately represented in the iconic memory of the display, but the fidelity with which the display is represented rapidly decreases as iconic memory decays away over time. Secondly, physical properties of the display are represented in iconic memory, but knowledge of higher-order features of items (e.g. whether they are letters or numbers) can only be attained after the items are transferred to a different form of memory.

*Masking and iconic memory*

The visual nature of iconic memory is emphasized by Sperling's finding that if the visual field in the interval between display offset and tone is dark rather than bright, iconic memory can last for about five seconds rather than for half a second. Furthermore, if the display is followed by a patterned stimulus such as 'visual noise' (a random pattern of black and white squares), there appears to be no iconic memory of the display (Sperling, 1963). This effect of an aftercoming visual stimulus on a visual display is referred to as visual backward masking.

One way of conceptualizing the effects of an aftercoming stimulus is to assume that the iconic memory of a display and the following stimulus are integrated, and that items present in iconic memory have to be picked out, if this is possible, from this composite stimulus. If the items are decaying they will soon reach the point at which they are not distinguishable when superimposed upon a bright background; it will take longer for them to fade sufficiently so as to be indistinguishable when superimposed upon a dark background; and they will be indistinguishable against an appropriately complex superimposed patterned stimulus as soon as this stimulus is presented. The pattern will camouflage the stimulus.

This view of how backward visual masking works was referred to by Kahneman (1968) as the integration theory of masking. An alternative view, the interruption theory, explains backward visual masking by saying that the subject ceases to process the display or its iconic memory and begins to process the stimulus which follows this display. Thus according to this theory processing of the original display is terminated by the onset of the masking stimulus. Evidence in favour of an integration theory is provided by Coltheart and Arthur (1972) and Eriksen and Eriksen (1971).

*What causes the report limitation?*

The question raised earlier (why can the subject report only four or five items when he can see them all?) remains to be answered. An explanation which seems appealing is that the subject can only report four or five items because he can only process so many items before the iconic memory of the display has decayed away. This explanation must be wrong, however. If a display lasting 70 msec is followed by a visual-noise mask, thus drastically limiting the time for which the display is visually available, about four items can be reported; the number of items which can be reported is only slightly increased by trebling the exposure duration (Sperling, 1963). Thus the limitation on the number of items which can be reported cannot be due solely to a limitation on the time available for processing the visual representation of the items.

In an attempt to measure the time it takes to process individual items, Sperling presented visual displays for various durations, with a visual-noise mask occurring at display offset. The amount reported as a function of exposure duration is shown in Figure 2. Sperling assumed that items are no longer visually available after mask onset. He therefore concluded from this experiment that the processing of a visual display proceeds at a rate of 10 msec per item, at least for the first four or five items.

There is considerable evidence that processing items is akin to naming them, and that the more durable form of storage in which processed items are represented uses an auditory code (Conrad, 1964; Sperling, 1960, 1963, 1967). However, we cannot name items at a rate of 10 msec per item; even to span a single syllable sub-vocally takes more than 100msec (Landauer, 1962). If items in iconic memory can be processed at a rate of one every 10

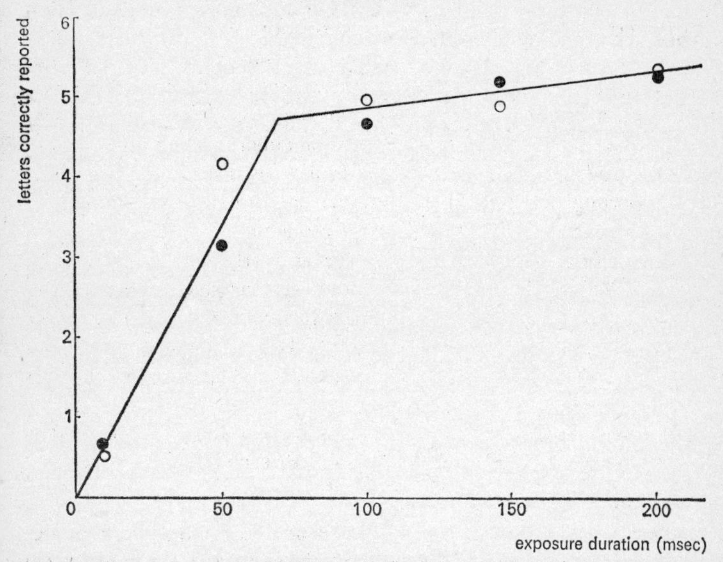


**Figure 2** Effect of exposure duration on amount reported (from Sperling, 1963)

msec, but can only be named at rate a of one every 100 msec, a simple model which identifies processing in iconic memory with naming must be inadequate.

Two attempts to solve this problem have been proposed. Sperling (1963, 1967) postulated an intervening store which accepts inputs from iconic memory at a rate of one per 10 msec, this acceptance of inputs corresponding to rapid setting-up of programs containing instructions for the pronunciation of items. These programs can subsequently be executed at leisure so as to transfer the items to the more durable auditory store. The limitation of four or five items might be a capacity limit of the intermediate store; it cannot be a fixed capacity limit of the auditory store, since we can remember more than four or five items under sufficiently favourable conditions.

Not only is this attempt to solve the problem a rather tortuous one, but it seems to raise many new problems. (Do items decay in the intermediate store? Can there be selection amongst the contents of this store?) An alternative proposal, briefly mentioned by Sperling (1963, footnote 5) and subsequently by Neisser (1967) and Kahneman (1968), is to reject the assumption that the availability of unprocessed visual information is terminated by the onset of the visual-noise mask. Eriksen and Eriksen (1971) have discussed this possibility in detail. The visibility of a brief stimulus is dependent on both stimulus duration and stimulus intensity. A decrease in intensity (I) can be compensated for by an increase in duration (T); this is expressed in the form of Bloch's Law, viz., $I \times T = C$. Thus doubling exposure duration is equivalent to doubling intensity. If we adopt the view that a visual—noise mask works because it is integrated with a target stimulus, then the more intense the target stimulus is relative to the mask, the easier it will be to pick out from the composite target-plus-mask. Since increasing duration is equivalent to increasing intensity, the results given in Figure 2 can be explained without assuming extremely rapid processing rates. What is being manipulated is the energy of the target relative to the mask, rather than the duration for which the target is visually available. Thus it may be possible to retain the idea that the mechanism by which the contents of visual displays are processed is, simply, naming, taking the view that a mask affects the quality, not the duration, of visual information.

Several facts concerning masking, however, suggest that this attempt to explain Figure 2 is no more successful than Sperling's. Firstly, if a masked display is simply a generally degraded form of an unmasked display, why is it that the introduction of a mask at stimulus offset impairs the report of items in the centre of a row of letters, but does not affect the report of end items (Merikle, Coltheart and Lowe, 1971)? Secondly, it is difficult to see why, on this view, a mask presented a full second after display offset impairs performance (Lowe, 1971). Thirdly, if target duration and intensity are both held constant, results like those in Figure 2 are obtained by varying the time between target offset and mask onset (van den Heijden, 1971), despite the fact that the relative energy of target to mask is fixed.

The most serious criticism of this sort of view, however, comes from experiments which used mask and target energies such that when the mask and target were exposed simultaneously for one second, none of the letters in the target could be read (Merikle, Coltheart and Lowe, 1971). Now when the mask was presented at target offset, the results given in Figure 3 were obtained. These results indicate a processing rate of 30 msec/item, slower than Sperling's but still very fast. Eriksen's explanation cannot be applied here. If the mask is such that a one-second target cannot be read when integrated with it, a target with lower energy (i.e. a target with duration less than 100 msec) would also not be discriminable when integrated with the mask. Therefore minor manipulations of the energy of such a low-energy target (i.e. varying exposure duration from 30 to 100 msec) could not affect performance; yet this did occur, as Figure 3 shows.

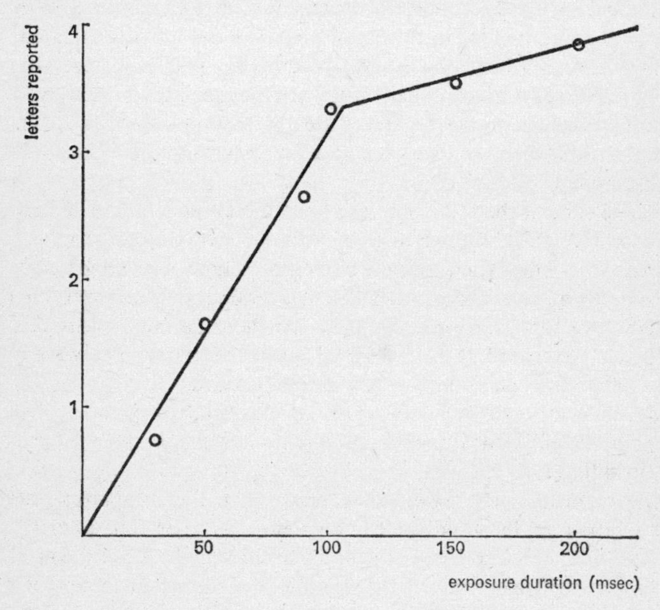


Figure 3 Effect of exposure duration on amount reported (replotting of data from Merikle, Coltheart and Lowe, 1971)

Figure 2 thus remains an enigma. A third attempt to account for it will be considered later.

**Posner's 'visual code'**

A quite different technique for studying the forms of visual memory has been developed by Posner (1969). Subjects are presented with a pair of letters and are asked to respond 'same' if these letters have the same name, and otherwise to respond 'different'. Sometimes letters with the same name are physically the same (e.g. AA); at other times letters with the same name are physically dissimilar (e.g. Aa). 'Same' responses to AA are significantly faster than 'same' responses to Aa. This must mean that subjects are not basing their responses purely on the names of the letters – they must be using the visual characteristics of the stimuli. However, this cannot be all they are using; otherwise they could never respond 'same' to Aa.

'Same' responses to physically identical stimuli are called 'physical matches'. 'Same' responses to stimuli which are physically different but have the same name are called 'name matches'. When the letter pair is presented sequentially, and the time between the presentation of the two letters is varied from 0 to 2 seconds, the time taken to make a name match is unaffected by the length of the inter-stimulus interval, but the time taken to make a physical match increases as inter-stimulus interval increases. The two types of response are about equally fast when the inter-stimulus interval is two seconds, whereas physical matches are about 90 milliseconds faster than name matches when the two letters are presented simultaneously, as shown in Figure 4.

These results suggest the following interpretation (Posner, 1969). When a letter is presented, it can be represented in memory in two ways – in a visual code and in a name code. When a second letter is presented, visual and name codes of this letter are also produced. The visual codes of the two letters are compared. If they match, the two letters must have the same name, and so the response 'same' is initiated. If the two visual codes do not match, however, neither the 'same' nor the 'different' response is justified.

The name codes of the two letters are also compared. If they match, the response 'same' is initiated; if the name codes do not match, the response 'different' is initiated.

The comparison of name codes takes longer than the comparison of visual codes. However, the visual code of a letter decays over time whereas the name code does not. The greater the decay of the visual code of the first letter, the longer it will take to match the visual code of the second letter to it. After two seconds' decay, matching visual codes will take longer than matching name codes, and so the response will always be initiated by the results of the name match.

Various experiments have suggested that the rate at which the visual code of an item decays is at least partly under the control of the subject.

Firstly, if an experiment is designed so that whenever two letters have the

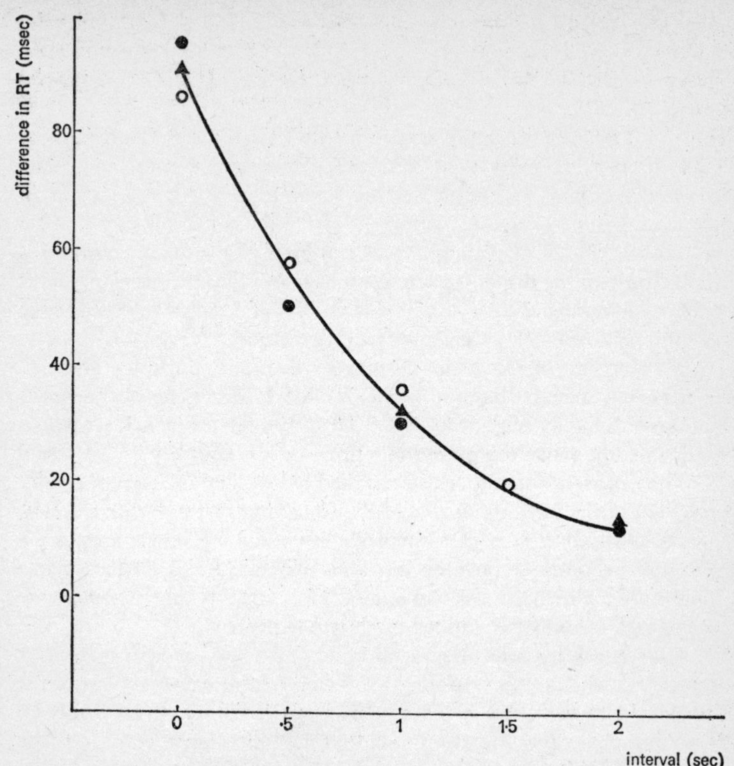


Figure 4 Effects of inter-stimulus interval on time taken to make physical and name matches (from Posner, 1969)

same name they are also physically identical, the subject no longer needs to use the name code; a comparison of visual codes is always sufficient to determine which response to make. This gives the subject a greater incentive to maintain the visual code if he can do so. It seems that he can, since under these conditions there is very little increase in the time taken to make physical matches as inter-stimulus interval is increased, which may be due to there being no decay of the visual code under these circumstances.

On the other hand, if the subject is given a pair of digits to add during the inter-stimulus interval, the advantage of physical matches over name matches is abolished, as if the visual code of the first letter is degraded or erased. These findings suggest that the subject can use his processing capacity to maintain the visual code. He will do this to a greater degree than usual, if there is some incentive to do so. Conversely, if his capacity is occupied with some other task, this will lead to poorer-than-usual maintenance of the visual code. This interpretation is complicated, however, by the fact that the material for the interpolated task was presented visually and by the lack of control over when the subject actually performed this task.

The visual code of a display, as studied by Posner's technique, and the iconic memory of a display, as studied by Sperling's post-cue technique and other similar techniques, appear to be separate and different forms of visual memory. A patterned stimulus following the display does not affect the visual code of the display, but does eliminate or drastically curtail the iconic memory of the display. There is no evidence that the decay of iconic memory is anything but passive, whereas the rate of decay of the visual code depends upon how much processing capacity the subject chooses to allocate to the maintenance of this code. Display luminance and display duration influence iconic memory but not the visual code. Iconic memory appears to have a large capacity (e.g. at least sixteen of the letters in a $3 \times 6$ array), whereas in some sense there are limitations on the capacity of the visual code. When a row of four letters is presented briefly, and then a probe letter is presented in the position of one of the four target letters, with the subject's task being to say whether the probe letter had the same name as the target letter in the same position, physical matches are faster than name matches only for the leftmost two letters. This suggests that a visual code was generated for only two of the four letters in the row.

The differences between the visual code and iconic memory are thus numerous and obvious. An unsolved problem of cognitive psychology is the relationship between these two forms of visual memory. It may only be because of the paucity of relevant data that the following attempt to relate these two forms of memory has any plausibility at all.

**A tentative model**

Let us return to the question of why subjects can report only four or five items from a brief display. If the display is an eight-letter row and exposure duration is 100 msec this result holds. If, however, the exposure duration is one second, all eight letters can often be reported. Moreover subjects in this situation report, firstly, that they are simply naming all eight letters, and, secondly, that they can get this job done before the letters go off. This agrees with estimates of the rate of implicit speech (Landaüer, 1962) which suggest a rate of about 100–150 msec per monosyllabic item. It is introspectively clear that sub-vocal naming is of great importance with exposure durations of one second. However, this cannot be the only mechanism by which items are processed, since about four items can be reported from a 50-msec display which is terminated by a visual-noise mask, and naming cannot proceed as rapidly as this.

Let us suppose that two forms of encoding are going on simultaneously.

Visual codes of the items in a briefly displayed letter row are constructed rapidly, but there is a limit on the number of items which can thus be encoded; suppose that it takes 20 msec per item and four items is the maximum. At the same time, name codes are being constructed, by naming the items; this process is slow (100 msec per item), but the number of items which can be encoded in this way is at least eight. We can plot these two processes as in Figure 5.

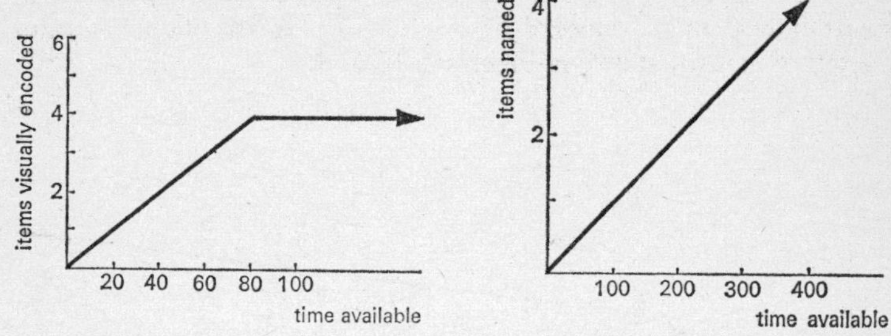


**Figure 5** Time courses of two hypothetical encoding processes

The function relating the number of items reported to the exposure duration can be obtained by combining these two functions, as follows.

Let $N$ = naming rate, in items per second.
$V$ = visual encoding rate, in items per second (until limit is reached).
$M$ = maximum number of items which can be visually encoded.
$I$ = number of items presented.
$D$ = processing time, in seconds (i.e. exposure duration, if a mask is used at display offset).
$R$ = number of different items encoded in at least one way.

The relationship between $R$ and $D$ rises sharply until the exposure duration at which $M$ items have been visually encoded ($M/V$ seconds) and then rises more slowly, since from this point on new items are added only by the slow naming process. The two segments of this function are:

(a) *If* $D < M/V$
Number of items named $= ND$.
Number of items visually encoded $= VD$.
Number of items encoded visually *and* named $= \dfrac{(ND \times VD)}{I}$
(assuming independence of the two processes).
Number of items encoded in at least one way (R)

$$= ND + VD - \frac{(ND \times VD)}{I}.$$

(b) *If* $D > M/V$

Number of items named $= ND$.

Number of items visually encoded $= M$.

Number of items encoded visually *and* named $= \frac{(ND \times M)}{I}$.

Number of items encoded in at least one way ($R$)

$= ND\,(1 - M/I) + M$.

In order to fit this two-limbed function to a set of data we need to estimate from the data the values of $N$, $V$ and $M$. The results of doing this for three sets of data are shown in Figures 2, 3 and 6.

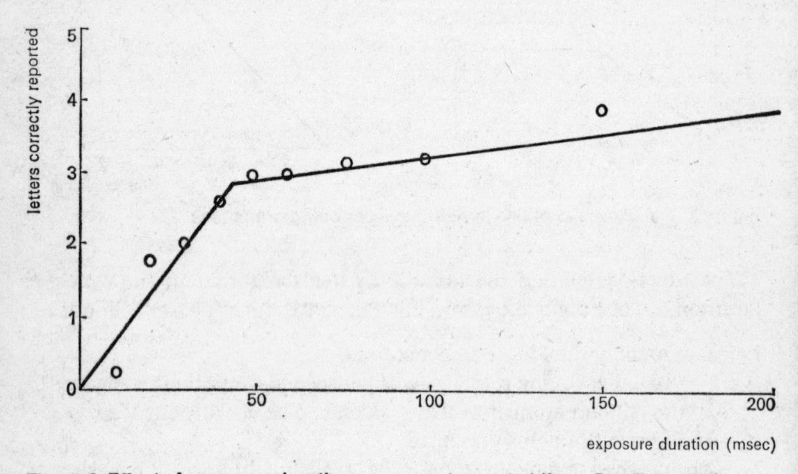


**Figure 6 Effect of exposure duration on amount reported (from Sperling, 1967)**

Clearly a two-limbed function with the first limb having a much greater slope than the second fits all three data sets well. The $N$ parameters for all sets of data are rather similar. The $M$ parameters for Sperling (1967) and Merikle, Coltheart and Lowe (1971) are equal. The differences which do exist between estimated values of the parameters may reflect differences in experimental conditions, but it is not possible to investigate this since the experimental conditions used by Sperling (1963, 1967) are not described in sufficient detail.

Extrapolation of these functions to larger values of $D$ yields the prediction that all the items in an eight-letter row will be encoded if exposure durations of the order of one second are used.

With relatively short exposure durations, performance is not affected by whether the display is switched off at the onset of a mask or some time before mask onset. The crucial variable is the time between display onset and mask onset, not the display duration. This implies that the construction of the visual code can continue after display offset. The simplest way to conceptualize this is to assume that the construction of visual and name codes occurs with either the visual display or its subsequent decaying iconic memory as data. This is schematized in Figure 7.

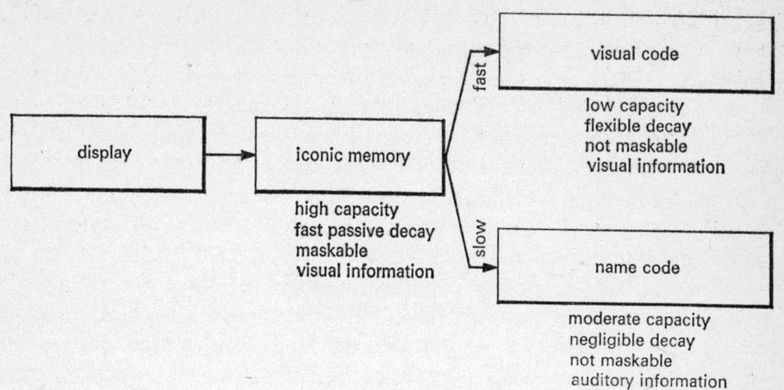


**Figure 7** A hypothetical organization of memory sub-systems involved in visual information-processing

One of the numerous assumptions upon which this scheme depends is that the recall of an item can be based upon a stored name code of the item or upon a stored visual code.

*Some relevant evidence*

These ideas are consistent with the results of various recent tachistoscopic experiments. For example, Colegate and Eriksen (1970) taught subjects different names for various nonsense forms. One group learned monosyllabic names; the other learned trisyllabic names. Following this training, the subjects participated in an experiment in which nonsense forms were exposed briefly, followed after a delay by an indicator pointing to the position which one form had occupied. The task was to give the name of the indicated form. The monosyllabic group performed better than the trisyllabic group. Presumably this is because, in the limited time during which the display plus its iconic memory was available, more monosyllabic items than trisyllabic items could be named. The difference in performance between the two groups was, however, smaller than would be expected on the simplest view of the naming process. A possible explanation for this is that the visual code might also have been used by the subjects in this experiment. Whenever this occurred no effect due to number of syllables would be expected. Thus reliance on both codes may have attenuated the difference between the two groups.

When a row of eight letters is presented for 100 msec, followed by a visual-noise masking pattern or by a blank white field, and subjects are asked to report as many letters from the row as possible, performance is of course worse in the mask condition that in the no-mask condition. However, Merikle, Coltheart and Lowe (1971) found that this was only true for letters near the centre of the row. The report of the letters at either end of the row is unaffected by the mask; some representative data are shown in Figure 8. This selective masking effect is consistent with the ideas being presented here. It is evident from Figure 8 that, with a 100-msec display, about three letters are not affected by the mask and the remaining five are. Since this exposure duration exceeds $M/V$, the duration beyond which the rapid construction of visual codes of items no longer occurs, there will be $M$ items visually encoded and therefore unmaskable, plus a small contribution from the name code (less than one item if $N < 10$). The remaining items would have to be named from iconic memory, and are therefore susceptible to a masking stimulus. What the selective masking effect shows in particular is that the items which are rapidly visually encoded are not a random selection from the letter row. Items at the ends of the row are the ones which are visually encoded.

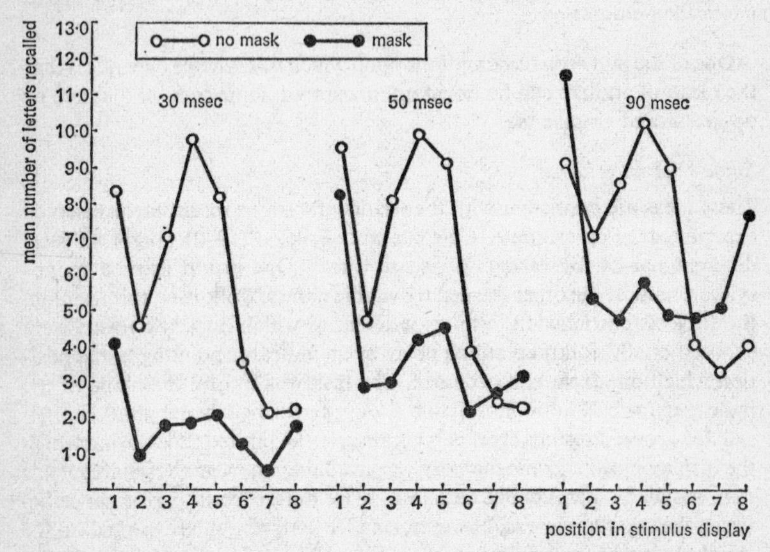


Figure 8 Relationship between item position and effect of backward masking at short exposure durations (from Merikle, Coltheart and Lowe, 1971)

This account of the selective masking effect generates a number of predictions, two of which will be considered here. Firstly, as exposure duration is increased from, say, 30 msec, the number of items unaffected by the mask should rapidly increase from about one to about three with an exposure duration of 100 msec or so, and then increase very slowly. That this is approximately the case is shown by a comparison of Figure 8 with Figure 9.

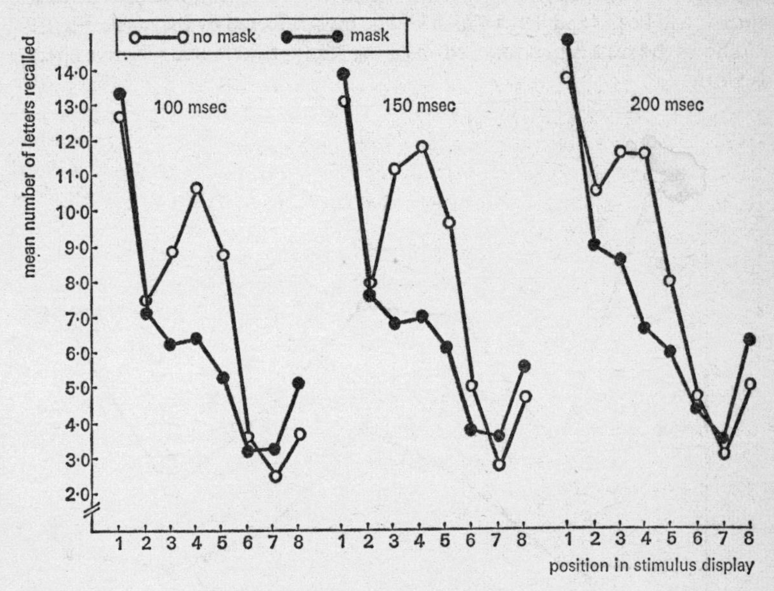


**Figure 9** Relationship between item position and effect of backward masking at longer exposure durations (from Merikle, Coltheart and Lowe, 1971)

The second prediction concerns the effects of forward masking, i.e., presenting the mask immediately before rather than immediately after the display. As mentioned earlier, one explanation of why masking (forward or backward) occurs is that the second stimulus is integrated with the decaying iconic memory of the first stimulus, thus producing a composite and therefore degraded stimulus. In the case of forward masking, it is the decaying trace of the mask which combines with the display and makes the display difficult to process. The strength of the mask's trace will be maximal at display onset and will decline during the display and after display offset. So the mask will have had a greater effect on processing which occurs early during the display and less effect on processing which occurs late in the display and on processing of the iconic memory of the display. Therefore if the first thing that happens after display onset is that the subject attempts to encode the end items, he will be attempting to process items which are degraded by the trace of the mask; if the middle items are processed later, when the mask trace is weaker, the mask will have less effect on the middle items.

If this is the temporal order in which the row is processed, it follows that forward masking will also have a selective effect on the letter row, but the effect will be reversed with respect to the backward-masking selective effect, since it will be the end items which will be most affected by the mask. Figure 10 shows the results of a forward-masking study; the reverse selective effect is clear.

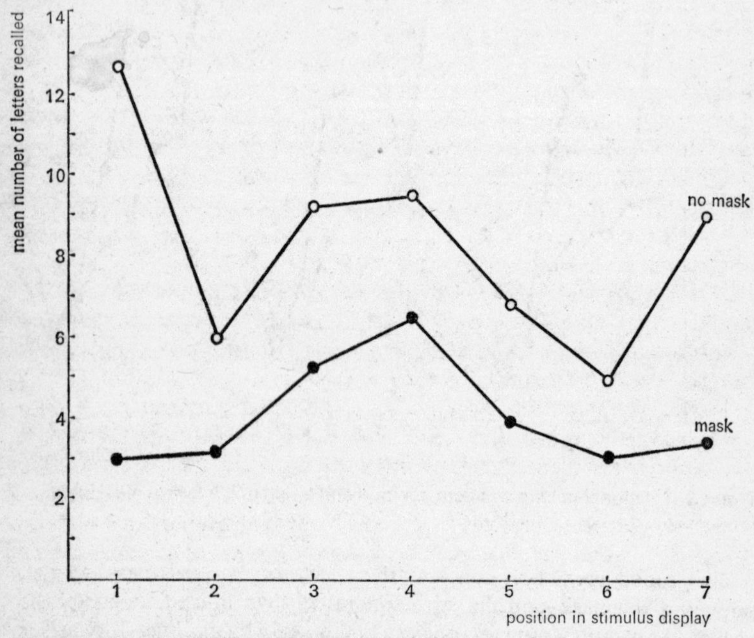


**Figure 10 The effects of forward visual masking as a function of position of item in stimulus display (from Merikle and Coltheart, 1972)**

A valuable technique for investigating visual and verbal memory codes has been used by Scarborough (1972). He presented his subjects with an auditory sequence of items, followed by a visual display, which in turn was followed by a post-cue which informed the subject whether he was to report the items he had seen or the items he had heard. The efficiency with which the visual display was reported was compared with how well it was reported when no auditory sequence was presented. Visual displays were always followed by a mask.

The pattern of results was as follows: with a 250-msec display duration, visual performance was unaffected by the presence of the auditory load.

However, with a 750-msec display, performance was worse with the auditory load.

Scarborough's interpretation of these results was that a limited number of items are rapidly stored in a visual memory, and that this process is unaffected by whether the subject is rehearsing an auditory sequence. Items from the visual display can also be stored by naming them, but the naming process cannot occur if an auditory sequence is being rehearsed (which explains the detrimental effect of auditory load with a 750-msec display). Auditory load has a small and insignificant effect with a 250-msec display because so little can be named in this short time that if naming is prevented performance is hardly affected at all. This interpretation is obviously very similar to the general view being discussed here, though some difficulty is encountered in attempting to give a quantitative account of Scarborough's data. If items are either named or in the visual memory, as he appears to suggest, then his data indicate that less than one item can be named in 750 msec; rate of naming appears to be about one item per second from his data. If we propose instead that naming and visual encoding are independent, so that some items are stored in both ways, the naming rate estimated from his data is still rather slow (about 400 msec per item). A faster rate would be consistent with the data if we assumed that there is some dependence between which items are named and which are encoded; but this assumption was not needed in fitting the data referred to earlier in this chapter.

Nevertheless, Scarborough's data are qualitatively consistent with the views being considered, and the technique of interfering with the naming mechanism so as to study pure visual encoding is clearly a very promising one. For example if subjects are given very brief displays (up to 100 msec) while the naming mechanism is occupied, a plot of amount reported against exposure duration should reveal the temporal properties of the visual encoding mechanism, uncontaminated by the additional contribution of naming. This would yield an independent estimate of the rate and the limit of visual encoding. It would also provide a test of the account given earlier of the selective masking effect. When the subject is prevented from naming the letters in an eight-letter row, this should mainly impair the report of items in the centre of the row, because the items at the ends are those which are encoded visually. Thus backward masking and preventing naming ought to have the same selective effect.

The existence of separate visual and name codes of tachistoscopic displays is also supported by the work of den Heyer and Barrett (1971). Their subjects had to report both the position of items in a display and the identity of the items. The view that the former information is maintained in a visual code and the latter in a name code was supported by the fact that a subsidiary visual task selectively impaired the report of item position, whilst a subsidiary verbal task selectively impaired the report of item identity.

**Word recognition**

The data discussed so far were all obtained with visual displays consisting of single letters or random letter rows. There is reason to believe that if the display is a word, this has some special effects on visual information processing.

Reicher (1969) and Wheeler (1970) presented subjects with brief visual displays which were then masked. A pair of letters was presented along with the mask. The subject's task was to say which of the two letters had been in the display. Subjects performed this task better when the display was a four-letter word than when it was a single letter, despite the fact that there are four times as many letters to process in the former situation. Performance with four-letter non-words was about the same as with single-letter displays.

Perhaps this result may not seem surprising. Words are more familiar, more meaningful and more pronounceable than non-words, and any one or more of these factors might have been responsible for the result. However, there are logical difficulties with this kind of explanation. It is difficult to see how the nervous system could have any information about the meaning of a display until after the display has been identified. How, then, can the time needed to identify the display be influenced by the meaning of the display? The same point can be made with respect to familiarity and pronounceability. Thus the view that meaning, familiarity or pronounceability influences the identification of visual displays is apparently paradoxical. Word recognition will only be understood when this logical problem is clarified, because it can be argued quite generally that we can only know whether a certain visual pattern is a word or a non-word after we have identified it, and so whether it is a word or a non-word cannot affect how easy it is to identify; yet words are more rapidly identified than non-words.

The same problem crops up in very many different situations, and some of these situations will be briefly described. Eriksen, Pollack and Montague (1970) measured the reaction time of the response of speaking the name of visually presented two-digit numbers. The more syllables there are in a two-digit number, the longer is the time between the onset of the number and the initiation of the subject's vocal response. For example, if you see 20 you can name it faster than you can name 63, and you can name 63 faster than 37. Eriksen *et al.* argue that this is because identification of the number involves naming it, and the more syllables there are in the number the longer it takes to name, and therefore identify it. Alternative explanations are possible, e.g., it may take longer to get a four-syllable response ready than a two-syllable response. The question of whether the effect was a stimulus effect or a response effect was studied by Pollack and Coltheart (1971). In this experiment subjects responded to a two-digit number by giving the number one greater than the one they saw. If the number of syllables in the *response* is important, then the response 27 to the stimulus 26 will be slower than the response 28 to the number 27. If it is the number of syllables in the *stimulus* which is important, the reverse result will occur. The results suggested that it was the number of syllables in the stimulus which is important, supporting the view of Eriksen *et al.* (1970) that the time it takes to identify a two-digit number is a function of the number of syllables in the number. (It is important to remember that in these experiments each extra syllable in the stimulus only adds about 11 msec to the reaction time, and 11 msec is far less than the time it takes to say a syllable, even sub-vocally. A suggestion given earlier may also be relevant here. Perhaps the number we see and the number we say are sometimes linked via the visual code of the number and sometimes via the name of the number. Syllable effects will only occur in the latter situation, and this will reduce the average increase in reaction time per syllable.) Again there is a paradox here: how can we name a number unless we already know what it is? So how can any property of its name influence the time it takes to identify it? Similar issues are involved in experiments by Posner (1970) and Treisman (1970); both have reported observations which seem to show that a stimulus can be classified as a letter or a digit prior to the subject knowing which letter or digit it is, or at least prior to naming the item.

Worthington (1964) had light-adapted subjects sit in a black room and look at an area marked out by four dim red lights. Within this area was a dim white light, too dim to be seen by the light-adapted eye. Subjects were told to press a button when they saw anything in this area; as they sat in the dark their eyes dark-adapted, becoming more sensitive, and eventually the dim white light was detectable, at which point the subject pressed the button and the light went off. The time elapsing before the button was pressed was measured.

Unknown to the subjects, the dim white light was a white disc with a word printed on it in black. No subject reported seeing anything on the white light, and this is not surprising, since detection of a light patch should occur earlier in the course of dark adaptation than detection of a small pattern on this patch, which would in turn occur earlier in dark adaptation than discrimination of the nature of this pattern.

Various words were used; some were obscene, some neutral, and there were various control conditions. The average time elapsing before the button press was the same for all conditions except for the obscene-word condition, in which this time was much longer. Why stimulus emotionality should have this particular effect is not relevant here. What is relevant is that behaviour was influenced by the meaning of a word when subjects reported that no word was present. Once again, information about the meaning of a word exists even when the word is not reported.

Wickens, Shearer and Eggemeier (1971) approached this topic from a different angle by using the semantic differential. This is a technique which allows one to represent the meaning of a word by giving it a value on each of three dimensions of meaning. In various situations this three-dimensional representation of meaning has proved to have surprising validity, e.g., in investigating the effects of meaning on memory (Wickens, 1970).

One of the meaning dimensions is evaluation. Examples of words which receive positive values on this dimension are 'mother', 'rose' and 'food'. Examples of words which receive negative values on this dimension are 'knife', 'black' and 'poison'.

In Wickens' experiment, a word from one extreme of a dimension (e.g. 'mother') is presented, too briefly for the subject to be able to report it. Then, after a brief masking stimulus, another word is presented for six seconds. This word is either also at the same extreme of the dimension (e.g. 'rose') or is neutral on that dimension (e.g. 'sand'). The subject is requested to give a yes or no answer depending upon his feeling whether or not the unrecognized and recognized words are similar. A chance matching score would be 50 per cent, but for both ends of the evaluative dimension performance proved to be significantly better than 50 per cent. Thus the subject must have had information about the meaning of the briefly presented word, even though he was unable to report it.

These findings compel us to take the view that being able to identify (i.e. being aware of) an item, and having information about its meaning or its pronunciation, are states which must be distinguished, however odd this may seem. Not only this, but having information about the meaning or pronunciation of an item is a state which can occur prior to being able to report the item, and even in the absence of being able to report it. If this view is taken, it is no longer *logically* peculiar to say that meaning or pronunciation can influence the efficiency with which we can become aware of an item, because information about meaning or pronunciation can be available prior to awareness of an item, and therefore it is logically possible for this awareness to be influenced by the meaningfulness or pronounceability of the item.

The notion of perception without awareness was frequently discussed in the early 1950s, although regarded with distaste by most experimental psychologists. Those who still experience this distaste are invited to propose alternative explanations of the findings which are discussed above.

To propose that information about meaning or pronunciation can be available prior to awareness is only a first step towards formulating an answer to the problem of word recognition. The next step would be to show how meaningfulness or pronounceability could increase the ease with which we can achieve awareness of an item.

In the case of meaningfulness, it could be argued that having information about the meaning of an item helps to eliminate some of the incorrect possible interpretations which might be offered of an impoverished representation of the item, and so increases the likelihood that the interpretation eventually chosen will be the correct one. As a crude example, if the visual representation of the word BIB is degraded by erasing the lower half of each letter, we will be more likely to identify it as BIB rather than PIP if we know that an associate of the word presented is 'baby'. Of course this implies that BIB has been registered at some stage in the nervous system well enough to generate such associations as 'baby', and yet the data available to awareness is so degraded as to be equally consistent with BIB and PIP.

This facilitation by meaning will not be available if the material displayed is meaningless, and so awareness of meaningful displays will be superior to awareness of meaningless displays.

It may be possible to relate these ideas to those expressed in the previous section by postulating a semantic code in addition to a visual code and a name code. (One could study the semantic code using Posner's technique, by presenting pairs of words and asking subjects to judge whether they were the same or different in meaning.) Thus when a meaningful item is presented, it is encoded by means of the simultaneous construction of visual, name and semantic codes.

**Summary**

I suspect that what Edward Teller enjoyed doing has been done in this chapter. A simple situation (a subject looks at a brief display of letters and writes down what he saw) has been made obscure. Three different forms of memory have been introduced, and so has subliminal perception. I hope I have shown, however, that these complications are mandatory, at least as far as one can tell at the moment. Sperling's original experiments show that the visual information present in a brief visual display is also present after the display is terminated, in the form of a rapidly decaying iconic memory. Posner's work also demonstrates the existence of a visual memory; but this memory has properties quite different from those of iconic memory. There is also abundant evidence indicating that at least some of the items in a brief visual display come to be stored in a non-visual, verbal memory.

The model sketched in this chapter is intended to incorporate these three forms of memory within the simplest schematization which is consistent with what is known at present about visual information-processing.

**References**

CLARK S. E. (1969), 'Retrieval of color information from preperceptual memory', *Journal of Experimental Psychology*, vol. 82, pp. 263–6.

COLEGATE, R. L., and ERIKSEN, C. W. (1970), 'Implicit speech as an encoding mechanism in visual perception', *American Journal of Psychology*, vol. 83, pp. 208–15.

COLTHEART, M., and ARTHUR, B. (1972), 'Evidence for an integration theory of visual masking', *Quarterly Journal of Experimental Psychology*, in press.

CONRAD, R. (1964), 'Acoustic confusions in immediate memory', *British Journal of Psychology*, vol. 55, pp. 75–83.

DEN HEYER, K., and BARRETT, B. (1972), 'Selective loss of visual and verbal information in short-term memory by means of visual and verbal interpolated tasks', *Psychonomic Science* in press.

ERIKSEN, C. W., and ERIKSEN, B. (1972), 'Visual perceptual processing rates and backward and forward masking', *Journal of Experimental Psychology*, vol. 89, pp. 306–13.

ERIKSEN, C. W., POLLACK, M. D., and MONTAGUE W. E. (1970), 'Implicit speech: a mechanism in perceptual encoding?', *Journal of Experimental Psychology*, vol. 84, pp. 502–7.

KAHNEMAN, D. (1968), 'Method, findings and theory in studies of visual masking', *Psychological Bulletin*, vol. 70, pp. 404–25.

LANDAUER, T. K. (1962), 'Rate of implicit speech', *Perceptual and Motor Skills*, vol. 15, p. 646.

LOWE, D. G. (1971), 'Components of memory for brief visual display', Ph.D. thesis, University of Waterloo.

MERIKLE, P. M., and COLTHEART, M. (1972), 'Selective forward masking', *Canadian Journal of Psychology*, in press.

MERIKLE, P. M., COLTHEART, M., and LOWE, D. G. (1971), 'On the selective effects of a patterned masking stimulus', *Canadian Journal of Psychology*, vol. 25, pp. 264–79.

MEWHORT, D. J. K. (1967), 'Familiarity of letter sequences, response uncertainty and the tachistoscopic recognition experiment', *Canadian Journal of Psychology*, vol. 21, pp. 309–21.

NEISSER, U. (1967), *Cognitive Psychology*, Appleton-Century-Crofts.

POLLACK, M. D., and COLTHEART, M. (1971), unpublished experiments, University of Waterloo.

POSNER, M. I. (1969), 'Abstraction and the process of recognition', in J. T. Spence and G. Bower (eds.), *The Psychology of Learning and Motivation*, vol. 3, Academic Press.

POSNER, M. I. (1970), 'On the relation between letter names and superordinate categories', *Quarterly Journal of Experimental Psychology*, vol. 22, pp. 279–87.

REICHER, G. M. (1969), 'Perceptual recognition as a function of stimulus material', *Journal of Experimental Psychology*, vol. 81, pp. 275–80.

SCARBOROUGH, D. L. (1972), 'Memory for brief visual displays: the role of implicit speech', *Cognitive Psychology*, in press.

SPERLING, G. (1960), 'The information available in brief visual presentations', *Psychological Monographs: General and Applied*, vol. 74, pp. 1–29.

SPERLING, G. (1963), 'A model for visual memory tasks', *Human Factors*, vol. 5, pp. 19–31.

SPERLING, G. (1967), 'Successive approximations to a model for short-term memory', *Acta Psychologica*, vol. 27, pp. 285–92.

TREISMAN, A. (1970), 'Perception and recall of simultaneous speech stimuli', *Acta Psychologica*, vol. 33, pp. 132–48.

TURVEY, M. T., and KRAVETZ, S. (1970), 'Retrieval from iconic memory with shape as the selection criterion', *Perception and Psychophysics*, vol. 8, pp. 171–2.

VAN DEN HEIJDEN, A. H. (1971), 'The processing of tachistoscopic displays as a function of effective stimulus duration', *Acta Psychologica*, vol. 35, pp. 233–42.

VON WRIGHT, J. M. (1968), 'Selection in visual immediate memory', *Quarterly Journal of Experimental Psychology*, vol. 20, pp. 62–8.

VON WRIGHT, J. M. (1970), 'On selection in immediate visual memory', *Acta Psychologica*, vol. 33, pp. 280–92.

WHEELER, D. D. (1970), 'Processes in word recognition', *Cognitive Psychology*, vol. 1, pp. 59–85.

WICKENS, D. D. (1970), 'Encoding categories of words: an empirical approach to meaning', *Psychological Review*, vol. 77, pp. 1–16.

WICKENS, D. D., SHEARER, W., and EGGEMEIER, T. (1971), 'Prerecognition processing of meaningful verbal material: an approach to successive multiple encoding', presented at Midwestern Psychological Association, Detroit.

WORTHINGTON, A. G. (1964), 'Differential rates of dark adaptation to "taboo" and "neutral" stimuli', *Canadian Journal of Psychology*, vol. 18, pp. 257–68.

# 4 Mathematics in Psychology

James G. Greeno

In this chapter I will try to report my impression of the current status of mathematical psychology. It goes without saying that this is a personal report, and reflects my biases about both methodology and substance. I will try to characterize mathematical psychology in a general way, and point to some trends that seem to be important regarding the role mathematical psychology has in the overall conduct of psychological science at the present time.

## General features

First, mathematical psychology is not very homogeneous. At least four major kinds of issues are studied. The oldest and best-known branch of mathematical psychology is psychometrics: the measurement of psychological variables such as abilities, attitudes, utilities and the like. A closely related area is the systematic study of experimental design, including investigation of the kinds of inferences that are justified on the basis of experimental data.

A third branch of mathematical psychology that has been actively developed during the last twenty years is the development of relatively rigorous models of psychological processes such as learning, perception, decision and problem solving. A majority of these models of processes involve the application of probability theory – hence, the phrase 'stochastic models'. However, many important process models use other sub-fields of mathematics, such as linear differential equations. The fourth branch of about the same vintage as mathematical modelling of processes is the simulation of psychological processes using computers.

A decade ago the boundaries between these sub-specialties were relatively distinct. They no longer are. Now, mathematical models are being used as bases for psychological measurement. Computer simulation is used to derive predictions from complex mathematical models, and experiments are conducted to determine the values of parameters that occur in both computer simulations and stochastic models. In many ways, the sub-specialties of mathematical psychology are losing their separate identities.

More importantly, the specialty of mathematical psychology is losing part of its identity. While it has always been clear that mathematical psychology is a collection of methods rather than a substantive field, mathematical psychologists have tended in the past to work on a different set of questions from those that other experimental psychologists were concerned with. For example, an experimentalist working on motivation might study the effect of stimulus complexity on subjects' preferences. Mathematical psychologists have been interested in relationships among probabilities of choice in preference experiments, such as whether choice probabilities are transitive, or whether constraints implied by Thurstone's (1927) or Luce's (1959) model of choice more nearly agree with observed proportions of preferences.

Another example of substantive difference was in the study of learning. Experimental studies (e.g., Underwood, Ham and Ekstrand, 1962) investigated the way in which subjects' selection of stimulus components is influenced by meaningfulness and other variables. Mathematical psychologists (e.g., Estes, 1964) wondered whether it was more accurate to say that stimulus elements are sampled independently (the 'linear model') or are perceived in configurations that vary from trial to trial, but always function as units (the 'pattern model').

It seems to me that recent studies by mathematical psychologists have dealt less with a distinctive set of theoretical questions than was the case a few years ago. There are many examples, some of which I will be discussing, in which quantitative analyses are being used to achieve a clearer and more decisive analysis of processes and structures that have been studied more informally by other methods. If my impression is correct, it is becoming increasingly true that mathematical psychology cannot be identified by what is studied but only by the ways of studying psychological processes and structures.

In our present state of development in psychology, the majority of mathematical psychologists spend most of their research time in experimental work, conducting tests of theories they have developed or implications of existing theories they have derived, or in putting new inference procedures to use. Thus, a discussion of mathematical psychology is about a set of scientific activities that a few scientists engage in nearly all the time, but most practitioners engage in only a small amount of their time.

On the other hand, many mathematical methods are accessible to investigators without special training, and a great many experimental psychologists spend some of their time working out the implications of new ideas in rigorous derivation or in devising modified statistical procedures to accommodate new experimental arrangements. Thus, it is also becoming harder to identify mathematical psychology as the work done by an identifiable subgroup of investigators. Mathematical psychologists have always been engaged in a lot of experimental work. And a lot of mathematical psychology is done by experimental psychologists.

Since mathematical psychology is not a field of study, nor a professional division, what is it? While many psychologists take it for granted that quantification represents scientific progress of a sort, others wonder what mathematics has to do with psychology at all. In my view, the contribution of mathematics to science is in the interface between theoretical ideas and empirical evidence.

In psychology, as in any science, a theory consists of some statements that describe hypothetical structures and processes that are postulated to be the nature of the system being studied. Scientific theories are empirical because they have implications that can be tested in observations. Thus, science consists of two main kinds of work: developing and refining ideas about the way things are (e.g., what memory is or how perception works), and carrying out studies that provide evidence to be used in improving our ideas about the way things are.

If theory and experiment are the two main building materials in the structure of science, then mathematics is the mortar that binds these materials together. Of the four sub-specialties of mathematical psychology mentioned earlier, psychometrics and experimental design are mainly concerned with the problem of inference – using data to decide about hypotheses. The use of mathematics in these fields provides analyses of assumptions that are needed to support various kinds of inferences and development of procedures for obtaining measurements and tests of hypotheses.

The sub-fields of mathematical modelling and computer simulation apply mathematics at the theoretical end – the concern is with the question of what empirical implications are contained in a set of theoretical assertions. Here the use of mathematics is in the development and analysis of theories that are sufficiently clear and precise that deriving their implications involves mathematics in a non-trivial way.

## Trends and developments

In the remainder of this chapter I will mention five general trends in the conduct of mathematical psychology that contribute to an understanding of the present status of the field, as well as allowing a projection of how the field may progress in the next few years. The investigations that I select to illustrate these trends are by no means exhaustive. The same points could be illustrated by a completely different set of studies.

### *Models of psychological processes*

The first trend in recent work has been increased psychological content in mathematical models of various kinds of processes. The assumptions of quantitative theories published recently are more detailed, and hence probably more realistic, than were models that were developed ten or twenty years ago. And the psychological content of a theory's axioms is often more explicit and direct than was the case with many earlier theories. Both kinds of development represent natural forms of growth in scientific theory. A more detailed theory often develops as an elaboration of an earlier theory. And the psychological content of a set of axioms is made more explicit when evidence allows the interpretation of the axioms to be less uncertain.

One important example is in the theory of choice and decision. Earlier work on the problem used a model taken from economics, where a person should choose an act that maximizes his subjectively expected utility. When the model deviated from data, as it did in many experiments where subjects chose between gambles, theorists noted that a property of the stimulus – the variance of the gamble – was systematically related to subjects' choices. The initial solution, then, was to postulate a preference function partly depending on a gamble's variance.

More recently a genuinely psychological postulate has been introduced to handle this problem. Coombs and his associates (Coombs and Huang, 1970; Coombs and Meyer, 1969) have developed a theory in which a subject is assumed to perceive some amount of risk in a gamble. Perceived risk relates to stimulus variables such as the expected value of a gamble, the amount that can be won or lost, and the probability of winning. The exact relationship between perceived risk and various factors can vary among individuals, and one purpose of experimentation is to determine both the functional relationships that seem to hold across subjects and the ways in which subjects differ in their perceptions of riskiness.

Just as Coombs' work has increased the psychological content of the theory of decision, it also has reduced the identifiability of psychometrics and modelling. Coombs' work is very much in the tradition of psychological measurement, and indeed directly uses ideas from his own theory of unfolding (Coombs, 1964), as well as concepts taken from the theory of conjoint measurement (Krantz and Tversky, 1971). But at the same time, definite postulates about the process of making a decision are tested in Coombs' experiments, so it is not clear whether the theory of risk belongs in psychometrics or in mathematical modelling.

A second example of increased psychological content in assumptions about a process is in the theory of memory. An important breakthrough in theorizing about memory occurred when Bower (1961) showed that a simple Markov chain gave predictions that described results of simple paired-associate memorizing. A Markov chain gives a particularly felicitous framework for theorizing, since it specifies a set of states and probabilities of transition between pairs of states that are independent of the system's history and constant over time. A considerable literature has been written using Markovian models to explain learning and problem solving. The operative concept in these analyses is the idea of a set of states, with each item occupying one of the states at any given time.

The states of various Markov models have been variously interpreted, but one of the earlier developments that put psychological flesh on the Markovian skeleton was Atkinson and Shiffrin's (1968) theory of short-term memory and rehearsal. The idea is that when an item is presented it enters (or may enter) a state in which the subject rehearses it actively. Each time a new item is presented, the contents of short-term memory may be changed, with the new item replacing one of the current occupants. And as long as an item remains in short-term memory, information about it is transferred to longer-term memory. On a test, retention is assured if the test item is in short-term memory; otherwise probability of recall depends on the amount of information that was transferred to longer-term storage.

Atkinson and Shiffrin's ideas are similar to those incorporated in other models, such as Bernbach's (1970) and Norman and Rumelhart's (1970). This class of short-term memory models is interesting partly because their mathematical structure involves time dependencies that depart from the elementary Markov assumptions used in other analyses. The idea of a storage buffer also provides a significant point of contact between mathematical modelling and computer simulation. But the main feature for the present discussion is that hypotheses about rehearsal and attention that these models postulate are definite psychological ideas that specify the psychological meaning of states that were relatively less substantive in earlier analyses.

A third example is in the use of reaction time to infer cognitive processes. A number of new developments in the use of reaction time have occurred, but one that particularly illustrates increased psychological content in models is by Trabasso, Rollins and Shaughnessy (1971). Earlier work used a stochastic model to estimate the number of stages in solving a problem (Restle and Davis, 1962) or identified rather general stages of processing, such as decision and response (e.g., Hohle, 1965).

But Trabasso *et al.* exemplify the trend towards more explicitly psychological models in postulating a specific sequence of decisions needed for each kind of problem used in an experiment. Their experimental task involved saying 'true' or 'false' when a picture was shown following a phrase that might or might not be satisfied in the picture. For example, if 'orange or triangle' were followed by a blue triangle, the subject should answer 'true'. The model assumes that the subject sets up a decision tree of the following kind:

1. Is the stimulus orange? If yes, respond true. If no, test shape.
2. Is the stimulus a triangle? If yes, respond true. If no, respond false.

Trabasso *et al.*'s work further illustrates the merging of computer simulation and mathematical modelling, as well as the merging of both these activities with experimental psychology. The notion of verifying a concept using a sequential decision tree came from Hunt's (1962) work, which was a blend of computer simulation and experimental investigation. But the main advance in Trabasso *et al.*'s study was the development of a model for reaction time using detailed hypotheses about just what stages are involved in processing information and deciding about the truth of a proposition.

*Relationship between processes*

Theories in psychology have usually been about single processes. We have theories of learning, theories of perception and theories of motivation. Recently analyses have been even more narrow, such as theories of short-term memory, theories of perceptual illusions and theories of risky decision. Of course these sub-systems do not operate in isolation. No one believes that we learn without perceiving, or that decision occurs without memory of past outcomes. But even severely restricted aspects of psychological processing have presented theoretical problems of considerable complexity and uncertainty. Attempts to cross territorial lines have been discouraged by the prospect of vacuous generality or overwhelming numbers of arbitrary assumptions.

We can take a step towards theorizing about two processes at once when we can give a precise characterization of the output of one hypothetical process and a similarly precise description of the effects of hypothetical input variables on another process. The situation is analogous to the need for carefully controlled stimuli in psychophysics. If experimenters did not control the physical properties of stimuli carefully, we would not have precise descriptions of the inputs to sensory systems, and we could not hope to test specific hypotheses about sensory processes. Just as a quantitative description of physical stimuli is needed to develop satisfactory theory in psychophysics, so quantitative descriptions of psychological processes are needed in order to develop satisfactory theories about the interactions between different psychological processes.

In a number of instances, investigators have begun to study relationships between different psychological processes, using mathematical models or computer simulation to provide the needed precision in hypotheses. A well-known example is the theory of signal detectability (e.g., Swets, Tanner and Birdsall, 1961), which specifies an hypothetical interaction between decision processes and sensory processes. The information in a stimulus is characterized as a ratio of likelihoods, and experimental analyses can be carried out to investigate the kinds of stimulus information that human subjects use. Motivational variables and expectations are assumed to determine a criterion $c$, with the subject's response determined by whether the likelihood ratio for the stimulus on a trial exceeds $c$.

An analysis of relationships between perception and memory has been given by Norman and Rumelhart (1970). Their model deals with recognition, storage and retrieval of verbal characters. Their model of perception is that of Rumelhart (1970), who characterized recognition as a process of feature extraction. Norman and Rumelhart postulated a system of memory storage that uses a naming process based on the perceived features, and storage of features that are in the background or context of the perceived characters. A retention test is assumed to partially reinstate the original context, and retrieval depends on the number of stored context features that match features of the test situation.

An investigation involving interaction between perception and reasoning was carried out by Evans (1968), in a study of artificial intelligence that has considerable psychological importance. Evans' program solves geometric analogies. Descriptions of stimulus figures are input to the program in a form that would result from available devices that carry out optical analyses. The solution of an analogy is accomplished by finding ways to transform the various stimulus figures into each other, and then constructing a kind of theory in which the similarity between sets of transformations can be evaluated. The response figure that is selected is the one whose transformation from one stimulus is most closely analogous, in the sense of similarity between transformations, to the transformation between the other two stimulus figures.

Each of these theories represents substantial progress on a hard problem, and other similar examples could be given. However, nearly all of the theories that I am familiar with that deal with interactions between processes represent first steps in an important sense. One kind of processing is assumed to occur, and then another kind of processing uses the first result. In a truly interactive system, processing of different kinds goes on simultaneously, with activity of each kind influencing the other kind of processing at all stages. It seems that we are far from the kinds of theories that would describe the kinds of interactions that probably occur between processes like perception, memory, reasoning and decision. But recent theoretical work has begun to explore relationships among processes in ways that seem interesting and fruitful.

### *Models of cognitive structure*

Although an attempt to distinguish rigorously between process and structure cannot succeed, there is a useful pragmatic distinction between hypotheses about the way stimuli and situations are represented in the mind and hypotheses about the ways various kinds of mental activity take place. Hypotheses about cognitive structure involving considerable increase in richness and rigour have been developed recently in many areas of psychological research.

Piaget's theory of cognitive structure and the many experiments carried out in exploring the properties of intellectual development at different ages are well known now, but it was not until quite recently (Flavell, 1963) that American psychologists were familiar with Piaget's ideas. Piaget's theory postulates the development of structures having formal properties like those of mathematical systems such as the theory of groups.

Another important contribution to recent psychological interest in cognitive structure was Chomsky's (1957) revolutionary linguistic theory of grammar. Some aspects of an early version of transformational grammar were given rigorous formal representation by Chomsky (1963), and important theoretical analyses have been carried out by Suppes (1969, 1970), exploring the relationships among linguistic theories, automata theory and psychological concepts.

A third issue in which new hypotheses about structure are involved in important new research is semantic information processing. Bobrow (1968) and Quillian (1968) developed formal models of semantic information processing with somewhat different emphases. Bobrow's program receives inputs in semi-natural language, coordinates the received information to linguistic forms, and translates the interpreted propositions into a form suitable for solving problems. Quillian took the rather different problem of simulating our knowledge of semantic concepts, particularly our ability to find relationships between concepts. Quillian postulated a network structure, with labelled arcs representing relationships between concepts. In theories that are closely related to Quillian's, Kintsch (1972) and Rumelhart, Lindsay and Norman (1972) have represented memory for semantic information in the form of propositions, using formalism like that of Fillmore's (1968) case grammar.

Psychological experiments about semantic information processing are neither as numerous nor as well developed as experiments about cognitive development or syntactic structures, but a few are available. Paige and Simon (1966) investigated solution of algebra word problems, and related their findings to Bobrow's (1968) theory. Kintsch (1972) and Rumelhart *et al.* (1972) showed relationships between their theories and phenomena of clustering in free recall. Collins and Quillian (1969, 1972) and Kintsch (1972) have measured reaction time for subjects to respond 'true' or 'false' to sentences requiring recall of information in semantic memory. Meyer (1970) has carried out extensive experiments on reaction time for deciding whether sentences are true or false, in connection with a model of semantic memory based on set relationships.

A final issue in which new structural hypotheses have been important is the analysis of serial concepts. Simon and Kotovsky (1963) used computer simulation and experimentation in their study of alphabetic sequence completion. Their model used structural hypotheses about a subject's understanding of a sequence and postulated a mechanism of searching for a pattern of relationships in a sequence of letters. Restle and Brown (1970) and Vitz and Todd (1967) have proposed hierarchical models for the structure of sequential concepts involving sequences of integers or binary events. Restle and Brown's model is particularly interesting, since it incorporates a recursive feature of the kind that has contributed considerable power in computer simulation and artificial intelligence (Reitman, 1965).

The psychological work accomplished thus far regarding cognitive structures is considerably less formal than that involving psychological processes. While hypotheses about structure have been stated with great rigour and considerable detail, a structure by itself does not generate observable performance. Therefore, the interface between theories and empirical evidence has been relatively weak. The need for more specific hypotheses regarding processing and acquisition of complex cognitive structures has been recognized by numerous writers, and it seems likely that development and test of such hypotheses will be a major activity of mathematical psychologists during the next few years.

*Analyses of existing theories*

Another important contribution of mathematical psychologists is the analysis of theories that have been developed earlier, in deriving new implications of older ideas, in developing new applications, or in finding new ways to obtain evidence on old questions. There are many examples of such analyses, and I will mention four cases.

In psychophysics, the concept of a threshold was made dubious by developments in signal detectability theory, particularly by the easily obtained finding that a proportion of detection response is influenced by motivational and other decision factors. Luce (1963) gave an analysis of the threshold concept that incorporates the idea of response bias in a way that is compatible with the main facts given in a receiver-operating characteristic (ROC). The ROC, a plot of proportion of 'yes' responses to signals versus proportion of 'yes' responses to noise trials, had been interpreted as evidence against threshold theory, as indeed it was for earlier versions of the hypothesis. Further extensions and refinements have been given by Krantz (1969) and Norman (1964).

A second analysis of existing theory involves work done by Restle (Restle and Greeno, 1970) on adaptation-level theory, originally developed by Helson (1964). Restle has derived a number of new implications of adaptation-level theory. In some cases the analyses show how the theory is compatible with experimental results earlier thought to be inconsistent with it. In other cases, Restle and his co-workers have found new ways to obtain experimental evidence distinguishing adaptation-level theory from alternatives such as the Gestalt theory of contour repulsion (Merryman and

Restle, 1970). And in other cases, Restle has used adaptation-level theory to provide a new analysis of a classical problem, such as the moon illusion (Restle, 1970).

A third kind of relationship between mathematical psychology and existing theory is seen in work that I and several co-workers have done on associative learning (Greeno, 1970; Greeno, James and DaPolito, 1971; Humphreys and Greeno, 1970). Our method has been to conduct standard experiments in paired-associate memorizing, varying meaningfulness, stimulus similarity, and other variables that are known to influence ease of learning and transfer. Then we analyse the data from these experiments, using a Markov model that enables us to measure the difficulty of learning in two stages. The results, showing which stage of learning is affected by various experimental variables, have given support to theories about association developed by Köhler (1947) and Koffka (1935). Our results have been inconsistent with more widely held views such as those of McGeoch (1942), Melton and Irwin (1940), Postman (1963) and Underwood and Schulz (1960).

A particularly impressive use of mathematical methods in connection with an existing theory is in concept identification. Restle (1962) gave a model of cue learning based on Lashley's (1928) classical theory. The idea used in Restle's model is that cue learning is mainly a process of selecting the correct stimulus properties to use in deciding on a response, and thus contrasts with the more commonly held view that in cue learning, subjects connect responses with stimulus features, with attentional processes governed by mediating responses (Kendler and Kendler, 1962). Bower and Trabasso (1964) conducted a series of powerful experiments that showed decisively that for adult human subjects, Restle's view is considerably closer to the truth than the mediating-response view. Additional empirical analyses and theoretical extensions were given by Trabasso and Bower (1968), and the model has been used in a large number of experimental analyses of human-concept identification (see, e.g., Levine, 1969).

*Measurement and inference*

Analyses of psychological measurement and procedures of inference have been a major continuing concern in mathematical psychology. Recent and current work has both contributed some new solutions to old problems, and has led to some relatively basic new concepts.

One important kind of contribution that mathematical psychologists sometimes make is devising a new experimental procedure that clarifies a theoretical idea and provides new evidence on a theoretical question. It often happens that alternative hypotheses cannot be differentiated clearly with data from standard experiments. But mathematical investigation of the hypotheses, often in more rigorous or specific form, can suggest new procedures for collecting data that afford considerable progress.

Estes has made particularly notable contributions of this kind. One example is in his and several co-workers' studies of information and reward in human learning (Humphreys, Allen and Estes, 1968; Keller, Cole, Burke and Estes, 1965). The problem of separating informational and incentive aspects of feedback given to subjects is difficult, of course, because positive feedback both encourages subjects to repeat what they did and informs them that their action was correct. Estes' solution to the problem was to give differing point values for choices in a verbal discrimination task. The results supported the idea that subjects responded on the basis of what they had learned about the points – the informational view. Results counter-indicated the incentive hypothesis, that subjects' individual responses were strengthened or weakened by positive and negative reinforcement.

Another example of an experimental innovation supported by mathematical analysis is in Estes' work on visual detection (Estes and Taylor, 1964; Wolford, Wessel and Estes, 1968). A serious difficulty of inference involves separating effects of limitation on input processing from interference with memory for perceived information produced when the subject gives a response. New information about the question was obtained in Estes' experiments where the subject had to report only one fact – which of two critical letters was in the display.

A second kind of innovation that can be made with the aid of mathematical analysis of assumptions involves finding ways to increase the information in data that can be used to answer theoretical questions. An example is in Sternberg's (1966) use of the form of the function relating reaction time to the size of a set of items in short-term memory. The subject's task was to decide whether a test item was in the set. With larger sets, reaction time was longer, but this fact is not very useful for theory. However, reaction time was a linear function of set size, and this fact is of considerable interest. The linear function is consistent with an hypothesis that the subject scans the contents of short-term memory serially, and it is inconsistent with a simple parallel processing assumption.

A significant increase in the power of data has been accomplished by analyses that use the distributions of empirical variables as data. In most psychological experiments conclusions are based on a single property of data in each condition – the mean or occasionally the median. The variance of scores within a condition is usually treated as a positive nuisance, and other properties of the distributions are ignored except to check on assumptions of normality. But with an appropriate mathematical model, the variance and other properties of distributions become useful data, providing information about hypothetical psychological processes.

There have been a number of instances in which distributions of reaction time have been derived from assumptions about response mechanisms. One interesting example is by LaBerge (1962), who assumed that a response occurs after the subject has sampled some criterion number of stimulus elements that are associated with responding in some way. The model permits use of the reaction-time distribution to obtain separate measurements of a motivational component and a sensory component of the psychological process. For example, in detection the incentive to respond would affect the criterion parameter and the ease of detection would affect the rate of sampling response-associated stimulus elements.

Another area where distributions of statistics have become important and useful is the study of learning. Since Bower's (1961) demonstration that a simple Markov chain can give a good approximation to results of a learning experiment, a number of investigators have used Markov models in their study of learning processes. An example is a study by Polson, Restle and Polson (1965), who used the distributions of two kinds of errors as evidence that paired-associate memorizing consisted of two relatively distinct stages – association and discrimination.

Another kind of contribution to psychological measurement and inference comes from analysis of assumptions needed to support certain kinds of inference, and development of procedures for measuring psychological quantities needing weaker assumptions than those required for procedures used earlier. A general problem in psychological inference is that quantitative variables like utility or perceived magnitude are not available for direct measurement. The result is that inferences about functional relationships among psychological variables remain uncertain to the degree that arbitrary correspondences between observable and theoretical quantities have to be assumed. There is considerable value, therefore, in developing procedures for measuring psychological quantities that require as weak a set of assumptions as possible about relationships between theoretical and observed variables.

One example is an important new procedure for scaling multi-dimensional stimuli, developed by Shepard (1962). Earlier methods (see Torgerson, 1958) used an assumption that variability in psychological quantities is normally distributed, and feasible methods also assume equal variance and independence. Shepard's procedure requires the much weaker assumption that empirical measures of distance between stimuli are monotonic with distances in the postulated psychological space. A number of computer programs have been written using Shepard's basic method, and the procedure has been used in many applications.

A major development in the theory of measurement was given by Luce and Tukey (1964). Earlier axioms for measurement depended on having an operation of concatenation, such as placing two objects adjacent to each other in measuring their combined length. Clearly no such operation is available for psychological measurement. Luce and Tukey found axioms for measurement that use properties of response when two empirical dimensions are jointly varied. If responses satisfy certain ordinal relationships, then inferences about underlying psychological variables are justified, involving assignment of values on psychological scales having desirable properties. Luce and Tukey's work extended earlier analyses along the same lines by Adams and Fagot (1959) and Debreu (1960). This line of analysis has been extended by a number of studies, and a general discussion is given by Krantz, Luce, Suppes and Tversky (1971). Applications of these principles of measurement to experimental design have been given by Krantz and Tversky (1971), who show how ordinal information about experimental factors can be used to infer the forms of rules by which theoretical variables influenced by the factors combine.

Another kind of analysis regarding inference from experimental results has been given by Anderson (1970) and Sternberg (1969). These are notable contributions, partly because after decades of using analysis of variance simply to decide whether empirical variables had any effect on performance, these analyses give a motivation for procedures of evaluating components of variance that are based on definite psychological hypotheses.

Sternberg's (1969) analysis is geared to observations of reaction time. The idea is that stages of processing that occur sequentially will take amounts of time that are additive. If different experimental factors affect the time needed for different stages of processing, then the effects of the factors should be additive – that is, there should be no interaction. Thus, analysis of variance in a factorial experiment provides a test of hypotheses about the stages involved in performing some task.

Anderson's (1970) analysis deals with numerical responses, such as magnitude judgements. One application of the analysis is in judgements made when several items of information must be combined by the subject, either because they are presented serially or because they involve different aspects of the situation being judged. Analysis of variance provides a test of hypotheses about the subject's manner of combining the information. If he averages the items, experimental factors should have no interaction. If judgement depends on a ratio of inputs, the interaction between factors should only be significant in the linear $\times$ linear component.

Most investigations of inference involve finding new procedures for obtaining measurements or making theoretical decisions from data. Sometimes, however, mathematical analysis is used to investigate certain kinds of limitations on the kinds of inference that can be made using data of specified kinds. When the problem is well defined, this is the question of identifiability. The question is whether data of a specified kind give definite estimates of all the parameters of a theory.

In psychology, analyses of identifiability have been carried out for three general kinds of theory. In psychometrics, multiple-factor analysis (Reiersöl,

1950) and latent-class analysis (McHugh, 1956; Madansky, 1960) have been studied. In learning, identifiability of Markov models has been studied (see Greeno, Millward and Merryman, 1971, for a review). In perception, Townsend (1970) has investigated the problem of distinguishing parallel and serial processing and has shown that if the models are described in reasonably general ways, there is a serial processor that will mimic the behaviour of any parallel processor, and there is a parallel processor that will mimic the behaviour of almost any serial processor. Townsend's results extend Christie and Luce's (1956) observation that parallel and serial systems will have similar observable properties, since Townsend has shown that with a more general but still reasonable characterization, the two kinds of system are identical in their temporal characteristics.

## Summary

I have tried to present a sketch of mathematical psychology as I see it in 1972. It includes many areas of activity, and provides an interface between theory and empirical evidence in many different ways. The sketch, therefore, is not very unified. Mathematical psychology is a chameleon that takes on the colour of the substantive problem for which mathematical analysis is used. In different fields of psychology, mathematics is used differently, and indeed different fields of mathematics are applied. As substantive investigations proceed, so will the development of formal models and procedures of inference to express and evaluate our understanding of psychological structures and processes. The unity of mathematical psychology is not likely to increase, but the importance of rigorous analysis is not likely to decline.

## Further reading

The following texts are all quite general, although they differ considerably in emphasis and approach to different substantive areas. The books marked with an asterisk are intended for beginning undergraduates. The others are appropriate for advanced undergraduates or beginning graduate students.

ATKINSON, R. C., BOWER, G. H., and CROTHERS, E. J., *Introduction to Mathematical Learning Theory*, Wiley, 1965.

BATCHELDER, W. H., BJORK, R. A., and YELLOTT, J. I., Jr, *Problems in Mathematical Learning Theory*, Wiley, 1966.

COOMBS, C. H., DAWES, R. M., and TVERSKY, A., *Mathematical Psychology: An Elementary Introduction*, Prentice-Hall, 1970.

*GALANTER, E., *Textbook of Elementary Psychology*, Holden-Day, 1966.

*GREENO, J. G., *Elementary Theoretical Psychology*, Addison-Wesley, 1968.

RESTLE, F. J., *Mathematical Models in Psychology*, Penguin, 1971.

RESTLE, F. J., and GREENO, J. G., *Introduction to Mathematical Psychology*, Addison-Wesley, 1970.

Major references in mathematical psychology are as follows:

LUCE, R. D., BUSH, R. R., and GALANTER. E. (eds.), *Handbook of Mathematical Psychology*, Wiley, 3 vols., 1962, 1963, 1965.

LUCE, R. D., BUSH, R. R., and GALANTER, R. (eds.), *Readings in Mathematical Psychology*, Wiley, 2 vols., 1963, 1965.

Major journals in the field are as follows:

*British Journal of Mathematical and Statistical Psychology*
*Journal of Mathematical Psychology*
*Psychometrika*

## References

ADAMS, E., and FAGOT, R. (1959), 'A model of a riskless choice', *Behavioural Science*, vol. 4, pp. 1–10.

ANDERSON, N. H. (1970), 'Functional measurement and psychophysical judgment', *Psychological Review*, vol. 77, pp. 153–70.

ATKINSON, R. C., and SHIFFRIN, R. M. (1968), 'Human memory: a proposed system and its control processes', in K. W. Spence and J. T. Spence (eds.), *The Psychology of Learning and Motivation*, vol. 2, Academic Press, pp. 90–197.

BERNBACH, H. A. (1970), 'Replication processes in human memory and learning', in J. T. Spence and G. H. Bower (eds.), *The Psychology of Learning and Motivation*, vol. 3, Academic Press, pp. 201–39.

BOBROW, D. G. (1968), 'Natural language input for a computer problem-solving system', in M. Minsky (ed.), *Semantic Information Processing*, MIT Press, pp. 135–215.

BOWER, G. H. (1961), 'Application of a model to paired-associate learning', *Psychometrika*, vol. 26, pp. 255–80.

BOWER, G. H., and TRABASSO, T. (1964), 'Concept identification', in R. C. Atkinson (ed.), *Studies in Mathematical Psychology*, Stanford University Press, pp. 32–94.

CHOMSKY, N. (1957), *Syntactic Structures*, Mouton.

CHOMSKY, N. (1963), 'Formal properties of grammars', in R. D. Luce, R. R. Bush and E. Galanter (eds.), *Handbook of Mathematical Psychology*, vol. 2, Wiley, pp. 323–418.

CHRISTIE, L. S., and LUCE, R. D. (1956), 'Decision structure and time relations in simple choice behavior', *Bulletin of Mathematical Biophysics*, vol. 18, pp. 89–112.

COLLINS, A. M., and QUILLIAN, M. R. (1969), 'Retrieval time from semantic memory', *Journal of Verbal Learning and Verbal Behavior*, vol. 8, pp. 240–47.

COLLINS, A. M., and QUILLIAN, M. R. (1971), 'Experiments on semantic memory and language comprehension', in L. W. Gregg (ed.), *Cognition in Learning and Memory*, Wiley.

COLLINS, A. M., and QUILLIAN, M. R. (1972), 'How to make a language user', in E. Tulving and W. Donaldson (eds.), *Organization and Memory*, Academic Press.

COOMBS, C. H. (1964), *A Theory of Data*, Wiley.

COOMBS, C. H., and HUANG, L. C. (1970), 'Polynomial psychophysics of risk', *Journal of Mathematical Psychology*, vol. 7, pp. 317–38.

COOMBS, C. H., and MEYER, D. E. (1969), 'Risk-preference in coin-toss games', *Journal of Mathematical Psychology*, vol. 6, pp. 514–27.

DEBREU, G. (1960), 'Cardinal utility for even-chance mixtures of pairs of sure prospects', *Review of Economic Studies*, vol. 26, pp. 174–7.

ESTES, W. K. (1964), 'Probability learning', in A. W. Melton (ed.), *Categories of Human Learning*, Academic Press, pp. 90–128.

ESTES, W. K., and TAYLOR, H. A. (1964), 'A detection method and probabilistic models for assessing information processing from brief visual displays', in *Proceedings of the National Academy of Sciences*, vol. 52, pp. 446–54.

EVANS, T. G. (1968), 'A program for the solution of geometric-analogy intelligence-test questions', in M. Minsky (ed.), *Semantic Information Processing*, MIT Press, pp. 271–353.

FILLMORE, C. J. (1968), 'The case for case', in E. Bach and R. T. Harms (eds.), *Universals in Linguistic Theory*, Holt, Rinehart & Winston, pp. 1–90.

FLAVELL, J. H. (1963), *The Developmental Psychology of Jean Piaget*, Van Nostrand.

GREENO, J. G. (1970) 'How associations are memorized', in D. A. Norman (ed.), *Models of Human Memory*, Academic Press, pp. 261–84.

GREENO, J. G., JAMES, C. T., and DAPOLITO, F. J. A. (1971), 'Cognitive interpretation of negative transfer and forgetting of paired associates', *Journal of Verbal Learning and Verbal Behavior*, vol. 10, pp. 331–45.

GREENO, J. G., MILLWARD, R. B., and MERRYMAN, C. T. (1971), 'Matrix analysis of identifiability of some Markov learning models', *Psychometrika*, vol. 36, pp. 389–408.

HELSON, H. (1964), *Adaptation-Level Theory*, Harper & Row.

HOHLE, R. (1965), 'Inferred components of reaction times as functions of foreperiod duration', *Journal of Experimental Psychology*, vol. 69, pp. 382–6.

HUMPHREYS, M. S., ALLEN, G. A., and ESTES, W. K. (1968), 'Learning of two-choice, differential reward problems with informational constraints on payoff combinations', *Journal of Mathematical Psychology*, vol. 5, pp. 260–80.

HUMPHREYS, M. S., and GREENO, J. G. (1970), 'Interpretation of the two-stage analysis of paired-associate memorizing', *Journal of Mathematical Psychology*, vol. 7, pp. 275–92.

HUNT, E. B. (1962), *Concept Learning: An Information Processing Problem*, Wiley.

KELLER, L., COLE, M., BURKE, C. J., and ESTES, W. K. (1965), 'Reward and information values of trial outcomes in paired-associate learning', *Psychological Monographs*, vol. 79, whole no. 605.

KENDLER, H. H., and KENDLER, T. S. (1962), 'Vertical and horizontal processes in problem solving', *Psychological Review*, vol. 69, pp. 1–16.

KINTSCH, W. (1972) 'Notes on the semantic structure of memory', in E. Tulving and W. Donaldson (eds.), *Organization and Memory*, Academic Press.

KOFFKA, K. (1935), *Principles of Gestalt Psychology*, Harcourt, Brace.

KÖHLER, W. (1947), *Gestalt Psychology*, Liveright.

KRANTZ, D. H. (1969), 'Threshold theories of signal detection', *Psychological Review*, vol. 76, pp. 308–24.

KRANTZ, D. H., LUCE, R. D., SUPPES, P., and TVERSKY, A. (1971), *Foundations of Measurement*, Academic Press.

KRANTZ, D. H., and TVERSKY, A. (1971), 'Conjoint-measurement analysis of composition rules in psychology', *Psychological Review*, vol. 78, pp. 151–69.

LABERGE, D. L. (1962), 'A recruitment theory of simple behavior', *Psychometrika*, vol. 27, pp. 375–96.

LASHLEY, K. S. (1928), *Brain Mechanisms and Behavior*, University of Chicago Press.

LEVINE, M. (1969), 'Neo-non-continuity theory', in G. H. Bower and J. T. Spence (eds.), *The Psychology of Learning and Motivation*, vol. 3, Academic Press, pp. 101–34.

LUCE, R. D. (1959), *Individual Choice Behavior: A Theoretical Analysis*, Wiley.

LUCE, R. D. (1963), 'A threshold theory for simple detection experiments', *Psychological Review*, vol. 70, pp. 61–79.

LUCE, R. D., and TUKEY, J. W. (1964), 'Simultaneous conjoint measurement: a new type of fundamental measurement', *Journal of Mathematical Psychology*, vol. 1, pp. 1–27.

MCGEOCH, J. A. (1942), *The Psychology of Human Learning*, Longman.

MCHUGH, R. B. (1956), 'Efficient estimation and local identification in latent class analysis', *Psychometrika*, vol. 21, pp. 331–47.

MADANSKY, A. (1960), 'Determinantal methods in latent class analysis', *Psychometrika*, vol. 25, pp. 183–98.

MELTON, A. W., and IRWIN, J. McQ. (1940), 'The influence of degree of interpolated learning on retroactive inhibition and the overt transfer of specific responses', *American Journal of Psychology*, vol. 53, pp. 173–203.

MERRYMAN, C. T., and RESTLE, F. (1970), 'Perceptual displacement of a test mark toward the larger of the two visual objects', *Journal of Experimental Psychology*, vol. 84, pp. 311–18.

MEYER, D. E. (1970), 'On the representation and retrieval of stored semantic information', *Cognitive Psychology*, vol. 1, pp. 242–99.

NORMAN, D. A. (1964), 'Sensory thresholds, response biases and the neural quantum theory', *Journal of Mathematical Psychology*, vol. 1, pp. 88–120.

NORMAN, D. A., and RUMELHART, D. E. (1970), 'A system for perception and memory', in D. A. Norman (ed.), *Models of Human Memory*, Academic Press, pp. 21–66.

PAIGE, J. M., and SIMON, H. A. (1966), 'Cognitive processes in solving algebra word problems', in B. Kleinmuntz (ed.), *Problem Solving: Research, Method and Theory*, Wiley, pp. 51–119.

POLSON, M. C., RESTLE, F., and POLSON, P. G. (1965), 'Association and discrimination in paired-associates learning', *Journal of Experimental Psychology*, vol. 69, pp. 47–55.

POSTMAN, L. (1963), 'Does interference theory predict too much forgetting?', *Journal of Verbal Learning and Verbal Behavior*, vol. 2, pp. 40–48.

QUILLIAN, M. R. (1968), 'Semantic memory', in M. Minsky (ed.), *Semantic Information Processing*, MIT Press, pp. 216–70.

REIERSÖL, O. (1950), 'On the identifiability of parameters in Thurstone's multiple-factor analysis', *Psychometrika*, vol. 15, pp. 121–49.

REITMAN, W. R. (1965), *Cognition and Thought*, Wiley.

RESTLE, F. (1962), 'The selection of strategies in cue learning', *Psychological Review*, vol. 69, pp. 329–43.

RESTLE, F. (1970), 'Moon illusion explained on the basis of relative size', *Science*, vol. 167, pp. 1092–6.

RESTLE, F., and BROWN, E. (1970), 'Organization of serial pattern learning', in G. H. Bower (ed.), *The Psychology of Learning and Motivation*, vol. 4, Academic Press, pp. 249–331.

RESTLE, F., and DAVIS, J. H. (1962), 'Success and speed of problem solving by individuals and groups', *Psychological Review*, vol. 69, pp. 520–36.

RESTLE, F., and GREENO, J. G. (1970), *Introduction to Mathematical Psychology*, Addison-Wesley.

RUMELHART, D. E. (1970), 'A multi-component theory of the perception of briefly exposed visual displays', *Journal of Mathematical Psychology*, vol. 7, pp. 191–218.

RUMELHART, D. E., LINDSAY, P. H., and NORMAN, D. A. (1972), 'A process model for long-term memory', in E. Tulving and W. Donaldson (eds.), *Organization and Memory*, Academic Press.

SHEPARD, R. N. (1962), 'The analysis of proximities: multi-dimensional scaling with an unknown distance function', *Psychometrika*, vol. 27, pp. 125–40, 219–46.

SIMON, H. A., and KOTOVSKY, K. (1963), 'Human acquisition of concepts for sequential patterns', *Psychological Review*, vol. 70, pp. 534–46.

STERNBERG, S. (1966), 'High-speed scanning in human memory', *Science*, vol. 153, pp. 652–4.

STERNBERG, S. (1969), 'The discovery of processing stages: extensions of Donders' method', *Acta Psychologica*, vol. 30, pp. 276–315.

SUPPES, P. (1969), 'Stimulus-response theory of finite automata', *Journal of Mathematical Psychology*, vol. 6, pp. 327–55.

SUPPES, P. (1970), 'Probabilistic grammars for natural languages', *Synthese*, vol. 22, pp. 95–116.

SWETS, J. A., TANNER, W. P., Jr, and BIRDSALL, T. G. (1961), 'Decision processes in perception', *Psychological Review*, vol. 68, pp. 301–40.

THURSTONE, L. L. (1927), 'A law of comparative judgment', *Psychological Review*, vol. 34, pp. 278–86.

TORGERSON, W. S. (1958), *Theory and Methods of Scaling*, Wiley.

TOWNSEND, J. T. (1970), 'Mock parallel and serial models: an observation on the methodology of model testing', unpublished MS, Purdue University.

TRABASSO, T., and BOWER, G. H. (1968), *Attention in Learning: Theory and Research*, Wiley.

TRABASSO, T., ROLLINS, H., and SHAUGHNESSY, E. (1971), 'Storage and verification stages in processing concepts', *Journal of Cognitive Psychology*, vol. 2, pp. 239–89.

UNDERWOOD, B. J., HAM, M., and EKSTRAND, B. (1962), 'Cue selection in paired-associate learning', *Journal of Experimental Psychology*, vol. 64, pp. 405–9.

UNDERWOOD, B. J., and SCHULZ, R. W. (1960), *Meaningfulness and Verbal Learning*, Lippencott.

VITZ, P. C., TODD, T. C. (1967), 'A model of learning for simple repeating binary patterns', *Psychological Review*, vol. 75, pp. 108-17.

WOLFORD, G. L., WESSEL, D. L., and ESTES, W. K. (1968), 'Further evidence concerning scanning and sampling assumptions of visual detection models', *Perception and Psychophysics*, vol. 3, pp. 439-44.

# Part Two
# Interest and Motivation: Normal and Abnormal

This second group of chapters may seem to be oddly assorted bedfellows, and indeed I must confess to a certain difficulty in knowing how best to classify them. They do have two important characteristics in common, however: all three chapters are in different ways concerned with questions about the sources of human action, about motivation, and all three demonstrate the application of careful experimental techniques to fields of inquiry which have tended to be regarded as less rigorous than those discussed in Part One.

In his chapter on experimental aesthetics, Professor Berlyne gives a fine historical review of the field, showing first how scientific methods have been introduced into the study of aesthetic behaviour and, secondly, how this is leading to the gradual assimilation of research on 'aesthetic' behaviour into a more general class of behavioural studies which concern themselves with motivational properties of stimuli. Indeed, Professor Berlyne has been the chief proponent of the desirability of such a change, at least in the English-speaking world.

The second chapter in this part, by Professors Heckhausen and Weiner, represents cooperation in two important senses. First of all, there is the obvious international cooperation of scholars from both sides of the Atlantic, but more importantly their chapter shows how fruitful the coming together of two different disciplines within psychology can be. Following up a theme developed in the Introduction to Part One of the book, one sees demonstrated in this chapter the general trend towards a very much more 'cognitive' view of human behaviour than was apparent ten years ago, in this case applied to questions of motivation. The field calls for ingenious research design, at times to a degree that some may feel goes beyond the bounds of mere ingenuity, harmless though the experiments themselves are. At a later stage we shall come up against the question of ethics in behavioural research: for now one may simply note that there are real problems to be faced if subjects in experiments have to be misled in any way as to the experimenter's purposes, or the conditions of the experiment. Yet certain sorts of important information can, apparently, only be obtained in this way.

The third chapter in this part, Dean Maher's chapter on psychopathology, is a departure from the general scheme of the book in being the only one devoted to studies of abnormal behaviour. It also has a somewhat more 'applied' flavour than most, since the problems of dealing with psychopathic behaviour cannot be divorced entirely from studying it. Yet once again one is impressed by the fact that a field which until comparatively recently was considered to be rather separate from the rest of scientific psychology is rapidly developing research methods and assimilating concepts from general behaviour theory which must lead to a considerable *rapprochement* between the two. This is particularly to be welcomed at a time when many people, including psychologists themselves, have been questioning the relevance of psychological research to the present human condition.

# 5 Experimental Aesthetics*

D. E. Berlyne

## The beginnings: Fechner's work

The psychological processes at work in the creation and appreciation of art have been studied for many centuries, both in the West and in the major Oriental cultures. Until the second half of the nineteenth century this study was a prerogative of art critics or, like the rest of psychology, of philosophers. Consequently, questions of interest to the modern psychologist were examined in conjunction with questions of quite different kinds, such as the criteria by which works of art should be appraised, the metaphysical status of art and of beauty, and how words referring to art and to aesthetic value should be used. Moreover, answers to questions of psychological aesthetics were either generalized from a writer's own experience and his everyday observation of other people's reactions, or deduced from principles that seemed to be self-evident or generally accepted.

Around the middle of the nineteenth century a different kind of psychology emerged, drawing its conclusions from experiments or from other forms of controlled observation and confining itself to questions that are amenable to scientific investigation. This new 'experimental psychology' grew up gradually, of course, as investigators applied experimental methods to one topic after another. But the first major work marking the definitive establishment of the discipline was the book *Elemente der Psychophysik* (*Elements of Psychophysics*), which was published by the German physicist, physiologist and philosopher G. T. Fechner in 1860. Fechner devoted himself for many years to psychophysics, the experimental study of the mathematical relations between the physical events that excite sense organs and the sensations to which they give rise. He then turned to aesthetics, publishing a substantial book, *Vorschule der Ästhetik* (*Prolegomenon to Aesthetics*), in 1876.

Fechner's contribution to experimental aesthetics, apart from the important step of proposing it as a field of study, was threefold. First, he carried out a few experiments that set important precedents. In one, first

* The preparation of this chapter was facilitated by a research grant (569–1073) from the Canada Council.

reported in 1865, he presented rectangles with different proportions between the lengths of their sides and asked subjects to say which one they liked best and which one they liked least. The rectangle that received more favourable votes, and fewer unfavourable votes, than any other was the one whose shorter side was 0·62 as long as the longer side, i.e., the famous 'golden-section' rectangle. Discussions of the mathematical and aesthetic significance of the golden-section ratio had already gone on for centuries, and its experimental investigation has continued among psychologists from Fechner's time to the present day. His second experiment used genuine works of art as stimulus material. Visitors to a museum, where two versions of a Holbein painting were exhibited side by side, were asked to state which version they liked more than the other. Of the few who recorded their judgements in the manner requested, opinion was about equally divided. So the findings were inconclusive and unenlightening. The experiment is, nevertheless, noteworthy because it initiated the practice of ascertaining the preferences of a representative sample of subjects rather than assuming one's own preferences to be either typical or exceptionally authoritative.

Secondly, Fechner put forward some fifteen principles, all psychological in content but speculative in origin. They are, however, close to the concerns of present-day specialists in motivation theory and therefore deserve careful examination. Martin reported experimental tests of some of them in 1906 and found some supportive evidence. Others fit in with more recent psychological and neurophysiological knowledge.

Lastly, and most important of all, Fechner formulated some methodological guidelines. He proposed an 'aesthetics from below', which concerns itself with the elementary determinants of 'liking' and 'disliking'. It contrasts with the 'aesthetics from above' that philosophers have always woven around lofty and abstract concepts. Most later experimental aestheticians have adopted this strategy of gradually working one's way up from the bottom. It has meant spending a great deal of time with simple visual and auditory patterns and artificial laboratory situations. It has exposed them to the derision of many people, who fail to understand that scientific inquiry must necessarily grope its way step by step from rudimentary prototypes to the complexities of everyday life.

Fechner went on to describe three methods for experimental aesthetics, akin to his famous three psychophysical methods. There was the *method of choice*, requiring subjects to select the stimulus object they liked best out of several presented to them; the *method of production*, requiring subjects to act on some object so as to bring it into conformity with their tastes; and the *method of application*, through which a sample of artifacts is examined as a source of information about the preferences of those for whom they are designed.

Variants of the method of choice have dominated experimental aesthetics from Fechner's day to the present. They now include the many sophisticated methods of data collection (ranking, rating, paired comparison, etc.), techniques of multi-variate statistical analysis, and ways of constructing mathematical models that modern scaling theory has made available. Experimental aesthetics has, in other words, been able to benefit from the technical progress made by the psychophysical tradition, launched by Fechner, and the social-attitude-measuring tradition, launched by Bogardus and Thurstone. The method of production has been used rather rarely, perhaps because it so often demands manual skills that are not possessed by everybody in sufficient measure. The method of application is the forerunner of modern content analysis, whose potentialities for aesthetics have barely been tapped.

**Early empirical studies**

From the time of Fechner until about the end of the Second World War experimental aesthetics stumbled along fitfully and haphazardly. It was an occasional sideline to which some experimental psychologists turned for sporadic relief from matters with stronger claims on their attention. They dabbled in it partly because Fechner's blessing had established it as a recognized area of experimental psychology and partly because of their spare-time interests in the arts. There were few, if any, experimental psychologists – certainly no prominent ones – who were primarily specialists in aesthetics.

These early investigators almost always followed Fechner's method of choice and his notion of 'aesthetics from below'. Their work was largely confined to having subjects indicate, by one method or another, how much they liked, or how highly they valued, particular stimuli. Now and then subjects were asked to select adjectives descriptive of moods or emotional states that seemed appropriate to the stimuli. Either way, verbal responses or their equivalents were recorded. These were the days when most psychologists still regarded conscious mental processes as their subject-matter, and 'aesthetic experience', 'aesthetic judgement' and 'aesthetic pleasure' seemed to be the most important mental processes resulting from exposure to works of art. As techniques for measuring physiological processes indicative of 'emotion' (e.g., changes in heart rate, electrical properties of the skin, electrical activity of the brain) came into use, psychological aestheticians began to utilize them as supplementary sources of information.

In this early work, subjects were occasionally exposed to genuine artistic material – reproductions of paintings, passages of music or of verse. Most experimenters, however, used simple stimuli such as may be found among the elements of works of art – visual forms, musical intervals, chords and, especially, colours and colour combinations. A substantial body of specific findings was accumulated (helpfully summarized by Valentine, 1962, and by

Francès, 1968). But all in all, little was done to piece these findings together into coherent theoretical structures or, in general, to illuminate the psychological roots of aesthetic appreciation.

Wide variations among individual tastes were, of course, revealed in the course of this research. Virtually any stimulus that was presented would receive a favourable rating from some subjects. Nevertheless, when fair-sized samples of subjects were tested, mean ratings, distributions of votes, and other indices of how stimuli were valued by the group as a whole showed some general tendencies with impressive regularity. Consistencies, as well as inconsistencies, have appeared between subjects belonging to different cultural traditions, social classes and age groups.

With the advent of personality theory and of multi-variate statistical techniques, such as correlational measures and factor analysis, differences between the aesthetic tastes of individuals began to be measured and related to personality traits. In studies of this sort, subjects were generally asked to judge artistic products rather than simplified patterns. A recurrent finding was that people can be classified along two dimensions with respect to their aesthetic preferences. First, there is a dimension or factor of general aesthetic appreciation: some people seem to be more appreciative of art in general, or to be more proficient judges of art, than others. There is the obvious problem of how to determine who is a better judge than somebody else. The two solutions that have been commonly adopted are correlation of an individual's judgements with those of the group as a whole and correlation with those of art experts. Judgements, even in experts, vary to at least some extent from society to society and from age to age. Nevertheless, art specialists of different cultures have been found to agree to some extent.

Apart from the dimension of general appreciation, a so-called 'bipolar' dimension has usually emerged. This reflects the degree to which individuals' tastes veer towards one pole or the other, e.g., how far their preferences favour 'classical' or 'romantic' art or how far they are dominated by form or by colour. Various links have been indicated between such bipolar dimensions and the more pervasive dimensions of personality such as introversion–extraversion.

### Theoretical contributions

By the end of the 1930s four important lines of theoretical analysis were under way. They grew up independently of the work in experimental aesthetics that was proceeding sporadically at the same time. They were based on deduction either from common experience or from empirical data on psychological phenomena outside aesthetics. Nevertheless, they contributed novel and ingenious ideas that later experimenters and theorists were able to build on.

*Analysis of communication through signs and symbols*

The book *The Meaning of Meaning*, published by Ogden and Richards in 1923, presented a highly influential account of how symbols work. It was really a formalization of some assumptions that already had wide currency, and indeed still have. Communication between human beings depends, according to this view, on symbols, which produce in the mind of the recipient some mental activity or 'thought' resembling what occurred in the originator's mind and prompted him to emit the symbols. A symbol is sometimes used 'emotively', i.e., to set up a replica of one person's emotional experience in somebody else. At other times, a symbol is used 'referentially' to stand for an absent object or 'referent'. It then serves to conjure up in the recipient's mind an experience resembling what the referent would have induced had it been present. The relevance of this to aesthetics is unmistakable, and Ogden and Richards discussed at some length the bearing of their analysis on this as on other subject-matters. Works of art clearly contain many symbols that are used emotively, as well as many referential symbols, e.g., in literature, representational visual art and programme music.

There are several grounds for holding the Ogden and Richards account to be inadequate. For one thing, it does not specify with sufficient clarity and precision how the mental events ('thoughts' or 'references') that bear the brunt of the whole process are related to observable behaviour. Consequently, this account has been superseded by others that recognize the crux of the symbolic function to lie in the effects of signs and symbols on behaviour. The outstanding contributor to this line of inquiry has been the American philosopher Charles Morris. He elaborated on elements found in the writings of two earlier philosophers, Peirce and Mead. But his approach was eminently compatible with that of neo-behaviourist learning theorists, such as Tolman, Hull, N. E. Miller, Mowrer, and especially Osgood. The last-named has contributed the 'semantic differential' technique for measuring emotional or affective aspects of meaning in terms of evaluative, activity and potency dimensions. This technique has found fruitful application in psychological aesthetics as in other fields.

The essence of the behavioural view of signs and symbols is that they evoke some, but not all, of the responses that would be evoked by the referent (or, to use a preferable term, the 'significate') if it were acting on the recipient's sense organs. The responses that occur when a sign or symbol is encountered, and that can therefore be identified with its 'meaning', are, however, mainly internal or covert. This means that a sign or symbol can give rise to quite different overt (visual or audible) behaviour from what the significate would have occasioned. In fact, the effect of a sign or symbol on behaviour may boil down to setting up a 'disposition', i.e., doing something to the recipient's internal state that makes him more likely to act in a certain way if and when he finds himself in a particular kind of stimulus situation in future.

Morris has discussed the connections between 'semiotic' (the study of signs and symbols) and aesthetics. He has taken up the necessary question of what distinguishes aesthetic signs and symbols from others. His conclusion is that they serve primarily for communication of values. By this, he means that they alert the recipient (or 'interpreter', as he calls him) to the importance of certain objects and events, their potential beneficial or noxious qualities, with reference to his needs or motives.

On examination, this is seen to be rather too broad. Not everything that communicates values is aesthetic. Aesthetic symbols communicate 'intrinsic' values. They transmit the artist's views regarding what will repay attention, what is worth looking at or listening to for its own sake, whether or not what we see or hear moves us to further action.

In one of his early writings Morris also put forward the interesting hypothesis that one element of a work of aesthetic pattern can symbolize another element of the same work, affecting the way the 'interpreter' reacts to the second element when he encounters it. This anticipates some recent discussions of aesthetic structure centering around the information-theoretic concept of redundancy.

### *Psychoanalysis*

Freud was deeply interested in, and knowledgeable about, the arts. He did not devote a large-scale monograph to aesthetics, but he wrote several articles on individual artists, works and artistic themes, as his followers have continued to do ever since. He referred more or less incidentally to problems of aesthetics in his writings on other matters, and what he said on the subject has been developed by many later writers. So a coherent psychoanalytic theory of art has grown up and has left a powerful imprint on thinking about aesthetics for most of the twentieth century.

According to the psychoanalytic account, the psychological functions of art are essentially the same as those of other phenomena that Freud studied, such as dreams, jokes, fantasies, neurotic and psychotic symptoms. Like them, art has a 'latent content' which is not apparent to the conscious part of the mind. It affords substitute satisfaction for wishes that have come into conflict with the pressures of external reality, transmitted through the ego, and the pressures of society's moral values, transmitted through the super-ego. These wishes, which are primarily of a sexual or aggressive nature, are consequently repressed and frustrated, so that only a disguised symbolic outlet may be open to them.

However, art, like dreams and fantasies, often portrays painful and frightening events, which seem the very contrary of dramatized wish-fulfilment. Freud and the Freudians have at one time or another entertained various ways of surmounting this problem. The solution that seems to have won most acceptance in the end is the suggestion that imagining, or thinking about, threatening events can be a way of dominating them and making them less fearsome.

Art, as Freud pointed out, differs from most other imaginative products in being presented to, and giving satisfaction to, a wide public. So it performs its psychological functions not only for its creator but for his audience also. It must, in other words, touch on conflicts and unfulfilled wishes that are common to a whole society, if not to the whole of humanity.

The entire edifice of psychoanalytic theory has, of course, been beset by controversy from the very beginning. The opposition stirred up by its original blows against human pride and prudery have since given way to methodological criticisms. It has not always been clear what observations could conclusively confirm or refute Freudian assertions. It has been questioned whether they are amenable to empirical test at all.

Nevertheless, the principles with which psychoanalytic writers have sought to explain aesthetic activity have a great deal in common with principles that have come out of other, more experimentally grounded, theoretical currents. For example, the Freudians are not the only ones to interpret many puzzling forms of behaviour as substitutes for biologically useful courses of action that have been blocked. Instances of such 'displacement' have been revealed by the experiments on animal behaviour of ethologists and learning theorists, as well as the pioneering work on human motivation of Lewin. Similarly, the Freudians are not alone in believing that emotional attitudes can spread from their original objects to other objects, including imagined or simulated objects, that resemble them or have often accompanied them. In this they come close, not only to the 'association by similarity and by contiguity' of the older philosophical psychologists, but also to the concepts of 'stimulus generalization' and 'emotional conditioning' that have grown out of experiments on animal and human learning.

It is evident that the Freudian theory of aesthetics is concerned almost exclusively with the content of art rather than with its structure. With regard to its all-important formal aspects, the Freudians had only the sketchiest of comments to make. They connected these aspects with forces within the personality that impose restrictions and constraints, e.g., with the need for order and regularity that is a by-product of toilet training in infancy. Quite apart from the doubts that such explanations have often raised, they do not tell us which forms or structures will be most satisfying and why.

### *Gestalt psychology*

The writings of the Gestalt school, like those of the psychoanalysts, contain a few relatively cursory treatments of aesthetic problems, as well as a great deal of other material that can be recognized as pertinent to aesthetics. The

Gestalt psychologists, staunch experimentalists though they were, did not engage directly in experimental aesthetics. What they contributed to aesthetics came from their experiments on perception and from their innovative theoretical orientation. However, one outstanding contemporary psychological aesthetician, Arnheim (e.g., 1954), has relied chiefly on Gestalt principles in analysing psychological reactions to painting and other arts.

The limitations of the Gestalt view were opposite to those of the psychoanalytic view. It had much that was enlightening to say about form, but little to say about content. About the only exception to this was the theory of 'physiognomic expression', holding that certain patterns are inherently expressive of certain emotional states because the patterns and the emotional states share a common structure.

Gestalt theory had the merit of introducing one crucial idea to experimental psychology, although it had many precursors in the philosophical writings of earlier centuries. This was the idea that certain perceptual structures, certain relations among the elements of a perceived pattern, can be disturbing and can consequently impel changes to restore 'equilibrium'. They thus anticipated a salient theme of recent motivation theory, namely that certain combinations or arrangements of elements (percepts, thoughts, attitudes, responses) are fraught with 'conflict', 'dissonance', 'incongruity', or 'inconsistency', that they induce 'discomfort', 'aversive states', 'drive', or 'arousal', and that other combinations or arrangements can be 'rewarding' or 'reinforcing'. The Gestalt psychologists did not, however, use such motivational language. They were partial to terms taken from physics, such as 'disequilibrium', 'tension' and 'stress'. For them, such language was not figurative. They meant what they said literally, since they believed that both behaviour and conscious experience depend on three-dimensional fields of electrochemical forces in the brain and on the way in which these fields sort themselves out in accordance with the laws of physics and chemistry. Accordingly, they tended to confine their attention to endogenous processes by which unbalanced or unstable structures are replaced by more stable ones, e.g., perceptual distortion, selection among alternative perceptual organizations, thinking. Later psychologists have paid more attention to forms of action on the environment through which disturbing patterns can be replaced by satisfying ones. Activities required for the creation and appreciation of works of art are, of course, prime instances.

In keeping with this line of thought, the Gestalt psychologists made much of a dimension of 'goodness' along which visual and auditory patterns were supposedly classifiable. They propounded the so-called 'law of Prägnanz', stating that 'worse' configurations tend to change into 'better' configurations when factors favouring veridical perception are weak. This happens when objects are seen briefly or in poor illumination and, especially, when they are recalled from memory. The validity of the law of Prägnanz, and thus the importance of the 'goodness' concept for perception in general, have been called in question by later investigators. But there is no mistaking the importance of such a concept for aesthetics, as later research has amply confirmed.

Unfortunately, the Gestalt psychologists left us badly in the lurch when it comes to specifying what exactly is meant by the 'goodness' of a pattern. It was said to include properties like 'regularity', 'symmetry' and 'simplicity', and their writings are replete with examples of 'better' and 'worse' patterns to give us an inkling of what they had in mind. But they provided no precise definition to tell us which is the 'better' of any two patterns we might encounter, and they did not explain how this eminently quantitative attribute could be measured. Since aesthetic value often hinges on where exactly the pattern is located along the 'goodness' dimension, precise measures are surely imperative.

The Gestalt theorists did another disservice to psychological aesthetics amid their meritorious contributions. They encouraged the mistaken belief that the 'best' patterns in their sense, i.e., simple, regular, geometrical forms, are the most aesthetically satisfying.* This is implied, for example, by Koffka's famous dictum, referring to the law of Prägnanz, that 'perception is artistic'. Subsequent work in experimental aesthetics has demonstrated quite consistently that it is not the case. 'Good' forms may be essential constituents of works of art in all cultures, but, when they stand alone, their aesthetic appeal is distinctly limited.

*Birkhoff*

The fourth important development of the period under discussion and the one that, in many ways, made the most direct contact with the work of the post-war period, was not the work of a psychologist. Its author was the distinguished American mathematician Birkhoff, who attempted a mathematical theory of aesthetic value in his book *Aesthetic Measure* (1933). Aesthetic value (M), he concluded, increases with 'order' (O), and varies inversely with 'complexity' (C). The crux of the theory is, in fact, the formula $M = O/C$.

O was identified with factors, like symmetry and repetition, that enable similarities and relations among elements to be discerned, and C with the amount of effort required to attend to a pattern and assimilate it. Birkhoff specified procedures for attaching numerical values to O and C, and consequently to M, for polygons, vase outlines, melodies and lines of verse. He did not, however, supply measures that would be applicable to all kinds of visual or auditory patterns.

* Arnheim, the foremost psychological aesthetician in the Gestalt tradition, repudiates this error. He insists (1954, pp. 24–6) that imbalance, productive of 'striving and activity', and balance are equally necessary in art as in life.

His theory had the additional flaw of being wrong. It implied that a pattern will have maximum aesthetic satisfaction when it has as much order or as little complexity as possible. This, like some interpretations of Gestalt theory, means that the most satisfying patterns of all will be simple geometrical forms or 'good configurations'. Experimental work, some of it done with the very polygons that Birkhoff published in his book as illustrations, has shown clearly enough that this is not so.

Be that as it may, Birkhoff's work was a substantial step forward, which no subsequent analyst of aesthetic value can afford to ignore. Birkhoff saw that a mathematical theory of aesthetics is indispensable, since aesthetic value always depends on the exact degree to which this or that factor is present. He saw the desirability of looking for mathematical formulations early, even though the first attempts are bound to be restricted in scope and naïvely oversimplified. His emphasis on the roles of order and complexity revive, in a modernized form, some recurrent themes in the older philosophical literature on aesthetics. His measures of order and complexity focused attention on two groups of factors that undoubtedly have much to do with aesthetic value, even though his characterization of these factors was limited and his specification of their mode of interaction was faulty. Several later writers have, in fact, proposed modifications of his formula to bring it more closely into line with experimental findings and with other bodies of psychological theory.

**Recent developments**

Since about 1960 experimental aesthetics has entered a new phase of unmistakable and unprecedented vigour in several different parts of the world. The pace of experimental work is quickening. Verbal scaling methods continue to render indispensable service, and they are being used to answer difficult, and perhaps more pertinent, questions than hitherto. A widening range of non-verbal measures is coming into use, so that the relations between verbal judgements and other forms of behaviour can be examined. New directions of theoretical analysis are pointing to new hypotheses, new variables and new objectives for experimental research to pursue. Significantly enough, they have come mainly from fields of inquiry that do not seem at first sight to have much to do with aesthetics, many of them from disciplines other than psychology. These recent developments are reviewed and discussed at length elsewhere (Berlyne, 1971).

*Statistical analysis and information theory*

Statistical analysis of literary and musical works has proved fruitful in attempts to characterize styles objectively, to settle disputes over attribution, and to simulate artistic creativity with computers. Theorists are beginning to use it to test predictions following from hypotheses about the psychology of art. These may be predictions about the historical course of changes in content or in style (e.g., Cohen, 1966; Martindale, 1972) or about the characteristics of societies that favour art with a particular style or content (e.g., Lomax, 1968).

However, statistical analysis has affected psychological aesthetics most profoundly through the concepts of information theory. These concepts are measures that can be computed from probability distributions. The most important of them, 'information content', 'uncertainty' and 'redundancy', are applicable to anything that can be thought of as a 'message' whose component 'signals' are selected from sets of alternatives with specifiable probabilities of occurrence. Any work of art can, of course, be regarded as a message in this sense, and its elements, whether they are present simultaneously or sequentially, as signals.

In the 1950s it was realized by Hochberg and McAlister (1953) and by Attneave (1954) that information theory held out hope of at last arriving at a precise definition, and even measure, for what the Gestalt school called 'goodness of configuration'. Their line of thought was developed more systematically by Garner (1962), who showed that the degree to which a pattern can be said to possess 'structure' depends on the amount of 'correlational redundancy' or 'internal constraint' that it possesses: if certain combinations of elements occur more frequently than others (e.g., because some combinations are debarred by the rules governing an artistic genre or style), the identification of some elements will help one to predict what other elements will be like. There will consequently be some recognizable similarities or other interdependences among elements, which is what we imply when we describe a pattern as 'structured' or 'orderly'.

The German school of information-theoretic aestheticians, led by Frank and Gunzenhäuser, has built an ambitious psychological theory of aesthetics on the assumption that aesthetic satisfaction reaches a maximum when the information-processing capacity of the human nervous system is fully used but not overstepped. If incoming information is too low, a perceived pattern is too dull to be satisfying. If the influx of information is excessive, the observer strives to reorganize the pattern by detecting redundancies, so that some information is discarded and an amount approximating the optimum is absorbed. These writers have also reinterpreted Birkhoff's theory with which their own views have clear affinities. They identify his 'complexity (C)' with the total information content of a pattern and his 'order (O)' with the amount of subjective (i.e. recognized) redundancy.

Apart from these applications, information theory can illuminate the communicative functions of art, paralleling, on a more abstract and widely generalizable level, the analyses of signs and symbols put forward by Ogden and Richards, Morris, and others. Information, clearly enough, flows from the creative artist to an audience member or appreciator through his work.

Much of this information can be traced further back to the external events and social influences that determined the artist's choice of form and content. Such a conceptualization helps us to analyse the network of reciprocal influences that link the artist with his audience and both of them with their social environment, with the external events in which they are both immersed, and with the physical characteristics of the medium (Moles, 1958). The competition between the various sources of information for the limited transmitting capacity of the artistic channel can also account for some of the stylistic differences between the artistic products of different ages and cultures (Berlyne, 1971).

*Neurophysiological findings*

Since the end of the Second World War revelations about the workings of the brain have been pouring out of neurophysiological laboratories. A great deal has been discovered, in particular, about the processes in the nervous system that underlie motivational and emotional states, including those that are of significance for aesthetics. Two currents of research have been particularly enlightening in this connection.

First, there is the work from which the notion of a fluctuating level of 'arousal' or 'activation' has arisen. Arousal level can be equated with an individual's momentary degree of 'alertness', 'attentiveness', 'emotional intensity' and 'excitement'. Much is now known about the events in the brain that are responsible for rises and falls in arousal level, about the many factors in the external evironment and inside the body that can raise or lower arousal, and about the psychophysiological changes through which fluctuations in arousal manifest themselves. These changes, which involve the electrical activity of the brain, the electrical properties of the skin, circulatory and respiratory functions, muscle tension, and the diameter of the pupil of the eye, provide ways of detecting and measuring emotional reactions that can supplement other, less direct methods, dependent on verbal reports and observations of motor activity. Many of these processes have long been recognized as bodily manifestations of 'emotion', and, as mentioned above, they were used relatively early to study reactions to art.

Secondly, it has been found that animals will learn to repeat a simple act, such as pressing a lever, at a high rate if this act has caused electrical stimulation to be delivered to certain areas in the lower brain. Such brain stimulation can, in other words, strengthen or reinforce an instrumental response that immediately precedes it. It is, that is to say, 'rewarding' in the sense in which this term is used by learning theorists. Rewarding events are usually reported by human subjects to be 'pleasant' or 'pleasurable'. And such is the case when neurosurgical patients have stimulation delivered to the appropriate areas of their brains. So, it would seem that experimenters have located processes in the brain that govern reward and pleasure or, to use an expression that covers both, 'positive hedonic value'.

There are evidently intimate links between these and the brain processes on which changes in arousal level depend. For one thing, there are abundant connecting fibres, and some degree of overlap, between the parts of the brain associated with the two. Secondly, the various properties that determine how rewarding or pleasurable a stimulus will be seem to coincide with those that determine how arousing or de-arousing it will be. There are, in fact, various indications that something will be rewarding and pleasurable if it either raises arousal moderately or brings arousal down from an excessively high level (Berlyne, 1967).

*Exploratory behaviour and collative stimulus properties*

Over the last twenty years there has been a rising tide of experimental and theoretical work on exploratory behaviour in animals and in human beings (Berlyne, 1960, 1966). This term denotes a multiplicity of activities, all of which serve to bring about, or prolong, or intensify exposure of sense organs to stimulus patterns that are not inherently beneficial or harmful.

Exploratory behaviour is exemplified by some of the activities observed or measured in what have become standard experimental techniques. Dogs stop whatever they are doing and turn around to look in the direction of some unaccustomed occurrence, while undergoing physiological changes indicative of momentarily increased arousal. Rats approach a strange object to look and sniff at it, or repeatedly press a lever that causes illumination to become momentarily brighter or dimmer, or tend to enter portions of a maze where novel and changing stimuli are likely to be found. Monkeys repeatedly push a heavily sprung door open to see what is going on outside the box in which they are confined. Human beings run their eyes over a picture that they are seeing for the first time, or operate the button controlling an automatic projector so that they look at each of a succession of slides for as long as they wish, or press one of two buttons to bring on one of two sound sequences. These forms of behaviour are sometimes motivated by curiosity and are cases of 'specific exploration'. The initial impact of an unaccustomed or puzzling event prompts efforts to obtain further information about it, to make sense of it, to classify it, to assimilate it. Human beings may often give way to 'idle curiosity', inquiring into matters of no practical, let alone vital, importance. But it is biologically understandable why specific exploration should replace other activities so readily whenever something occurs to interrupt a normal, expected course of environmental events. Anything strange may betoken impending danger, or else impending opportunities for gratification, that an animal cannot afford to ignore.

There is, however, also the category of 'diversive exploration', covering much that everyday parlance would label as 'play' or 'entertainment'.

Diversive exploratory behaviour seeks exposure to any event, regardless of content, that will offer a rewarding and pleasurable level of stimulation, variability, information inflow. It is, we may suppose, a matter of obtaining stimuli that will generate a moderate arousal boost, within the rewarding and pleasurable range, and also of avoiding the deleterious effects to which a complex nervous system is evidently liable when the inflow of stimulation and information from the environment is either excessive or sparse.

Postural changes (e.g., eye movements, head movements, sniffing) and locomotion are the only forms of exploratory behaviour available to animals, apart from the limited ability of some higher species to manipulate, or otherwise act on, objects so as to change their appearance or to extract sounds and tactual sensations from them. In contrast, the manual, imaginative and verbal capacities of human beings enable them to gain access to curiosity-alleviating or optimally variable stimulation by radically transforming portions of their environments. They can achieve this aim by creating artifacts, by decorating their implements, their buildings and their persons, by generating appropriate sequences of bodily movements, words and sounds.

The study of exploratory behaviour thus merges with experimental aesthetics. What we call aesthetic behaviour can be regarded in large part as a highly elaborate kind of exploration. This is true of forms of behaviour that bring about exposure to works of art. It applies to the behaviour of the artist who works on his medium until he has produced stimulus patterns that content him. It also applies to the actions that bring members of his audience into contact with his works, e.g., everything that must be done before reading a novel, settling into a seat in a theatre or concert hall, stationing oneself in front of a painting. The parts of aesthetic behaviour that do not qualify as exploration consist of the reactions, internal or externally observable, that follow the impact of a work.

Apart from this relationship, research on exploratory behaviour has had one outcome that bears much of the responsibility for the current revitalization of experimental aesthetics. It has drawn attention to the motivational effects of 'collative' stimulus properties. These are properties involving comparison or collation of distinct stimulus elements or items of information. They include novelty, surprisingness, complexity and ambiguity. They appear to determine more than anything else how likely it is that exploration will replace other activities, to what portions of the environment it will be directed, how vigorous it will be, and how long it will last.

It gradually became clear, however, that the motivational effects of collative properties are by no means confined to their influence on exploratory behaviour. In some conditions, they can make stimulus objects frightening and repellent, rather than curiosity-inducing or entertaining. Their significance for motivational aspects of personality, species-specific behaviour in lower animals, child development, psychopathology and social psychology is beginning to be appreciated. Most important of all for our present topic, the collative stimulus properties are the essential constituents of aesthetic 'form', 'composition' or 'structure'. They, more than any other factors, determine the 'intrinsic' values of sights and sounds (see our discussion of Morris's views, above).

*The new experimental aesthetics*

The study of exploratory behaviour and related phenomena has had various offshoots. One of them is a flourishing area of experimental investigation that deserves to be called the 'new experimental aesthetics'. Its exponents have not generally thought of themselves as contributors to psychological aesthetics. Nevertheless, what they are doing comes closer, if anything, to the central psychological problems of aesthetics than much of the older experimentation that was supposedly aimed in that direction.

The new experimental aesthetics contrasts with the old in three principal respects:

1. It concentrates on collative stimulus properties. Aesthetic reactions can certainly depend on many stimulus properties, including those that the older experimenters took up, and the objects that have been classed as 'artistic', 'beautiful' or 'aesthetically satisfying' at one time or another are bewilderingly varied. If one asks what they all have in common, it is surely that they all depend, in some degree at least, on form or structure, which means on collative variables, for their effects.
2. There is still a heavy reliance on verbal judgements to supply data through which 'subjective', 'latent' or 'intervening' variables can be scaled, but such data are sought in conjunction with data on non-verbal responses, including measures of exploratory behaviour and of psychophysiological processes.
3. Whereas the older experimental aestheticians pursued aesthetic problems in isolation, doing little to connect them with the rest of psychology or even with the rest of their own work, their successors are open to influences from many directions and strive to integrate their subject-matter with the main body of psychology.

There have been experiments on effects of novelty (the variable that received most attention in the early days of research on exploratory behaviour), as well as on surprisingness, incongruity and ambiguity. But most of the research with human subjects that we are now discussing has been concerned with effects of variations along the simplicity–complexity dimension. This dimension is evidently very close to the 'goodness' dimension that loomed so large in Gestalt theory, with the 'best' patterns approaching its 'simple' pole.

Judged complexity has been found to reflect, often in an astonishingly precise and direct way, the number of elements in a pattern and the degree to which its elements are similar or otherwise interdependent. This one variable determines reactions, both verbal and non-verbal, to a very large extent, at least when relatively simple, non-representational material is used. It has been found to retain a great deal of influence over them even when reproductions of paintings and passages of genuine music are presented.

It is difficult to sum up all the findings that have so far accrued from this kind of research. It is, however, possible to distinguish two groups of interrelated measures that both vary with complexity, but in different ways.

One group consists of measures that increase steadily as complexity rises (whether one thinks of subjective or judged complexity or of some objective criterion). They include judgements along an 'uninteresting–interesting' dimension and duration of exploration (how long a subject looks at a visual pattern or listens to a sequence of sounds when duration is under his control). Various indices of arousal likewise increase with complexity, and, in at least some circumstances, subjects faced with a choice between patterns are likely to seek exposure to the more complex one.

The second group includes judgements that indicate how 'pleasing', 'pleasant', 'liked' or 'preferred' a pattern is. Such judgements seem to be highly correlated with one another and to be non-monotonically related to complexity. A large number of experiments have produced inverted U-shaped curves, indicating that these attributes reach maxima when patterns fall within an intermediate range of complexity. Occasionally, curves with several peaks have been obtained. In view of the early experimental aestheticians' almost exclusive concentration on this kind of judgement, and considering its prominence in everyday conversation about the arts, it is rather paradoxical that the behavioural correlates of pleasingness, etc., are far from clear. As we have seen, there are clear and well-established links between exploratory behaviour and interestingness. In certain conditions, pleasingness, separated from interestingness, governs exploratory choice (i.e., which of two familiar patterns a subject chooses to be presented to him) and reward value (the ability of a stimulus to reinforce an instrumental response). But pending further research, little more than this can be said.

*Steps towards theoretical synthesis*

Each of these new approaches has imparted its own salutary fillips to the study of psychological aesthetics. Even more encouraging are the theoretical junctions that are being established between them. We are still far from the day when our knowledge about psychological reactions to art will coagulate into a clear and comprehensive theoretical picture. But the particles are beginning to cohere.

Let us review some of the points of contact briefly:

1. The collative stimulus properties, which have been brought to the fore by experiments on exploratory behaviour and have been scaled through verbal judgements, possess intimate connections with the measures used by information theory. As we have seen, the complexity of a pattern increases with the number of independently selected elements. When the number of elements is held constant, it is reduced by the presence of similarities or interdependencies among elements. This means that the more complex a pattern, the greater its information content and the greater the uncertainty associated with the class of patterns to which it belongs. In general, the more novel, surprising or incongruous the stimulus, the more improbable it is, which means the greater the amount of information contained in it. An ambiguous or unclear pattern admits of several mutually exclusive interpretations, classifications or hypotheses, which implies a commensurate degree of uncertainty.

2. In his book *Emotion and Meaning in Music* (1956) Meyer argued that structural properties of perceived patterns could suffice to induce emotion. He expatiated on the implications of this hypothesis for music, which, in the usual absence of representational content, has nothing but its structure to exert an affective impact. His copious examples showed how musical passages that violate expectations or that leave the listener without a firm expectation can induce emotional disturbance, which is assuaged when what follows brings clarification. Meyer was clearly discussing factors that can be specified either in information-theoretic terms or in terms of collative stimulus properties. He was the first to propound plainly and incisively, with special reference to aesthetics, a principle that, as we have seen, had been adumbrated by the Gestalt school, that emotion can result from the structural relations contained in a perceived pattern. This principle is receiving corroboration as a steady flow of experiments demonstrates that collative and information-theoretic variables – novelty, surprisingness, complexity, uncertainty – can have significant effects on various indices of arousal.

3. As we have already noted, there is plentiful evidence of intimate connections between arousal and hedonic value. Several experiments have by now shown how exploratory responses can be reinforced by visual or auditory patterns that appear immediately after they have been performed. Furthermore, there is plenty of evidence that the reward value of these patterns depends on their collative properties. Similarly, experiments with verbal evaluative judgements confirm that collative properties can determine how 'pleasing', 'pleasant', etc., a pattern will be judged.

4. Many writers, going back at least two and a half centuries, have asserted that beauty or aesthetic pleasure depends on the interplay of two antagonistic and mutually compensating factors. Various pairs of terms have been used to designate these factors – 'diversity' and 'unity', 'complexity' and 'order',

etc. – but none of these pairs of terms has been sufficiently inclusive to cover all cases. We can now see that these writers were referring to factors that tend to raise arousal and factors that tend to moderate arousal. We can also understand, in the light of recent developments in both psychology and neurophysiology (Berlyne, 1967), why appropriate combinations of arousing and de-arousing factors should produce pleasure. They may generate a jump in arousal to an uncomfortable level followed by relief, or they may jointly ensure a rise in arousal that is mild enough to be within the pleasurable range.

5. Many recent experiments have shown stimulus patterns to be judged most favourably when they fall within an intermediate range of novelty or complexity. Patterns that are too novel or complex are apt to be shunned as too confusing or startling. Those that are too familiar or simple are apt to be condemned as insipid and dull. Several earlier experiments, relating pleasure to stimulus intensity, produced similar inverted U-shaped curves. Psychologists interested in the information-processing aspect of the nervous system, including the information-theoretic aestheticians, have noted the disturbing effects of deficient or excessive intake of information. Recent work on the brain functions governing arousal and hedonic value helps to make these findings intelligible. Some stimulus patterns are incapable of heightening arousal. Others drive arousal up to uncomfortable heights without prospects of early relief.

Psychological aestheticians are now equipped to venture beyond the old questions of how people look at, listen to and react to works of art towards the deeper question of why they do so. They can, in other words, begin to attack the inescapable question of why aesthetic activities, which do not at first sight seem necessary for survival, exist at all and have existed through the whole range of human history and geography. Progress in these directions will not only help us to understand art. It will help us to understand human psychology in general.

## References

Arnheim, R. (1954), *Art and Visual Perception*, University of California Press.

Attneave, F. (1954), 'Some informational aspects of visual perception', *Psychological Review*, vol. 61, pp. 183–93.

Berlyne, D. E. (1960), *Conflict, Arousal and Curiosity*, McGraw-Hill.

Berlyne, D. E. (1966), 'Curiosity and exploration', *Science*, vol. 153, pp. 25–33.

Berlyne, D. E. (1967), 'Arousal and reinforcement', in D. Levine (ed.), *Nebraska Symposium on Motivation, 1967*, University of Nebraska Press.

Berlyne, D. E. (1971), *Aesthetics and Psychobiology*, Appleton-Century-Crofts.

Birkhoff, G. D. (1933), *Aesthetic Measure*, Harvard University Press.

Cohen, J. (1966), *Structure du langage poétique*, Flammarion.

FECHNER, G. T. (1860), *Elemente der Psychophysik*, Breitkopf & Härtel.
FECHNER, G. T. (1865), 'Über die Frage des goldnen Schnitts', *Archiv für die zeichnenden Künste*, vol. 11, pp. 100–112.
FECHNER, G. T. (1876), *Vorschule der Ästhetik*, Breitkopf & Härtel.
FRANCÈS, R. (1968), *Psychologie de l'esthétique*, Presses Universitaires de France.
GARNER, W. R. (1962), *Uncertainty and Structure as Psychological Concepts*, Wiley.
HOCHBERG, J., and MCALISTER, E. (1953), 'A quantitative approach to figural "goodness"', *Journal of Experimental Psychology*, vol. 46, pp. 361–4.
LOMAX, A. (1968), *Folk Song Style and Culture*, American Association for the Advancement of Science.
MARTIN, L. J. (1906), 'An experimental study of Fechner's principles of aesthetics', *Psychological Review*, vol. 13, pp. 142–219.
MARTINDALE, C. E. (1972), *The Romantic Progression*, Temple University Press, in press.
MEYER, L. B. (1956), *Emotion and Meaning in Music*, University of Chicago Press.
MOLES, A. (1958), *Théorie de l'information et perception esthétique*, Flammarion. Translated as *Information Theory and Aesthetic Perception*, University of Illinois Press, 1966.
OGDEN, C. K., and RICHARDS, I. A. (1923), *The Meaning of Meaning*, Harcourt, Brace.
VALENTINE, C. W. (1962), *The Experimental Psychology of Beauty*, Methuen.

# 6 The Emergence of a Cognitive Psychology of Motivation

Heinz Heckhausen and Bernard Weiner

Perhaps the oldest and most central controversy in the study of motivation is whether behaviour should be conceptualized as 'mechanistic' or 'cognitive'. These two theoretical approaches differ in the extent to which higher mental processes are inferred and employed to account for the initiation, direction and persistence of behaviour.

In the recent history of psychology, mechanism has been declared the winner of this quarrel. During the 1920–60 era psychology was dominated by the mechanistic behaviourism of Watson and the neo-behaviourism of Hull and Spence. The goals of this mechanistic psychology were 'to predict, given the stimulus, what reaction will take place; or given the reaction, state what the... stimulus is that causes the reaction' (Watson, 1924, p. 11). It is certainly true that psychology 'first lost its soul, and then its mind'.

The elegance, precision and success of the predictions generated by the Hull–Spence models of behaviour in part provided the validity for a mechanistic conceptual approach to the study of motivation, and resulted in Hullian theory having an all-powerful position in the academic study of motivation. While some psychologists publicly or privately may have questioned the ability of a mechanistic conception to account for the variety and complexity of human action, most agreed that drive theory as formulated by Hull and Spence did provide an acceptable framework to understand the 'simple' behaviour of infrahumans.

The mechanistic movement in psychology has now abated. The current trend in the study of motivation is towards the inclusion of higher mental processes as determinants of action. In contrast to the S-R (stimulus-response) formula of Watson and other associationists, and the 'empty organism' theories of Hull and Spence, the general format of a cognitive model of motivation is: S–Cognition–R. That is, an antecedent stimulus, viewed as a source of information rather than stimulation, is conceived as encoded and transformed into a 'belief'. The meaning imposed upon the environment then determines the subsequent behavioural response. Psychology thus is regaining its mind!

Our task in this paper is to document the challenge of a cognitive psychology of motivation. Rather than pointing out the inadequacies of drive theory by discussing data which fall beyond its usual boundary conditions, or referring to the cognitive dissents of Lewin and Tolman, we have chosen first to review recent studies bearing upon the very empirical foundations of Hullian theory. The data we consider were generated by experimental paradigms associated with cognitive approaches to motivation, and concern food and water consumption, the expression of fear and emotion, the effects of anxiety on learning, the frustration–aggression hypothesis, and resistance to extinction. We will conclude that even within these traditional terrains a mechanistic or S-R approach cannot account for the empirical evidence. In the second part of the paper theoretical developments in the area of achievement motivation are recounted in detail. The growth of a systematic cognitive psychology is perhaps best illustrated within the context of achievement-related behaviour. And finally, some present gaps in motivation research and illustrative examples of the study of cognitive processes in motivation are examined.

## The empirical foundations of drive theory

### *Hours of deprivation, drive and consummatory activity*

As conceived by Hull (1943), drive is a non-directive energizer of behaviour which activates and augments all potential behavioural responses. The strength of drive has been generally operationalized as hours of food or water deprivation, or other causes of tissue injury, such as the strength of an electric shock or the intensity of a puff of air to the eye. A number of investigations have demonstrated that the speed, latency, intensity, etc. of an instrumental response, and the amount of consummatory activity, vary directly as a function of drive level (hours of deprivation, etc.). This work is cited extensively as supporting the Hullian conception of motivation (see Brown, 1961).

*The cognitive determinants of drive states.* It now appears that the strength of drive is not simply determined by the amount of deprivation or the magnitude of a shock. Rather, drive level is dependent upon the person's perception of his state of need.

Perhaps the most interesting evidence demonstrating the cognitive determinants of drive was generated by Festinger's (1957) theory of cognitive dissonance. According to Festinger, two cognitions are dissonant if their implications are mutually exclusive. One oft-cited example of such a dissonant relationship is the cognition that 'smoking causes cancer', coupled with the knowledge that one likes to smoke. Festinger states that when a state of incompatible cognitions exists, the person is motivated to bring the cognitions into a more consonant relationship. Thus, the individual may convince himself that he does not like to smoke, disbelieve the smoking–cancer relationship, try to get others to smoke to bolster his own belief system, etc.

A 'forced-compliance' paradigm has been used to produce cognitive dissonance in laboratory situations. In this experimental paradigm an unpleasant request is made of the subject, and the reward offered to comply is insufficient, given the nature of the solicited behaviour. Because engagement in the action and the small amount of reward are dissonant, it has been predicted that the individual may bring his cognitions into harmony by revaluing the perceived aversiveness of the request. A decrease in the subjective unpleasantness of dissonant behaviour has been reported by many investigators (see Festinger and Carlsmith, 1959, for the prototypical experiment).

Brehm (1962) extended this paradigm to investigate the determinants of hunger and thirst. Brehm asked some of his subjects to undergo continued food or water deprivation, without providing an appropriate incentive for their actions. The lack of incentive for voluntary deprivation creates a state of dissonance. As predicted by dissonance theory, individuals who agreed to this deprivation rated themselves as less hungry or thirsty, and drank less water when given the opportunity, than subjects given adequate compensation for their compliance.

A related finding is reported by Grinker (1967) (see Zimbardo, 1969). Grinker demonstrated that subjects given no 'reason' to undergo continued avoidance conditioning are less likely to display an avoidance response (eyelid closure prior to a puff of air to the eye) than subjects not burdened with the dissonant cognition. It is as though the experimental subjects experience the aversive stimulus as less painful than control subjects, and thus are less motivated to avoid the air puff.

In other words, to activate behaviour a state of deprivation or tissue injury must be cognized as a 'need'. The cues from the viscera provide the organism with one source of evidence concerning its need state, while 'higher centres' provide yet another source of knowledge. In the experiments by Brehm (1962) and Grinker (1967) the 'higher-order' or dissonance-generated information contradicts the cues of the viscera, and in part controls the behaviour.

### *Fear as a learned drive*

Most human behaviours apparently are initiated when the organism is not deprived of a commodity necessary for survival. We work when not hungry, affiliate when sexually satisfied, etc. These observations seem to contradict the simplified conception of drive presented above. Hull was aware of this difficulty, and in his later writings broadened his thinking about drives. He postulated (1951) that any neutral stimulus could acquire drive properties, if it were contiguously paired with the rapid onset and offset of a drive. In the classic experiments of Miller and Mowrer, it was demonstrated that cues paired with shock energize behaviour and lead to new learning when later unaccompanied by the shock. Hence, it was postulated that fear or anxiety is a learned drive, having the same functional properties as the unlearned drive activated by shock. Fear was believed to be elicited automatically in situations resembling those in which the shock was experienced.

*The cognitive determinants of fear.* The conceptualization of a conditioned drive of anxiety is called into question by a series of studies conducted by Lazarus (1966) and his colleagues. Lazarus suggests that in situations of threat the individual reappraises the potential harm of a feared stimulus. Emotion and subsequent action are then based upon this cognitive evaluation.

In the general experimental paradigm employed by Lazarus, a 'threat' film (an accident, a primitive circumcision rite) is shown to subjects. A psychological defence or coping mechanism is introduced, either prior to or during the film presentation, which is intended to reduce the threat value of the film. For example, a soundtrack accompanies the film which assures the viewer that the circumcision is not painful, that the people in the accident film are actors, etc. While subjects watch the film autonomic indicators of fear, such as heart-rate, are monitored continuously. Lazarus finds that facilitation of the mechanisms which enable an organism to cope with threat reduces fear. That is, relative to a control group, viewers receiving defensive orientations such as denial or intellectualization exhibit less fear reactions. The drive properties of aversive stimuli therefore are dependent upon how a person cognizes perceived threat.

*Cognitive determinants of other emotions.* There is evidence that emotions other than fear are a function of the individual's perception of his immediate stimulus situation. In a well-known study by Schachter and Singer (1962), subjects were injected with epinephrine, an activating agent. While under this induced arousal they were placed in a social situation in which another person acted either angry or euphoric. The epinephrine-activated subjects not aware of the arousal properties of the drug acted more euphoric in the euphoria-producing situation, and more angry in the anger-producing situation, than subjects given a placebo pill. Schachter and Singer propose a two-factor theory to explain these data. They postulate that emotional expression requires both arousal and an appropriate label for one's arousal state. Hence, they argue that there is a lability in the experience of emotions; perceived feelings are dependent upon cognitions concerning the causes of one's internal state.

Other data, however, suggest that arousal is not a necessary antecedent for emotional expression. In one pertinent experiment, Valins (1966) gave subjects false information concerning their internal arousal. While viewing slides of nude females, males overheard false heart-rate feedback which indicated that they were excited by some of the pictures, but not by others. The subjects subsequently rated the slides paired with the false arousal information as more attractive, and were more likely to select them for further viewing, than slides associated with a normal heart-rate. The subject apparently infers: 'My heart is beating rapidly; I must like this picture.' Thus, the cognition of an internal state, whether veridical or non-veridical, appears to be a sufficient condition for emotional feelings.

### *Anxiety and learning*

Inasmuch as anxiety is conceptualized as a drive or energizer within the Hullian system, its presence theoretically augments all the behavioural responses elicited in a given stimulus situation. Thus, anxiety may facilitate the speed of learning when correct responses to task stimuli are dominant, for the added drive level due to anxiety further increases the likelihood of responding correctly. On the other hand, anxiety may cause decrements in learning if incorrect task responses are dominant, or if many responses are competing for expression. The expected interaction between level of anxiety and the difficulty of a task has been reported by many investigators (see Spence, 1958). In these experiments an easy or complex verbal learning (paired-associates) task is administered to the subjects. Anxiety (drive) level is inferred from the score on an individual difference measure (the Manifest Anxiety scale). The results of these investigations reveal that individuals classified as high in anxiety learn an easy task, in which correct responses are pre-potent, faster than persons low in anxiety. Conversely, on a difficult task in which many competing responses are aroused, subjects high in anxiety take longer to learn than subjects who are relatively non-anxious. These data confirm the predictions of drive theory, and apparently demonstrate the capability of this mechanistic conception to explain relatively complex human behaviour.

*The cognitive determinants of the anxiety–learning relationship.* When learning a task rapidly, one may infer that he is performing well, or succeeding. On the other hand, when learning is progressing slowly, one might conclude that he is performing poorly, or failing. In the paired-associate tasks employed by Spence and his colleagues, the easy task is learned quickly, while the difficult task is mastered relatively slowly. Thus, the data cited by Spence may indicate that the learning of highly anxious subjects is facilitated at the easy task because there is success feedback, but relatively retarded at the difficult task due to the subjective failure.

To test this mediational interpretation of the verbal-learning data, Weiner (1966) and Weiner and Schneider (1971) severed the inherent relationship between task ease and subjective achievement evaluation. These investigators informed subjects performing an easy verbal-learning task that they were failing relative to others. Conversely, false norms conveyed that subjects attempting a difficult task were doing well. The data revealed that subjects high in anxiety learn the difficult (successful) task faster than subjects low in anxiety, but are slower at learning the easy (failed) task than the low-anxiety subjects. These results, which contradict the data cited by Spence, indicate that the Anxiety × Task Difficulty interaction is mediated the person's cognitions concerning the adequacy of his performance.

*Frustration and aggression*

The hypothesis that frustration causes aggression was first advanced by Dollard *et al.* (1939). These investigators attempted to explain aggressive behaviour by employing the constructs of Hullian learning theory, such as drive, stimulus, response and reward. A great deal of research generated by this theoretical approach has provided evidence that aggression is a function of the magnitude of the frustrated desire, that aggression may be displaced to other stimuli and modes of responding, that the occurrence of aggression may reduce the immediate tendency to aggress, and that the likelihood of aggressive expression is inversely related to the amount of punishment expected as a consequence of the action. In short, the S-R analysis of aggression has been heuristic and received substantial empirical support.

*The cognitive determinants of aggressive expression.* There is a growing literature which suggests that hostile feelings and aggressive behaviour are strongly affected by cognitive processes. In a pertinent investigation by Mallick and McCandless (1966), frustration was induced by having a stooge prevent subjects from completing tasks, thus causing the subjects to lose a monetary reward. In one experimental condition it was explained that the frustrator was 'sleepy [and] upset'. Subjects given this interpretation were less likely to aggress against the stooge than others not provided with a reasonable explanation of the stooge's behaviour. In an associated experiment guided by the cognitive approaches of Schachter and Singer (1962) and Valins (1966), Berkowitz, Lepinski and Angulo (1969) arranged for a stooge to anger subjects. The subjects then were given false autonomic feedback supposedly revealing their anger towards the stooge. These non-veridical perceptions of emotion systematically influenced the subsequent tendency to punish the stooge. Subjects informed that they were angry displayed more aggressiveness towards the stooge than subjects believing they were not overly upset. Thus, the two experiments briefly outlined here demonstrate that cognitions concerning the cause of frustration and beliefs about one's internal state mediate between frustrating events and the likelihood of aggressive expression.

*Resistance to extinction*

Resistance to extinction has been a popular dependent variable in the testing of Hullian theory. It has been demonstrated that the time to extinction is in part a function of the number of rewarded trials during learning, and the hours of deprivation during the testing period. These findings confirm predictions from Hullian theory. In addition, extinction is most retarded when there is intermitted or partial reinforcement during acquisition. A number of theories of extinction derived from the S-R approaches of Hull and Spence explain this phenomenon with some success.

*The cognitive determinants of extinction.* Three recent cognitive conceptions of motivation examine resistance to extinction, and have generated data not readily amenable to a mechanistic explanation. They are dissonance theory, social-learning theory and attribution theory.

1. Cognitive dissonance and experimental extinction. Instrumental actions towards a goal and the non-reception of a reward are dissonant cognitions (see p. 127). Hence, Lawrence and Festinger (1962) reason that partial reinforcement creates dissonance, for some of the instrumental acts are not followed by a reward. Further, these investigators suggest that one way to reduce this dissonance is to perceive 'extra' rewards in the situation. They infer that the perceived extra reward value of a goal is responsible for the relative slowness of extinction when there is partial reward during learning. In support of this position they demonstrate that resistance to extinction is a function of the number of non-rewarded or dissonance-creating trials during the learning period, rather than being determined by the percentage of reinforcement, as associationists had specified.

In a similar manner, Lawrence and Festinger argue that experimental manipulations such as the delaying of reinforcement or the requirement of an effortful instrumental response also create dissonance, and thus should retard extinction. In a series of experiments supporting the hypothesis concerning effort, they report that resistance to extinction is positively related to the steepness of an incline which rats must climb to receive food.

2. Social-learning theory, locus of control, and extinction. Social-learning theory as formulated by Rotter (1954) specifies that the strength of the tendency to engage in some behaviour is in part a function of the expectancy that a reinforcement will follow the response. The expectation of the goal event, in turn, is a function of two determinants: a specific expectancy, based upon the reinforcement contingency between the response under consideration in a specific stimulus situation, and a generalized expectancy, which is a higher-order belief concerning the probability of a reinforcement for a class of related behaviours across a variety of stimulus situations.

Locus of control, or the actual or potential allocation of responsibility for an outcome, is postulated to affect the strength of the generalized expectancy of reinforcement. On one end the locus of control dimension is anchored by internal (personal) factors, while at the other it is anchored by external (environmental) causes. Internal control refers to the perception of positive and negative outcomes as a result of one's own actions, while external control refers to events as being unrelated to one's own behaviour, or beyond personal control.

It has been hypothesized that internal versus external perception of control differentially influences shifts in expectancy, or the subjective probability of attaining a goal. The most straightforward test of this hypothesis is reported by Phares (1957). Phares instructed half of his subjects that performance at a task is only a matter of luck (external control), while subjects in a second experimental condition received instructions that performance is determined by skill (internal control). The data revealed that increments in the expectancy of future success after a success experience, and increments in the expectancy of failure following a failure experience, were more frequent and of greater magnitude in the skill than chance condition. That is, the preceding outcome was believed more likely to recur given internal rather than external perception of control.

In addition, a series of experiments has examined the relationship between locus of control, schedule of reinforcement, and resistance to extinction (see Rotter, 1966). Subjects in these experiments are given chance or skill task instructions, and either continuous (100 per cent) or partial (50 per cent) reward during the initial phase of the experiment. Then the reward is withheld, and resistance to extinction assessed. The data in these studies indicate that extinction is faster in the 100 per cent than 50 per cent schedule given chance instructions. On the other hand, in contrast to prior findings in the extinction literature, extinction is faster in the 50 per cent than 100 per cent reward condition given skill instructions. This programme of research again demonstrates the cognitive control over behaviour; time to extinction is in part affected by one's interpretation of the cause of an outcome.

3. Attribution theory, the conceptual analysis of causality, and extinction. Attribution theory concerns the allocation of responsibility for an event. Attribution theorists such as Heider (1958), who is most reponsible for the current interest in this area, assume that man is motivated to find the causes of events, and to understand his environment. Although incorrect or motivated inferential errors may be made, man is conceptualized as a rational organism, acting as a scientist, testing and discarding hypotheses about the world.

To reach causal inferences one must search for information, assemble and process this knowledge, etc. According to Kelley (1967), information about the consistency and social consensus of events is especially necessary to reach appropriate causal inferences. For example, let us assume one sees that another individual has enjoyed a film, and that one must decide whether to go to that film. This decision may in part depend upon the attribution of the enjoyment to the person (easily pleased, in a good mood), or to the film (a 'good' film). If all other individuals watching the film also enjoy it, and the particular person likes the film over repeated occasions, then it is likely that ascription of the enjoyment will be to the properties of the film. This may result in film-going behaviour. On the other hand, if *only* that particular person enjoys the film, the attribution is likely to be to the person, and the decision is likely to be to forgo the film. Hence, the attribution of causality has a functional significance (see also Jones *et al.*, 1972).

A taxonomic scheme for the allocation of causality in achievement-related contexts has been outlined by Weiner *et al.* (1971). Guided by the work of Heider (1958), these investigators propose that success or failure is primarily attributed to four causal elements: ability, effort, task difficulty and luck. These four elements can be comprised within two causal dimensions: locus of control (internal versus external), and the stability of the causal element (fixed versus variable). Ability and effort are properties of the person, while task difficulty and luck are environmental sources of causality. Further, ability and task difficulty remain relatively unchanged over time, while effort and luck may vary from moment to moment. According to Weiner *et al.*, locus of control determines the affect (not expectancy, as Rotter, 1966, specified) associated with an outcome. In one test of this hypothesis, Weiner, Heckhausen, Meyer and Cook (1972) allowed children to reinforce themselves for their achievement performance. Subjects could take an unspecified number of 'chips' following a success, and return an unspecified number of these chips following failure. The data indicated that ascription of success to effort heightens self-reward, while attribution of failure to lack of effort is associated with the greatest amount of self-punishment.

Affective reactions also are a function of locus of control in non-achievement-related contexts. In a prototypical demonstration of this relationship, Nisbett and Schachter (1966) informed some subjects that their naturally occurring fear symptoms towards an impending shock were due to a pill which they had taken. These subjects then manifested less fear than subjects ascribing their symptoms to the fear of shock. In a similar manner, Schachter and Singer (1962) had previously demonstrated that attribution of arousal to a pill rather than to the immediate social situation modulated feelings of anger or euphoria.

In opposition to Rotter (1966), Weiner *et al.* (1971) also postulate that the stability of the attributional dimension, rather than locus of control, influences expectancy shifts. In support of this hypothesis, Weiner, Heckhausen, Meyer and Cook (1972) report that following failure expectancy decrements are directly related to task difficulty and low-ability attributions, and inversely related to ascriptions to a lack of effort and bad luck. That is, if one believes that failure is due to bad luck or lack of effort, then he might expect the future outcome to differ from the past performance. On the other hand, attribution of failure to low ability or task difficulty implies that the past and future will be consistent. Weiner *et al.* (1971) report that extinction in an achievement-related context is hastened when attributions during non-reward are to stable factors, and retarded when ascriptions are to unstable factors. Random reinforcement schedules are therefore expected to retard extinction, for randomness of outcomes is a cue used to infer luck (unstable) attributions.

### *General summary*

Evidence has been reviewed that: (i) cognitions concerning deprivation states determine their psychological effects; (ii) anxiety reactions are influenced by the manner in which one cognitively copes with threat; (iii) the anxiety–learning relationship is mediated by perceptions of success and failure; (iv) aggressive responses are a function of perceptions of the frustrator and beliefs about one's anger; and (v) extinction is affected by causal ascriptions for the non-attainment of a goal. These data have been respectively generated by experimental paradigms involving: (i) forced compliance; (ii) introduction of defensive mechanisms; (iii) manipulation of success and failure; (iv) misinformation concerning one's internal arousal and feeling state; and (v) skill and chance instructions, and the assessment of causal attributions and subjective expectancies. In addition, theories pertaining to cognitive dissonance, emotionality, social learning and causal ascriptions have been introduced. The data, experimental paradigms, and theoretical advances in cognitive psychology reveal that a mechanistic psychology of motivation is neither dominant nor viable. Sophisticated cognitive conceptions of behaviour which attempt to relate systematically the structure of thought to action are evolving to explain our newly acquired knowledge (see Weiner, 1972).

## Research in achievement motivation

We now turn to examine the influence of cognitive psychology on achievement motive research. In the area of achievement motivation, psychology never completely lost its mind. Looking back, we now see that the twenty-year-old history of research in the area of achievement motivation, initiated with the publication of *The Achievement Motive* (McClelland *et al.*, 1953), represents an integration of inputs from mainstreams of psychology which have been traditionally segregated: psychoanalytic theory, mentalism and behaviourism. We can discern three overlapping stages in the research development which increasingly take into account the different kinds of cognitions which intervene in the motivating processes of behaviour.

*The stages in achievement research*

*The evolving of motive measures.* The first stage, extending from the late 1940s to the early 1960s, was preceded and guided by a definition of the achievement content area. The achievement motive was conceived to be involved whenever there is 'competition with a standard of excellence'. This simple definitional shortcut did not help resolve the problem of constructing a taxonomy of motives (see McDougall, 1908; Murray, 1938). It did, however, open the way for a more heuristic approach to the study of the person by singling out and delimiting *one* important area of human concerns.

In addition to a qualitative definition, the achievement motive had to be assessed quantitatively to have explanatory power in predicting and postdicting behaviour. The main and initial input to solve the problem of measurement was psychoanalytic and clinical in origin. It was Freud who considered fantasy the best place to look for unfulfilled wishes and intentions. Accordingly, Murray (1943) developed the Thematic Apperception Test (TAT) to diagnose the strength of individual needs. In this test persons tell stories to a set of standardized pictures portraying situations that intuitively tap one's motives. Guided by Murray's contribution, to assess the achievement motive four or six thematically cued pictures generally are presented on slides, to which stories are written. The analysis of the protocols with a carefully constructed scoring key of proven coding reliability became the *via regia* of achievement motive assessment (McClelland *et al.*, 1953). The fantasy measure even is able to discriminate between approach (hope of success) and avoidance (fear of failure) achievement tendencies (Heckhausen, 1963). There have been many attempts to supersede the TAT projective index of the achievement motive with an objective measure – but without clear success. Some self-report anxiety scales, however, do validly reflect achievement avoidance tendencies.

The European tradition of the psychology of consciousness, doomed to have died under the attacks of behaviourism, also was revived in the new motive measure. The achievement scoring key delineates cognitive entities, such as intentions and goal anticipations, and uses these thoughts as mentalistic brickstones which sum to a total achievement score. This seemed to many hard-nosed psychologists like a late resurrection of the Würzburg school and its mentalism or, even worse, like a re-establishment of the condemned introspectionism. But now this initial disrespect has been replaced by the simple insight that stimulus-controlled story-telling gives rise to observable cognitive behaviour, i.e. to thought samples, which are indicative of behaviour. In their integrative ingenuity the founders of the motive measure also succeeded in wedding European mentalism to American functionalism. The scoring units of the story unravel the content as conceived in the problem-solving sequence proposed by Dashiell (1949), a leading American functionalist.

With its psychoanalytic ancestry the TAT method of motive measurement inherited another suspicion. If fantasy gives rise to unfulfilled or repressed wishes, then a high achievement motive score should be a substitute expression for a low strength of actual achievement behaviour, and vice versa (Lazarus, 1961; see also Heckhausen, 1963). Empirical results, however, show the contrary to be true. Apperceptive fantasy concerning a motive which is not socially tabooed is directly related to overt action tendencies.

But is the measure really a valid index of the need for achievement? Initially, investigators examined whether the TAT was sensitive to increments in motive arousal *within* individuals. This sensitivity would be reflected in the increment in the achievement motive scores when the stories are written under 'arousal' conditions. The so-called 'shift' studies of motive arousal employed two different research procedures. On the one hand, the researchers were guided by the deprivation paradigm manipulating drive strength (see p. 127), with subjects 'aroused' by inducing failure (non-attainment of a goal). However, to deprive human subjects of achievement goals by having them fail in tasks has proved to be a questionable equivalent to depriving rats of food. The effects of prior success and failure on motive arousal and the achievement motive score remain somewhat ambiguous. On the other hand, a second shift paradigm contrasting the effects of relaxed versus ego-involving pre-test task instructions has been more successful. The data indicate that ego-involving task instructions clearly increase subsequent achievement-related content on the TAT. In sum, it appears that manipulating immediate cognitions with the experimenter structuring the meaning of the task is more effective in motive arousal than variation in the prior 'deprivation' history of the organism.

The second strategy to validate the thematic procedure was to relate the motive scores *between* individuals to various criterion data which were thought to be indices of motivated behaviour. This experimental work, heavily influenced by the mental-testing movement, was conducted to create networks by correlating the motive measure with a variety of dependent variables. This allowed for the further development and refinement of the measure, while the reported correlations also demonstrated the empirical validity of the fantasy procedure. Diverse areas of motive manifestation, such as choice, judgement, perception, memory, performance, time experience, bodily activation, etc., were employed both to develop and validate the TAT measures (Heckhausen, 1963, 1967).

*The motive construct placed within a theory of interacting forces.* Thus far, motive measures have been discussed as evolving via an integration of hitherto segregated mainstreams of psychology, yielding a measure with both scoring reliability and validity. Of course, the psychology of personality has developed a plethora of tests with similar characteristics. However, these tests, at times constructed with the aid of factor-analytic techniques, frequently did not further our understanding of personality dynamics and remained primarily descriptive in nature, reminding one of static structuralism. The achievement measure escaped this fate when Atkinson introduced his risk-taking model in 1957. He placed the need for achievement construct within the framework of an Expectancy × Value theory. Thus, as opposed to other indices of personality traits such as the two big 'A's' of that period (Authoritarian Personality and Anxiety), need for achievement was conceived within a quantitative and cognitive context as one force of a person × environment interaction. This step opened the second stage in the achievement motivation research.

According to Atkinson (1957), motive arousal (here the strength of an achievement tendency) was conceived to be a multiplicative function of the strength of the achievement motive, the probability of success (task difficulty), and the incentive value of success. Success probability and incentive value are linked in an inverse linear relationship (i.e. low probability of success indicates a high incentive value of success, and vice versa). Atkinson's risk-taking theory thus stands in the tradition of the expectancy theory which Tolman (1955) formulated (demand for the goal × expectancy of goal attainment); the level of aspiration theory which Lewin *et al.* (1944) proposed (valence of the goal × probability); and the decision theory which Edwards (1954) outlined (utility × probability). The contribution of Atkinson's formulation to these Expectancy × Value theories was the introduction of an individual difference parameter based on the newly developed motive measure.

Atkinson's model stimulated much research, particularly in the level of aspiration area, for the model led to differential risk-preference predictions among individuals differing in achievement motive strength. Persons high in achievement needs were expected to (and do) prefer tasks of intermediate levels of difficulty, while persons low in achievement needs were predicted relatively to (and do) prefer tasks of high or low difficulty level (see also Atkinson and Feather, 1966). The model has not been static, and more recently a number of revisions and extensions have been formulated. Some of these revisions were guided by evidence that persons high in achievement needs appear to prefer somewhat lower success probabilities than predicted by the theory (Heckhausen, 1968). In addition, other empirical data which led to theoretical modifications suggest that motivational tendencies persist until satisfied, as Freud had postulated many decades before (Weiner, 1970). And the model's conceptualization of fear of failure as being only an inhibitory force also is being reconsidered (Birney, Burdick and Teevan, 1969).

*Elaboration of cognitions involved in achievement-related behaviour.* Atkinson's risk-taking model today is one of the most prominent theories of motivation. It is in the best tradition of hypothetico-deductive theory formation advocated by Hull, and is strongly influenced by the mechanistic tradition of Hull. The main cognitive component in Atkinson's theory is the subjective probability of success. But this cognitive construct is conceived within the general framework of body-mind parallelism, where cognitive events are merely unreliable accompaniments of underlying motivational processes (Atkinson and Birch, 1970). In addition, the theory neglects all mental events other than expectancy which might have motivational impact, such as information scanning and processing, causal judgements, self-evaluations, etc.

After the extensive integrative convergence in the achievement motive research area over the last two decades, we now expect a departure which will re-establish contact with the more positive aspects of phenomenology. In this new path cognitions will be treated as observables which influence action, rather than as epiphenomena. Thus, research in the area of achievement motivation may completely regain its mind in a third stage of the achievement motivation research.

One recent step in this direction is exemplified in the introduction of causal attributions as determinants of achievement-related behaviour (Weiner, Heckhausen, Meyer and Cook, 1972; Weiner *et al.*, 1971). This work (see p. 133) has resulted in a re-analysis of the springs of achievement-related behaviour. Achievement motive differences have been related to different preoccupations with causal attributions. Persons with a stronger hope of success than fear of failure tend to ascribe success to ability and effort (properties of the self) and failure to a lack of effort. On the other hand, individuals with a predominantly fear-of-failure orientation relatively ascribe success to good luck and failure to a lack of ability. These attributional tendencies are important because causal ascription determines the affective and expectancy-change consequences of success and failure. When internal factors are believed to be influential in determining achievement outcome, affect (as exhibited in self-reinforcement, verbalized feelings of pride and shame, etc.) is augmented. Further, as already discussed, when fixed causal factors are considered to be more influential in causing an outcome, the decrease in the expectancy of success after failure is magnified. It therefore follows, for example, that individuals high in fear of failure are especially likely to expect further failure after non-attainment of a goal, inasmuch as they ascribe failure to the fixed factor of low ability. They might then tend to quit the task because of this judgement. Furthermore, the causal attribution pattern depends, in part, on the perceived difficulty of the task. Outcomes of tasks of intermediate difficulty are believed to be most influenced by effort expenditure (Weiner, Heckhausen, Meyer and Cook, 1972). Thus, the essential risk-preference predictions of Atkinson's risk-taking model are amenable to reinterpretation within the framework of causal attribution theory (see also Weiner *et al.*, 1971).

### *Some present gaps as promises for future research*

*Cognitive dimensions and encoding patterns.* An old notion in psychology is that people differ in apperceiving and structuring the identical objective situation. We would now prefer to talk about information processing, and assume that individual differences in motive dispositions relate to different encoding patterns in evaluating situations. The TAT could be a useful tool to examine individual differences in these encoding patterns. Further, a configural analysis of the scored cognitive elements, along with the recognition of neglected cognitive dimensions and processing strategies, might greatly enhance the predictive power of the TAT. For example, story protocols might be scored for the causal concepts now known to influence achievement striving.

Attempts at achievement motive change have been guided by the impact of cognitive concepts and encoding patterns on achievement-related behaviour. In the achievement change programmes exemplified in the work of McClelland and Winter (1969), new cognitions are instilled, in part, by having the course participants learn to score the TAT for achievement motivation. There is inferential evidence that through this technique the participants actually come to think and feel like business entrepreneurs. For example, the participants become more sensitive to the probability of attaining feedback and to the possibility of taking responsibility in achievement-related situations. The view of motivation as a set of cognitions comes close to Kelly's (1955) notion of personal constructs.

*Cognitive styles, concepts and schemata.* It can be argued that a person's transactions within his dominant motive system are characterized by sharper, more discriminative and more abstract understanding of relevant situations. That is, cognitive styles of information processing and concept encoding develop which allow the individual to function efficiently in situations of his cardinal motive type. The distinction made by Harvey, Hunt and Schroder (1961), for example, between abstractness and concreteness in thought, which relates to the manner in which the environment is meaningfully decoded, might prove useful in the understanding of motivational processes.

It is a short step from cognitive styles to the concepts and the schemata underlying the cognitions which mediate between situational cues and responses, and between response outcomes and new responses. Schemata refer to higher-order encoding patterns or to implicit theories which a person holds about the 'nature' of his transactions with the environment. Although, for example, concepts such as ability and effort are employed in the study of achievement motivation, the perceived nature of these concepts, and their schematic interactions, has not been examined in any detail.

*Anticipatory cognitions and future orientation.* One oversimplification coupled with laboratory situations is that an experiment has a final outcome which is the end of a short episode, generally divorced from the person's long-term goals. For the subject, working in the laboratory is a 'closed' as opposed to an 'open' task (Nuttin, 1953). Outside the laboratory, however, virtually all achievement-related activities are future-oriented, with both immediate and long-term consequences. The delayed consequences must take into account the fact that the event is intermediate in a chain of activities extending into the future. This overlapping of time-structuring activities has been labelled a 'serial' by Murray (1951). Raynor (1969) recently has formalized the impact of long-term goals on immediate action within Atkinson's model of achievement behaviour. Applied researchers concerned with behaviour outside the laboratory previously had constructed achievement models taking into account the future consequences of present activities. Vroom (1964), for example, includes the perceived 'instrumentality' of a goal within an Expectancy × Value frame work. In Vroom's conception perceived instrumentality connects the immediate ('first-order') outcome of present activities with delayed consequences, or 'second-order' outcomes, where outcomes are construed as individual preferences or valences.

**Illustrative investigations of intervening cognitive processes**

Causal attributions and reappraisal studies (see pp. 133–5) demonstrate the mediating nature of different types of cognitions in motive arousal and their influence on performance. We now examine other areas of investigation which also are of fundamental importance for a cognitive psychology.

*Intentions*

The cognitions most influencing action according to 'naïve' inner experience are 'intentions'. Intentions were a main object of psychological consideration for many years, but they vanished from psychology with the rise of behaviourism. The last time this construct was of central influence was during the turn of the century, in the Würzburg school of Külpe, Watt and Ach. Now, however, intentions, and even 'will', are making a comeback. For example, Locke and his colleagues (Locke, 1968; Locke, Cartledge and

Knerr, 1970) have shown that conscious goals and intentions regulate task performance. These investigators find that persons choosing hard rather than easy goals, or accepting hard goals when assigned by the experimenter, expend relatively great effort and have a high level of performance. Evidence that this augmented performance is mediated by higher-order intentions has been shown in other studies demonstrating that level of aspiration choice is dependent upon pre-choice commitment to varying 'behavioural intentions'. Intentions of 'just succeed', 'get as great a sense of personal achievement as possible' or 'overcome the greatest possible challenges' respectively increase preference for more difficult goals as well as performance output. Moreover, it appears that incentives *per se*, such as monetary reward, do not affect performance independently of intentions.

It has been hinted that applied research interests may be particularly conducive to a more cognitive view of motivation. Kanfer (1971), for example, arguing from the perspective of a behavioural therapist, conceptualizes behaviour as a three-stage process. The stages consist of self-monitoring, or the attainment of feedback about one's ongoing behaviour; self-evaluation, or the comparison of outcome with performance standards; and self-reinforcement, or the positive or negative evaluation of the self. Within such a self-regulative process, statements of intent are necessary precursors for the initiation of new behaviours which may come to dominate initially stronger responses in the person's habit-family hierarchy. The new behaviours are instigated by 'performance promises' or 'contracts' made with oneself, often in communication with another person, such as a therapist. Kanfer and Karoly (1971) point out that these intentions alter the self-reinforcing consequences of action by changing the performance standards which provide a basis for self-evaluation.

### *Expectations*

Expectations are determined by both an individual's generalized or motive-linked expectancies and by the concrete cues of a given situation. While both personality and the situation always interact, the question arises under what conditions one or the other of these two factors will be a more potent determinant of expectations.

Ertel (1964), for example, has demonstrated that the announcement of an intelligence test arouses expectations which are consistent with an individual's predominant motive. Ertel first independently established the semantic profiles of two types of tasks. One task was given the description 'One hopes to achieve success in the end', while the other task was described as eliciting the reaction that 'One is afraid of not achieving success despite the efforts made'. The ratings of an impending intelligence test by individuals high in hope of success were similar with the semantic profile of the 'success' task. Conversely, persons whose achievement motivation was failure-oriented anticipated the forthcoming intelligence test in a manner characterized by the semantic profile of the 'failure' task. In sum, generalized expectancies of success brought into the situation by the person determined his immediate expectancy.

As opposed to Ertel, Reiss (reported in Heckhausen, 1968) demonstrated the dominance of situational cues in determining expectation. She used the Zeigarnik effect as a behavioural index, for it has been demonstrated that task recall is in part a function of generalized expectancies of success. The usual empirical finding in this area is that persons high in hope of success recall more unsolved tasks than solved tasks, while more solved than unsolved tasks are recalled by persons high in fear of failure. Reiss induced daydream activity between task performance and recall in a Zeigarnik-type situation by instructing subjects to have a vivid daydream involving either a success or failure experience. Following the success induction, subjects recalled more unsolved than solved tasks, while with the failure induction this pattern of recall was reversed. These findings characterized subjects in the success and failure arousal conditions regardless of the individual motive dispositions. In other words, the situational cues or the immediate arousal expectancy was a more potent determinant of recall than the motive-dependent expectancies brought into the situation by the person.

### *Daydreaming*

The Freudian notion that imaginative behaviour primarily has the function of drive reduction has been called into serious question (Klinger, 1969, 1971; Singer, 1966). Daydreaming appears to be a normal activity of an 'active brain' when the channel capacity for processing information from the outside world and from the monitoring of one's activity is not fully utilized. Under these conditions the 'inner channel' is available and processes self-generated contents which provide varied stimulation (Fiske and Maddi, 1961), elaborate the person's current concerns (Klinger, 1971), and aid him in coping with his environment.

The role of daydreaming in a goal-directed action sequence has not been seriously studied. It is reasonable to assume that daydreaming may have arousal or motivational properties, be a rehearsal of planned instrumental activities, or involve the calculation of future action possibilities. In addition, daydreaming may have a retrospective directedness and heighten the awareness of errors in past instrumental actions. In short, daydreaming may be interpolated at various segments of an action sequence: it may be preparatory to the action, occur during the behaviour, or follow the attainment or non-attainment of the goal. Further, the daydream may focus upon intents, expectations, long-term goal consequences, causal attributions, etc.

### A process model of self-regulation

Different kinds of cognitions influence the course of behaviour within an action sequence. An action sequence may be subdivided into four temporally sequential stages: the foreperiod, the performance period, the immediate post-performance or self-evaluation period, and the delayed post-performance period. Cognitive events are not distributed evenly or stochastically over this whole sequence. The foreperiod perhaps gives rise to the most diverse cognitive activity. There may be appraisal of the situation, planning of the action to be taken, intentions, fixing the standard against which performance is to be evaluated, prospective causal attributions to possible sources of performance outcome, expectations of success and failure, search for relevant performance information, etc. During the performance period there may be continuous monitoring of one's behaviour, alteration of planned instrumental sequences, re-evaluation of expectancies, appraisal of one's internal states, etc. In the immediate post-performance or self-evaluation segment of action the performance outcome is compared with the personal standard for that performance (see Diggory, 1966). The perceived outcome is determined via self-monitored feedback or via information provided by outside sources. If feedback is incomplete, then there is likely to be a search for feedback information. The standard in self-evaluation may be deduced from generalized expectancies of the motive system, although they are often set by an intention made during the foreperiod. (It has been shown that general standards are more resistant to reappraisal and change than specific intentions; see Diggory, 1966). The last of the 'cognitive segments', the delayed post-performance period, also includes a variety of possible cognitions. A reappraisal may take place altering the causal ascriptions; intentions (standards), instrumental planning, and expectations may be reconsidered; and so on. Further, the delayed post-performance period may be the most likely time that daydreaming occurs about further delayed consequences and their contingencies.

### Summary

It is evident from the review in this paper that the empirical and theoretical foundation of a cognitive theory of motivation already has been set. More concentrated analysis of motivational phenomena from a cognitive point of view is the promising challenge for future research and understanding in the field of motivation.

### References

Atkinson, J. W. (1957), 'Motivational determinants of risk-taking behavior', *Psychological Review*, vol. 64, pp. 359–72.

Atkinson, J. W., and Birch, D. (1970), *The Dynamics of Action*, Wiley.

Atkinson, J. W., and Feather, N. T. (eds.) (1966), *A Theory of Achievement Motivation*, Wiley.

Berkowitz, L., Lepinski, J. P., and Angulo, E. J. (1969), 'Awareness of own anger level and subsequent aggression', *Journal of Personality and Social Psychology*, vol. 11, pp. 293–300.

Birney, R. C., Burdick, H., and Teevan, R. C. (1969), *Fear of Failure Motivation*, Wiley.

Brehm, J. W. (1962), 'Motivational effects of cognitive dissonance', in M. R. Jones (ed.), *Nebraska Symposium on Motivation*, University of Nebraska Press, pp. 51–77.

Brown, J. S. (1961), *The Motivation of Behavior*, McGraw-Hill.

Dashiell, J. F. (1949), *Fundamentals of General Psychology*, Houghton Mifflin.

Diggory, J. C. (1966), *Self-Evaluation: Concepts and Studies*. Wiley.

Dollard, J., Miller, N. E., Doob, L., Mowrer, O. H., and Sears, R. R. (1939), *Frustration and Aggression*, Yale University Press.

Edwards, W. (1954), 'The theory of decision-making', *Psychological Bulletin*, vol. 51, pp. 380–417.

Ertel, S. (1964), 'Die emotionale Natur des "semantischen Raumes"', *Psychologische Forschung*, vol. 28, pp. 1–32.

Festinger, L. (1957), *A Theory of Cognitive Dissonance*, Row, Peterson.

Festinger, L., and Carlsmith, J. M. (1959), 'Cognitive consequences of forced compliance', *Journal of Abnormal and Social Psychology*, vol. 58, pp. 203–10.

Fiske, D. W., and Maddi, S. R. (eds.) (1961), *Functions of Varied Experience*, Dorsey.

Grinker, J. (1967), 'The control of classical conditioning by cognitive manipulation', unpublished doctoral dissertation, New York University.

Harvey, O. J., Hunt, D. E., and Schroder, H. M. (1961), *Conceptual Systems and Personality Organization*, Wiley.

Heckhausen, H. (1963), *Hoffnung und Furcht in der Leistungsmotivation*, Hain, Meisenheim/Glan.

Heckhausen, H. (1967), *The Anatomy of Achievement Motivation*, Academic Press.

Heckhausen, H. (1968), 'Achievement motive research: current problems and some contributions towards a general theory of motivation', in W. J. Arnold (ed.), *Nebraska Symposium on Motivation*, University of Nebraska Press, pp. 103–74.

Heider, F. (1958), *The Psychology of Interpersonal Relations*, Wiley.

Hull, C. L. (1943), *Principles of Behavior*, Appleton-Century-Crofts.

Hull, C. L. (1951), *Essentials of Behavior*, Yale University Press.

Jones, E. E., Kanouse, D., Kelley, H. H., Nisbett, R. E., Valins, S., and Weiner, B. (eds.) (1972), *Attribution: Perceiving the Causes of Behaviour*, General Learning Press.

Kanfer, F. H. (1971), 'The maintenance of behavior by self-generated stimuli and reinforcement', in A. Jacobs and L. B. Sachs (eds.), *The Psychology of Private Events*, Academic Press.

KANFER, F. H., and KAROLY, P. (1971), 'Self-regulation and its clinical application: some recent considerations', in R. C. Johnson, P. R. Dokecki and O. H. Mowrer (eds.), *Conscience and Social Reality: Theory and Research in Behavioral Science*, Holt, Rinehart & Winston.

KELLEY, H. H. (1967), 'Attribution theory in social psychology', in D. Levine (ed.), *Nebraska Symposium on Motivation*, University of Nebraska Press, pp. 192–238.

KELLY, G. A. (1955), *The Psychology of Personal Constructs*, 2 vols., Norton.

KLINGER, E. (1969), 'Development of imaginative behavior: implications of play for a theory of fantasy', *Psychological Bulletin*, vol. 72, pp. 277–98.

KLINGER, E. (1971), *Structure and Function of Fantasy*, Wiley.

LAWRENCE, D. H., and FESTINGER, L. (1962), *Deterrents and Reinforcement*, Stanford University Press.

LAZARUS, R. S. (1961), 'A substitute-defensive conception of apperceptive fantasy', in J. Kagan and G. S. Lesser (eds.), *Contemporary Issues in Thematic Apperceptive Methods*, C. C. Thomas, pp. 51–71.

LAZARUS, R. S. (1966), *Psychological Stress and the Coping Process*, McGraw-Hill.

LEWIN, K., DEMBO, T., FESTINGER, L., and SEARS, P. (1944), 'Level of aspiration', in J. McV. Hunt (ed.), *Personality and Behavior Disorders*, vol. 1, Ronald Press, pp. 333–78.

LOCKE, E. A. (1968), 'Toward a theory of task motivation and incentives', *Organizational Behavior and Human Performance*, vol. 3, pp. 157–89.

LOCKE, E. A., CARTLEDGE, N., and KNERR, C. S. (1970), 'Studies of the relationship between satisfaction, goal-setting and performance', *Organizational Behavior and Human Performance*, vol. 5, pp. 135–58.

MCCLELLAND, D. C., ATKINSON, J. W., CLARK, R. A., and LOWELL, E. L. (1953), *The Achievement Motive*, Appleton-Century-Crofts.

MCCLELLAND, D. C., and WINTER, D. G. (1969), *Motivating Economic Achievement*, Free Press.

MCDOUGALL, W. (1908), *An Introduction to Social Psychology*, Methuen.

MALLICK, S. K., and MCCANDLESS, B. R. (1966), 'A study of catharsis of aggression', *Journal of Personality and Social Psychology*, vol. 4, pp. 591–6.

MURRAY, H. A. (1938), *Explorations in Personality*, Oxford University Press, Inc.

MURRAY, H. A. (1943), *Thematic Apperception Test Manual*, Harvard University Press.

MURRAY, H. A. (1951), 'Toward a classification of interactions', in T. Parsons and E. A. Shils (eds.), *Toward a General Theory of Action*, Harvard University Press, pp. 434–64.

NISBETT, R. E., and SCHACHTER, S. (1966), 'Cognitive manipulation of pain', *Journal of Experimental Social Psychology*, vol. 2, pp. 227–36.

NUTTIN, J. (1953), *Tâche, réussite et échec*, Presse Université de Louvain.

PHARES, E. J. (1957), 'Expectancy changes in skill and chance situations', *Journal of Abnormal and Social Psychology*, vol. 54, pp. 339–42.

RAYNOR, J. O. (1969), 'Future orientation and motivation of immediate activity', *Psychological Review*, vol. 76, pp. 606–10.

ROTTER, J. B. (1954), *Social Learning and Clinical Psychology*, Prentice-Hall.

ROTTER, J. B. (1966), 'Generalized expectancies for internal versus external control of reinforcement', *Psychological Monographs*, vol. 30, no. 1, pp. 1–26.

SCHACHTER, S., and SINGER, J. E. (1962), 'Cognitive, social and physiological determinants of emotional state', *Psychological Review*, vol. 69, pp. 379–99.

SINGER, J. L. (1966), *Daydreaming: An Introduction to the Experimental Study of Inner Experience*, Random House.

SPENCE, K. W. (1958), 'A theory of emotionally based drive (D) and its relation to performance in simple learning situations', *American Psychologist*, vol. 13, pp. 131–41.

TOLMAN, E. C. (1955), 'Principles of performance', *Psychological Review*, vol. 62, pp. 315–26.

VALINS, S. (1966), 'Cognitive effects of false heart-rate feedback', *Journal of Personality and Social Psychology*, vol. 4, pp. 400–408.

VROOM, V. H. (1964), *Work and Motivation*, Wiley.

WATSON, J. B. (1924), *Behaviorism*, People's Institute, New York.

WEINER, B. (1966), 'The role of success and failure in the learning of easy and complex tasks', *Journal of Personality and Social Psychology*, vol. 3, pp. 339–44.

WEINER, B. (1970), 'New conceptions in the study ot achievement motivation', in B. A. Maher (ed.), *Progress in Experimental Personality Research*, vol. 5, Academic Press, pp. 67–109.

WEINER, B. (1972), *Theories of Motivation: from Mechanism to Cognition*, Markham.

WEINER, B., FRIEZE, I., KUKLA, A., REED, L., REST, S., and ROSENBAUM, R. M. (1971), *Perceiving the Causes of Success and Failure*, General Learning Press.

WEINER, B., HECKHAUSEN, H., MEYER, W. U., and COOK, R. E. (1972), 'Causal ascriptions and achievement motivation: a conceptual analysis of effort and re-analysis of locus of control', *Journal of Personality and Social Psychology* vol. 21, pp. 239-48

WEINER, B., and SCHNEIDER, K. (1971), 'Drive versus cognitive theory: a reply to Boor and Harmon', *Journal of Personality and Social Psychology*, vol. 18, pp. 258–62.

ZIMBARDO, P. G. (1969), *The Cognitive Control of Motivation*, Scott, Foresman.

# 7 Experimental Psychopathology*
Brendan Maher

Experimental psychopathology has come to refer to that growing body of research that employs experimental or other controlled methods in the study of abnormal behaviour. Although Kraepelin had urged the use of the techniques of experimental psychology in the field of psychopathology nearly a century ago, it is only in the past two or three decades that this movement has become widespread. However, these years have seen an exponential growth of activity in experimental psychopathology: a brief review such as this must therefore be highly selective in coverage. The writer has limited himself to discussion of certain problem areas in which notable progress has been made along systematic lines. Inevitably some important lines of investigation have been slighted, but it can be hoped that any imbalance may be redressed in part through the additional readings suggested at the end of this chapter.

## Psychopathy

Cleckley's seminal book *The Mask of Sanity* (1964) has proved to be an enduring influence upon experimental research directed at the problem of psychopathy. His clinical observations, coupled with his general hypothesis of a deficit in the mechanisms that produce emotional experience, has been cited by many recent workers as the basis for experimental study of autonomic nervous system reactivity in psychopathic patients. The most systematic work has been reported by the Canadian psychologist Hare (see Hare, 1970, for a summary of this).

### *Autonomic reactivity*

Several possibilities exist with respect to the autonomic reactivity of the psychopath. It might be the case that the patient is under all circumstances operating at a lower level of activity than does the normal. Alternatively, it might be the case that the major deficiency is in responsivity to marked stress. Following up this general question, Hare (1968) compared a group of

* This chapter was prepared while the writer was on leave of absence at the Institute of Clinical Psychology of the University of Copenhagen. Acknowledgement is made to Professor Lise Østergaard for access to the facilities of the Institute in the course of this work.

penitentiary inmates who conformed to Cleckley's criteria for psychopathy with a group whose characteristics were ambiguous in this regard and with a third group that was relatively free from psychopathic features. Measurements were taken of cardiac, respiratory and electrodermal activity. The psychopathic and ambiguous groups showed lower resting levels of electrodermal activity, but there were no differences between any of the groups on the other two measures. These results are congruent with earlier findings by Fox and Lippert (1963), Hare (1965a, 1965b), and Lippert and Senter (1966). They are consistent with the hypothesis that the psychopath has a lower level of autonomic arousal than normal. Hare (1968), in the same study, also found that his psychopathic group showed little cardiac response to a novel stimulus, introduced into a series of repeated stimuli. One interpretation of this, offered by Hare, is that the psychopath is less attentive and sensitive to changes in environmental stimulation – a characteristic to be expected if he is in a low state of arousal.

*Avoidance learning*

It is a long-established observation that the psychopath appears to be deficient in learning avoidance responses. Punishment does not appear to lead to the changes in behaviour that occur in normal people. Indeed its failure to produce these effects is one of the diagnostic definitions of psychopathy. One explanation of this is that the patient may be deficient in acquiring anticipatory anxiety in the presence of the cues for punishment. In normal individuals it appears that the degree of anxiety experienced increases with the temporal proximity of the punishment. Hare (1970) has hypothesized that the gradient of anxiety for the psychopath does not begin to rise as soon as in the normal person.

This hypothesis has been supported by his own work (Hare, 1965c) in which psychopaths were compared with non-psychopathic criminals and normal non-criminals in a task in which electric shock was delivered concomitantly with the display of the number 8 in a memory drum, on which the numbers 1 to 12 were displayed in sequence over a number of trials. Subjects were warned of this in advance. Figure 1 shows the differences in reactivity between psychopaths and other subjects. The latter show a gradient of increasing skin conductance as the number 8 approaches, the effect increasing as trials continue. On the other hand the psychopathic group shows little in the way of anticipatory reaction, even when the number 7 is shown just before the crucial shock cue. Much the same findings have been reported by the Swedish workers, Schalling and Levander (1967).

*Empathetic responsivity*

Clinical descriptions of the psychopath have drawn attention to the callous ness and indifference with which the psychopath views the distress of others

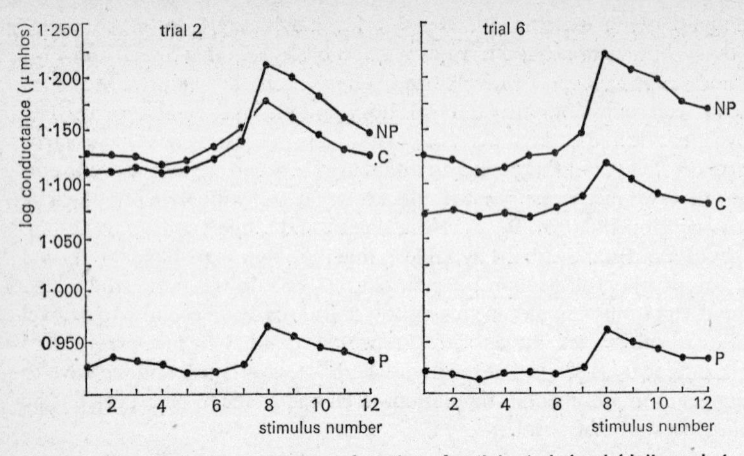


**Figure 1** Log conductance level as a function of anticipated shock (delivered at stimulus number 8). P = psychopathic criminals; NP = non-psychopathic criminals; C = normal controls. The lack of anticipatory gradient in the psychopathic group can be seen from the lack of increase in conductance from stimulus 1 to stimulus 7. No change takes place in this from trial 2 to trial 6 (from Hare, 1965c)

including his own victims. Sutker (1970) has reported an ingenious experimental investigation of this question. Psychopathic and normal subjects were placed in a situation in which the subject was required to observe the apparent delivery of electric shock to another person. The latter was, in fact, a confederate of the experimenter and merely acted the part of a shock-recipient. No shock was actually employed at any point in the study. Each genuine subject observed the simulated delivery of shock when the number 4 was uttered, in a sequence of uttered numbers, 1 to 7. However, he could prevent the delivery of shock by placing a coin (twenty-five cents) into a device near by. Any coins not used in this way were available for the subject to keep personally. Coins were supplied sufficient to prevent shock on each trial but not in excess of this.

Baseline data were obtained from a series of trials in which this empathetic prevention of shock was not available. Psychopaths showed a significantly smaller gradient of anticipation in their galvanic skin responses (GSR) to the shock delivery. There was no difference in their resting levels, nor was there any difference in the number of coins surrendered to secure the safety of the supposed 'victim'. The author concluded

> that sociopaths (psychopaths) seem to have a difficulty in experiencing anticipatory autonomic responses relative to imminent unpleasant or perhaps pleasant situations seems consistent with these data. Perhaps the problem they encounter is not a difficulty in recognizing emotional cues in others and in experiencing

these emotions themselves but is an inability to respond in anticipation of emotional situations in time to check impulsiveness and an overreactivity when these situations occur (Sutker, 1970, p. 385).

Her interpretation is clearly supportive of Hare's hypothesis of a retardation of the gradient of anticipatory autonomic reaction.

*Etiology: family history*

From a psychodynamic point of view the most popular explanation of the etiology of psychopathy has been that of Bender (1947). She alleged that the major cause is

emotional deprivation in the infantile period due to a serious break in parent–child relationships, for example the child who spent a considerable time in infancy or early childhood in an institution without any affectional ties, or a child who has been transferred from one foster home to another with critical breaks in the continuity of affectional patterns . . . the defect is in the ability to form relationships, to identify themselves with others, and consequently, in conceptualization of intellectual, emotional and social problems (p. 362).

This hypothesis is in two parts, one of which states that the major disorder is in the formation of interpersonal relationships and the second part of which attributes this to a break in, or lack of, stable parent–child relationships in the early life of the patient. Empirical evidence bearing on this has been reported by Oltman and Friedman (1967). Their data are given in Table 1. Although nearly half of all of the psychopaths included in the study

Table 1 **History of frequency and kind of parental loss in various psychiatric patients (from Oltman and Friedman, 1967)**

| *Group* | *N* | *Type of parental loss (per cent)* | | | |
|---|---|---|---|---|---|
| | | *Death* | *Separation* | *Mental illness* | *Total* |
| Psychopaths | 301 | 20·6 | 27·9 | 0·7 | 49·2 |
| Drug addicts | 69 | 23·2 | 20·3 | 0 | 43·5 |
| Psychoneuroses | 363 | 25·3 | 14·9 | 0·3 | 40·5 |
| Alcoholic states | 1103 | 29·3 | 7·9 | 0·6 | 37·9 |
| Organic conditions | 341 | 22·9 | 11·4 | 2·3 | 36·7 |
| Neurotic depressions | 377 | 20·4 | 13·5 | 1·3 | 35·3 |
| Schizophrenia | 2921 | 23·4 | 8·9 | 2·8 | 35·0 |
| Affective psychoses | 829 | 23·9 | 7·1 | 2·4 | 33·4 |
| Normal subjects | 350 | 26·9 | 7·4 | 0 | 34·3 |

had experienced the loss of a parent, this must be set against the fact that 34 per cent of normal control subjects had similar histories. Further doubt is cast upon the specific pathogenesis of psychopathy from a history of broken homes in childhood by a report by Robins (1966) to the effect that while 67 per cent of a group of 94 psychopaths came from broken homes, 63 per cent of 342 patients with other disorders also came from broken homes. All in all the most parsimonious conclusion is that a broken home may well precipitate psychological disturbance, but there is no basis for supposing that psychopathy is more likely to result than any other diagnostic category.

*The later careers of psychopaths*

Several leading textbooks in psychiatry have affirmed that psychopaths tend to mature and settle down in later life, the supposed age range of this being variously given as from the mid-twenties to the mid-forties. Cleckley (1964), on the other hand, has maintained that the prognosis for improvement is very pessimistic. Maddocks (1970) has conducted one of the very few systematic follow-up studies of this problem and apparently the only such study of untreated patients. Beginning with a sample of 59 adult psychopaths he was able to obtain data on their status five years later for all but 7 of them. His source of information on their status was either personal interview (14), report from another hospital or physician (31), from parent or social worker (5) or letter from patient (2). Of this total group, 3 had committed suicide, 10 appeared to have developed stable social-life patterns, while 39 evidenced a variety of psychological problems of which the chief were alcoholism and hypochondriasis. Criminal convictions were found in 60 per cent of the patients. Although there are several difficulties with this study (five years is not a long time to test out a 'slow maturity' hypothesis, and the investigator does not report the chronological age range of his sample) it does not support any optimistic view of psychopathic prognosis. This problem is one in which long-term, large-sample controlled studies are still badly needed.

*Summary*

Experimental techniques have begun to provide a picture of the psychological processes of the psychopath that have both consistency and reliability. The evidence strongly suggests an impairment of the autonomic component of emotional responding and especially in those situations where anticipatory responding is important in determining acceptable behaviour. Hypotheses of an etiology stemming from lack of parent–child affectional relationships have gained, as yet, no support from controlled investigation. The same holds true for the hypothesis of late maturation leading to ultimate psychological stability.

## Schizophrenia

By far the greatest bulk of experimental research has been devoted to the problem of schizophrenia. A review confined to this topic alone could well exceed the space available for the whole chapter, and here we must be even more selective.

*Genetics*

After a period of scepticism and hostility towards the genetic explanation of schizophrenia there has been a revived effort to conduct investigations using either the twin-method or the adoptee method. The essence of the twin method is, of course, the comparison of the incidence of schizophrenia in the second members of twin pairs where the first members have already been so diagnosed. This comparison is made between identical (single ovum and hence identical genetic constitution) twins on the one hand and fraternal (separate ovum) twins on the other. Many factors operate to affect the empirical rates of concordance. The older the sample the more time has passed to permit the second twin to develop psychological disorder: different countries have differing diagnostic standards for schizophrenia; and so forth. The work of Kallmann (1946) was greeted very critically and it was not until the 1960s that the topic of twin studies was taken up again on a large scale. Table 2 illustrates the concordance rates for all twin studies reported since Kallmann's. We see that, with the exception of Tienari (1963, 1968), all investigators report significantly higher concordances for identical than for fraternal twins.

Table 2 **Concordance rates for schizophrenia as reported from twin studies since 1950**

| | | *Monozygoitc* | | *Dizygotic* | |
|---|---|---|---|---|---|
| *Investigation* | *Sample* | *Number of pairs* | *% concordant* | *Number of pairs* | *% concordant* |
| Slater (1953) | England | 37 | 65–74·7 | 115 | 11·3–14·4 |
| Inouye (1961) | Japan | 55 | 36–60 | 17 | 6–12 |
| Tienari (1963, 1968) | Finland | 16 | 0–6 | 21 | 4·8 |
| Gottesman and Shields (1966) | England | 24 | 41·7 | 33 | 9·1 |
| Kringlen (1967) | Norway | 55 | 25–38 | 172 | 8–10 |
| Fischer *et al.* (1968) | Denmark | 16 | 19–56 | 34 | 6–15 |
| Hoffer *et al.* (1968) | US veterans | 80 | 15·5 | 145 | 4·4 |

A second technique that has been employed in recent studies is the examination of the fate of children born of parents one or both of whom are schizophrenic but where the child is adopted early in life into a normal home. Such children are compared with either the other children of the adoptive parents, or with other adopted children whose biological parents have no history of schizophrenia. Two studies have used this latter method. Rosenthal *et al.* (1968) examined a sample of eleven thousand Danish biological parents who had given up their children for adoption. Approximately one thousand were omitted because of uncertainty as to the identity of the father. Of the remaining group those whose parents had a history of schizophrenia or manic-depressive psychosis were regarded as index cases, and matched with other adopted children of normal parents, the matching being for sex, age, age at adoption and socio-economic status of the adopting family. Each child was examined intensively for psychiatric assessment and received a range of objective psychological tests. As neither the child nor the examiner could know the child's status (index or control) all examining was free from contamination. This study is still in progress on a long-term basis, but as of the moment (Hoffer, *et al.*, 1968) 10 of 39 index cases have been diagnosed as suffering from some variety of schizophrenic disorder – one being hospitalized – compared to one control case diagnosed as borderline schizophrenic. Rosenthal concludes that these preliminary figures 'provide strong evidence indeed that heredity is a salient factor in the etiology of schizophrenic disorders'.

Somewhat earlier than this study, the American psychiatrist Heston (1966) studied the careers of the adopted children of 47 schizophrenic mothers, compared to those of 50 normal mothers. The children had been separated from their mothers at birth and placed in foundling homes, adoptive homes, or raised by the family of the father. These children were born between the years 1915 and 1945, and were of a mean age of about thirty-six years at the time of follow-up. Heston reported that at the time of his study 5 of the index cases were hospitalized with a diagnosis of schizophrenia, 3 being 'chronic deteriorated', while none of the control group had met this fate. Of further interest was his finding that the ratio of other disorders showed greater pathology in the index cases. Psychopathic diagnoses were made for 9 index cases to 2 controls; military discharge for psychiatric or behavioural reasons occurred in 8 index cases compared to 1 control; neurotic personality disorder showed a ratio of 13 to 7, and conviction for felony 7 to 2. These figures raise the question of what is inherited, schizophrenia or a general liability to psychopathology? However, they add one further element to the evidence of a genetic factor in schizophrenia.

### *Vulnerability*

The data from genetic studies implies the existence of vulnerable individuals who might be identified in childhood on the basis of a parental history of schizophrenia. This fact, coupled with the methodological problems arising from the use of retrospective data obtained from adults who are already schizophrenic, has pointed to the necessity and feasibility of longitudinal investigation of the pre-schizophrenic child. The pioneering use of this method has been the initiation by Mednick and Schulsinger (1968) of a study of a sample of children born of schizophrenic mothers in Copenhagen. These children stand a higher-than-average chance of ultimate schizophrenic breakdown. The investigators have compared them to a matched group of controls on a variety of measures including autonomic responsivity, conditionability and generalization, word-association responses and the like. Once the initial measurements have been made it is necessary to wait for the group to grow to maturity and for some to develop overt psychological disorder. This research is still proceeding and it is as yet too early to draw conclusions. However, some members of the vulnerable group have developed psychiatric disorders, and in a recent report from the project (Mednick, 1970) it is suggested that those who do may be distinguished from the vulnerable subjects who do not develop difficulties, on the basis of a history of pregnancy or birth complications. At this time, however, such a statement can merely be noted for future reference when more data are in.

*Attentional difficulties*

Bleuler long ago characterized a deterioration of attention as one of the primary symptoms of schizophrenia. This observation has been followed up in several ways over the past few decades, as for example in the case of Shakow's conclusion that the patient suffers from an inability to maintain mental set (e.g. Shakow, 1962). Until recently such attempts were necessarily at a behavioural-descriptive level as there was no articulated theory of the process of attention to which a psychopathologist might have recourse in the matter. Experimental general psychology has made considerable progress in this regard, and we also have a broad understanding of the neurophysiological mechanisms that appear to be involved in the maintenance of attention and inhibition of distracting sensory input.

Venables (1964) offered a systematic integration of both behavioural and biopsychological data as well as making use of the phenomenological reports from patients gathered and published by McGhie and Chapman (e.g. McGhie and Chapman, 1961; McGhie, Chapman and Lawson, 1964). In essence, Venables' formulation is that the patient suffers from a very low level of arousal and that low levels of arousal lead to broad attention spans. This has the effect of keeping the sensory channels of the patient excessively open – both to relevant and irrelevant stimulation – with a concomitant inability to concentrate or to perform well in any task calling for a narrowed and continuous attention.

There are some problems with this formulation. One of them relates to the incompatibility of the very evident intense anxiety of acute schizophrenics and the assumption that they are in a low state of arousal. Strictly speaking, the assumption is not necessary if we are prepared instead to assume that the relationship of arousal and attention is described by an inverted U-curve, as is the relationship between arousal and behavioural efficiency. It is quite possible that unusually high or unusually low levels of arousal may have similar effects upon attention to those postulated by Venables for low arousal alone.*

From a methodological point of view there are many technical problems associated with the test of an arousal–attention hypothesis, chiefly the selection of a measure of arousal. Most investigators have turned to autonomic measures, but these do not have very high test–retest reliabilities and the intercorrelation between different measures (such as EMG, GSR, heart-rate, etc.) are unacceptably low – this latter fact making it somewhat a question of the experimenter's judgement as to which is used to differentiate high from low arousal. A recent attempt by Spohn, Thetford and Woodham (1970) to relate arousal to attention span in schizophrenic patients is worthy of description here. Thirty-two hospitalized adult male schizophrenic patients were compared with 16 volunteer controls, local firemen who were paid for participation. The experimental task was the recognition and written recording by the patient of an array of six consonants displayed tachistoscopically at varying intervals from 50 to 1000 msec. Several measures of arousal were used, the main data reported being from heart-rate (HR) and skin resistance. Schizophrenic patients showed the predictable deficit in performance at all exposure durations, but no correlation was found in either normal or patient groups between standard autonomic measures and performance. However, the authors did obtain a significant correlation between some measures of autonomic variability over the duration of the whole experiment and level of performance in the attention task. Those subjects who showed most variability also showed better performance. The investigators speculate, rather tentatively, that variability might reflect general sensitivity or 'alertness' of attention that would contribute to better task effectiveness.

### *Language and thought*

A particular interest has developed recently in the experimental investigation of language and thought in schizophrenia by experimental means. One significant group of studies has concentrated on the perception of language by the patient. The preferred technique in these studies has been the manipulation of the degree of contextual restraint provided in a language passage. Lawson, McGhie and Chapman (1964) reported the results of an investigation in which schizophrenic and normal subjects were presented with passages in English in which the transitional probabilities of word sequences were varied from low to high. That is to say, the predictability of one word following another in normal English usage varied from minimally predictable to more so. Normal subjects were able to utilize this factor in a recall task,

* In this connection, the reader may refer to the study by Fenz and Velner (1970) reporting that chronic schizophrenic patients were either under-aroused or over-aroused, with controls falling in the middle.

whereas schizophrenics were not. Their recall was as poor with high probability texts as with low. Levy and Maxwell (1968) and Raeburn and Tong (1968) using the same general procedure found that their schizophrenic subjects were unable to benefit from the increase in transitional probability.

However, the passages used in this technique have no additional grammatical constraints, i.e. they are not formed into sentences. Gerver (1967) added grammatical form to test passages in an experiment wherein subjects listened to passages in which the variables of grammatical–ungrammatical form and meaningful–meaningless were varied independently. Passages were presented against a background of white noise at various signal-to-noise ratios. In this investigation the schizophrenic subjects were inferior to normals in performance under all conditions, but within the schizophrenic group there was evidence to show that syntax and meaning both aided in recall.

Following this series of studies, Truscott (1970) examined the effects of four kinds of text: normal sentences, e.g. *Snug rings bind chubby fingers*; anomalous sentences, *Snug olives spread splintered subdivisions;* anomalous but related-word sentences, *Rings snug chubby fingers bind;* and random five-word strings with neither sentence structure nor meaning. Her results indicated that, as expected, schizophrenic subjects were inferior to normals under all conditions but especially in the normal-sentence condition.

These data are amenable to interpretation in several different ways. One possibility is that there is a deficiency in short-term memory. This hypothesis has been advanced by Yates (1966). Yates and Korboot (1970) have summarized it as proposing

> that schizophrenic deficit may occur, not because of the distracting effect of irrelevant (internal or external) stimulation which the schizophrenic is unable to screen out, but because the schizophrenic cannot process *relevant* incoming information in short-term memory per unit of time as can other persons (p. 453).

Another hypothesis has been advanced by Salzinger (1972). Stated in general form it is that schizophrenic behaviour is primarily controlled by stimuli that are immediate in the environment. Applied to speech, or memorizing generally, this implies that the perception of a single word in a text is most likely to be influenced only by words in immediate proximity. Extra increments of probability provided by sentence structure, chains of transitional probabilities, etc. would be ineffective in determining behaviour because they would require attention to words relatively remote from each other.

The present writer (Maher, 1968, 1972b) has suggested that the language processes of the schizophrenic are subject to interference from associations (which may be quite normal in themselves) and hence will intrude into the patient's utterances. By the same token they are liable to occur in the patient's monitoring of language produced by others and disrupt the process of storage – and hence the accuracy of recall. This associative interference can be seen as entirely analogous to the interference effects found in monitoring sensory input, and might be attributed to a failure of inhibitory mechanisms.

There are experimental data bearing on each of these hypotheses. Yates and Korboot (1970) tested the short-term memory deficit hypothesis in an experiment in which schizophrenic patients were faced with a task that required them to inspect and then report on material that was visually displayed. Inspection was measured by the amount of time the subject illuminated the display. The results of this study indicated that schizophrenic subjects generally took longer to inspect the display than did neurotic control groups, and that this difference grew more marked the more complex was the material displayed. The authors attribute this difference to slowness in processing the visual information, in line with Yate's hypothesis. While the data are congruent with the notion of a retardation of processing time they are not unequivocal on the matter. No steps were taken to minimize external distraction in the experimental situation and, as in most cases of schizophrenic deficit, it is equally plausible that the results reflect distractibility, which would become more marked in tasks requiring longer concentration of attention. As the complex displays took longer inspection times by the controls we would expect them to be most vulnerable to distraction in schizophrenic performance.

The Salzinger immediacy hypothesis has been tested by Salzinger *et al.* (1970). They obtained speech samples from 10 schizophrenic subjects and from 10 normals, matched on age and education. These samples were then submitted to 230 judges. From the samples a specific type of word was selected (e.g. a noun, pronoun, article, etc.). The selected word was eliminated from the sample, which was then given to the judges with a number of the surrounding words provided as clues to the identity of the word omitted. To the extent that a word is uttered under the influence of only one or two proximate words, the provision of longer segments should not substantially increase the ease with which it can be guessed. Thus the immediacy hypothesis demands that normal speech can be increasingly easily estimated when longer contexts are provided, but that this advantage would not be found in schizophrenic utterances. The hypothesis was supported but only with regard to 'function' words (articles, prepositions and conjunctions). A comparison for 'lexical' words (nouns, pronouns, verbs, adverbs and adjectives) did not produce significant differences.

Data bearing on the failure of inhibition of association have been reported by Smith (1970). He used a task developed by Rosenberg and Cohen (1966). In this task the subject is presented with two words, such as *robber* and *thief*, with the task of determining which one of them is correct. A third word, for example *baron*, is given as a clue indicating in this case that *robber* is the correct choice. Smith modified the task to require his subjects to examine the two words, one of which was marked as correct, and then select an associative clue such that a listener might guess the correct member of the pair. This task required that the subject be capable of producing normal associations and editing them to select for utterance that one that is likely to be informative to a listener. In this experiment the subjects were provided with clues from which to choose, the clues varying in their normative associative strength to the members of the word pairs. In one series of items one clue had strong associative value to both words – and hence was less discriminative – while the other clue had low associational relation to the correct word, but less or none to the incorrect choice. Good performance thus depended upon inhibiting the tendency to utter the strong association and choosing instead the weaker, but more discriminating associative clue. Smith's data indicated that the schizophrenic group in his study

> communicated poorly, not because they produced deviant associations nor because they were unable to properly assess the relative strengths of associative relations, but because they failed to edit adequately their responses by considering the relation between what they did not want to communicate and what they were about to say (p. 186).

At the present time it is clear that several hypotheses are tenable within the limits of the data available from studies of schizophrenic speaking and listening. We are far from having any crucial evidence to enable us to choose between them. However, the most important aspect of this kind of approach is that all three hypotheses place the problem of schizophrenic language rather firmly in the realm of attention or memory deficit – and out of the previous rubric of psychodynamic or unconscious motivational explanation. It is clear also that all three are susceptible to experimental test in a way that has been unavailable for exclusively clinical formulations of these disturbances.

### *Thinking disorder*

Experimental psychopathologists have found it useful to make an operational distinction between disorders of language and disorders of thinking in schizophrenia. The latter are generally defined by tasks of deductive reasoning, object-sorting or proverb interpretation. For many years the Von Domarus principle (Von Domarus, 1944) was regarded as the established explanation of the cognitive disorder underlying delusions.* However, two

* The question of whether or not delusional thinking can be quantitatively differentiated from normal thinking is far from clear. Smith (1968) has examined this question in general terms and the present writer (Maher, 1972a) has pointed out the alternative possibility that the delusional patient is reasoning normally about abnormal experiences.

developments have arisen to cast doubt upon this. The first of these is a series of studies dealing with the vulnerability of schizophrenic patients to the error of reasoning described by Von Domarus. In brief, this is the classic logician's 'error' of the excluded middle. The deluded patient is presumed to reason thus: The Prime Minister is a man: I am a man: Therefore I am the Prime Minister. Experimental investigation of logical reasoning has not supported the hypothesis that schizophrenics are unusually prone to this error.

A new attempt to measure thinking disorder has been reported by Braatz (1970). He has turned to the use of preference intransitivity as a possible index. Preferences may be said to be transitive if a subject who prefers choice A to choice B, and choice B to choice C, also prefers A to C. Intransitivity of preferences would lead to inconsistencies in this kind of ordering. Braatz reports that a schizophrenic sample showed much higher intransitivity scores on a paper and pencil test of this than did other psychiatric subjects or normal controls. However he considers the possibility that the results may reflect affective rather than cognitive processes, although this would not detract from the measure as an index of the extent to which affective variables have produced illogical ordering of choices, and hence a *de facto* cognitive disturbance. Although there are many unresolved questions raised by Braatz's research, it opens up a new angle of attack upon the vexed question of the illogicality of schizophrenic thought.

**Behaviour therapy**

While the contribution of the experimental method was once nearly exclusively in the domain of etiology and pathological process, the past two decades have seen its extension to the field of treatment in the form, mainly, of the behaviour therapies. Here again, the literature is of great size and it is possible only to discuss some of the many developments that have taken place. We may turn first to individual treatment techniques.

*Systematic desensitization*

The literature on systematic desensitization is already prolific and most interest attaches to its application to specific disorders. Lanyon (1969) has reported the use of this technique with stuttering in a twenty-five-year-old male. A hierarchy of speaking situations was compiled, ranging from a low-anxiety item (*talking out loud when nobody else can hear*) through to a maximum anxiety item (*being introduced as a speaker in a large lecture hall*). Desensitization was conducted via imagery of the hierarchical scenes. Improvement was measured by three indices of stuttering taken both immediately at the end of treatment and nine months later on follow-up. Improvements were recorded on all indices. Lanyon compared the percentage improvement in this case with the mean percentages from a speech-therapy group at the University of Iowa and finds his client to have achieved more success. He points out cautiously that this case must be regarded as a demonstration of the use of this technique in stuttering but not firm evidence for its efficacy.

This caution appears perhaps a little too severe as he did obtain pre- and post-therapy measures of an objective kind. As much experimental work in systematic desensitization has been done, so far, on minor phobias (snake phobia, etc.) the treatment of stutterers appears as an opportunity to conduct further research with this technique on a problem that is common but severely distressing.

*Implosive therapy*

The rationale underlying systematic desensitization is one of the elimination of conditioned anxiety by exposure to graded and tolerable threatening stimuli under conditions (muscular relaxation) incompatible with an anxiety response. Directly contrary to this, Stampfl and Lewis (1967) have developed what they refer to as *implosive* therapy. They assume that extinction of anxiety will proceed most rapidly when the subject is exposed to the direct CS (a very threatening stimulus) without primary reinforcement. It is assumed that as the anxiety response occurs, but with no aversive consequences associated with the CS, extinction will occur. This is accomplished by requiring the client to visualize very threatening scenes repeatedly until the anxiety response is extinguished. Barrett (1969) has conducted a study of the relative efficacy of implosive therapy (IT) and systematic desensitization therapy (SDT) with snake-phobic adult subjects. Three groups were used. One, a control group, was placed on a waiting list, a second group was treated by SDT and a third group by IT. Efficacy of the treatment was tested by the ability of the subject to hold a live snake. Both kinds of therapy produced reduction of the phobia. Eleven of 12 SDT subjects and 10 of 12 of IT subjects held the snake. One control subject passed this test. At six-months' follow-up, these differences were maintained. Barrett points out that the amount of time required to complete IT procedures was only 45 per cent of that required for SDT and that the latter is thus less efficient. On the other hand there were two incidents of personal distress in IT subjects between therapy sessions, requiring persuasion on the part of the therapist for attendance at the next session. Presumably the therapist will want to weigh the gain in efficacy (about five hours per subject in this experiment) against the problem of intersession distress, where the therapist is not present to take any necessary action.

Research on implosive therapy is still rather limited in amount and many problems remain for study. However, it poses important issues of theory and practice for behaviour therapists which will undoubtedly receive increasing attention.

*Cognitive therapy*

Behaviour therapists have begun to show more interest in the question of internal mediating responses and their role in determining overt behaviour. Beck (1970) has pointed out the many common features of cognitive and behaviour therapies, but identifies the major difference as residing in concepts used to explain the dissolution of maladaptive responses through therapy. Where most usual behaviour therapies invoke the principles of counter-conditioning or reciprocal inhibition to account for therapeutic changes, the cognitive therapist emphasizes changes in attitudes or modes of thinking. Beck, for example, hypothesizes that many anxiety attacks are preceded, and triggered, by a cognition of some kind rather than by an external stimulus of fixed characteristics. Therapy then consists of the discovery of these cognitions, a goal achieved through extensive examination and analysis of the cognitions of the patient before his actual attacks, as recalled by the patient. Once identified, the irrationality of the cognition is dealt with in discussion with the patient and, in effect, is extinguished by processes not unlike systematic desensitization. The important difference is that the cognitive element is treated rather than the anxiety response.

**Institutional and milieu treatment**

The principles of behaviour therapy have been applied increasingly to the treatment of large groups of patients in hospital or community settings. Perhaps the most systematic kind of approach is through the use of comprehensive schedules of reinforcement for a variety of adapative responses. Such plans have become known as *token economy* programmes.

*Token economy*

Atthowe and Krasner (1968) have provided a clear and quantitative report of the effects of a token economy programme in the Veterans Administration Hospital, Palo Alto, California. Their report covers a two-year period (1963–5) and deals with the results of the programme in a closed, 'chronic' ward. The ward accommodated a maximum of 86 patients, whose median age was 57 and of whom one-third were over 65. Median length of hospitalization of this group was 22 years and the majority bore diagnostic labels of chronic schizophrenia. A sample of 60 of these patients was followed over the two years for research purposes. Tokens were paid for a variety of activities. If a patient adequately cared for his personal needs, attended scheduled activities, helped on the ward, interacted with other patients or showed increased responsibility in any way, he was rewarded with tokens. In turn these were required for the purchase of cigarettes, money, passes, watching television, etc. Before the introduction of the programme, a six-month baseline was recorded for various adaptive behaviours on the ward.

After tokens had been introduced, the frequency of these activities increased, as shown in Figure 2 below. Other measures of the effectiveness of this

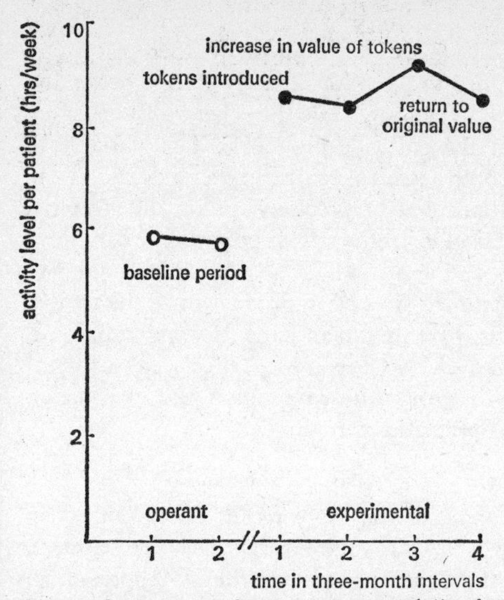


Figure 2 Increase in adaptive responses (attendance at group activities) following introduction of token reinforcements. The role of the reinforcement in maintaining this behaviour is shown by the rise in rate following a temporary increase in token reward at the third month (from Atthowe and Krasner, 1968, p. 39)

programme included significant increases in the number of patients going out of the hospital on pass, 24 discharges and 11 transfers to pre-discharge wards compared to figures of 11 and zero for the pre-programme period. Care was taken to ensure that the token system was responsible for these changes by increasing the value of certain kinds of activities and noting an increase in the performance of them, followed by a slight decrease when the original value was reinstated (see also Figure 2).

*Volunteer therapists*

The other major innovation in institutional treatment in recent years has been the employment of non-professional volunteers as therapists. There is already a substantial literature reporting observations made about such programmes but little in the way of controlled investigation of their efficacy. Recently Verinis (1970) has investigated the effects of a volunteer-therapist programme upon the status of chronic psychotic female patients in a psychiatric hospital. Two groups of such patients were matched for age, education and length of hospitalization. One group received no treatment, while the other was assigned to a group of volunteers. The volunteer group consisted of nine housewives and four college students. None had any formal training in psychology: all were given a brief orientation urging them simply to talk to their assigned patient and try to be 'a friend'. They were asked to avoid making interpretations or suggestions. Half of the therapist group were told that the patient assigned to them was already getting better and needed only this extra attention to get out, while the other half were given pessimistic expectations about the patient's prognosis. This variable of optimism–pessimism provides both a control against expectancy effects and also deals with previous suggestions that it is precisely this kind of effect that accounts for the reported success of volunteers. This programme continued for five months, each therapist seeing his patient once a week. Ratings of behaviour before and after treatment showed improvement in the treated group compared to the controls. Five treatment patients were discharged, no control patient was discharged. No expectancy effects were found: improvement was as evident in the group whose therapists were given pessimistic prognoses as those given optimistic expectations.

## Summary

This chapter has pointed to some of the more recent developments in experimental psychopathology. Necessarily the coverage has been selective. It is evident, however, that the experimental-quantitative approach in psychopathology has expanded into many areas of abnormal behaviour and already has a significant influence upon current thinking about etiology, pathology and treatment. There is good reason to believe that this will continue and lead the study of abnormal behaviour into the rubric of general biopsychology, where it belongs.

## Further reading

HARE, R. D., *Psychopathy: Theory and Research*, Wiley, 1970. A brief but comprehensive synthesis of the empirical data available from research into psychopathic states.

ROSENTHAL, D., and KETY, S. S., *The Transmission of Schizophrenia*, Pergamon, 1968. A collection of papers presented at the Second Research Conference of the Foundations' Fund for Research in Psychiatry. It provides good reviews and original research reports from genetic, social, cultural and interpersonal studies of the etiology of schizophrenia.

YATES, A. J., *Behaviour Therapy*, Wiley, 1970. A complete textbook and research review in the behaviour therapies.

## References

ATTHOWE, J. M., and KRASNER, L. (1968), 'Preliminary report on the application of contingent reinforcement procedures (token economy) on a "chronic" psychiatric ward', *Journal of Abnormal Psychology*, vol. 73, pp. 37–43.

BARRETT, C. L. (1969), 'Systematic desensitization versus implosive therapy', *Journal of Abnormal Psychology*, vol. 74, pp. 587–92.

BECK, A. T. (1970), 'Cognitive therapy: nature and relation to behavior therapy', *Behavior Therapy*, vol. 1, pp. 184–200.

BENDER, L. (1947), 'Psychopathic behavior disorders in children', in K. M. Lindner and R. V. Seliger (eds.), *Handbook of Correctional Psychology*, Philosophical Library.

BRAATZ, G. (1970), 'Preference intransitivity as an indicator of cognitive slippage in schizophrenia', *Journal of Abnormal Psychology*, vol. 75, pp. 1–6.

CLECKLEY, H. (1964), *The Mask of Sanity*, 4th edn., Mosby.

FENZ, W., and VELNER, J. (1970), 'Physiological concomitants of behavioral indexes in schizophrenia', *Journal of Abnormal Psychology*, vol. 76, pp. 27–35.

FISCHER, M., HARVALD, B., and HAUGE, M. (1969), 'A Danish twin study of schizophrenia', *British Journal of Psychiatry*, vol. 115, pp. 981–90.

FOX, R., and LIPPERT, W. (1963), 'Spontaneous GSR and anxiety level in sociopathic delinquents', *Journal of Consulting Psychology*, vol. 27, p. 368.

GERVER, D. (1967), 'Linguistic rules and the perception and recall of speech by schizophrenic patients', *British Journal of Social and Clinical Psychology*, vol. 6, pp. 204–11.

GOTTESMAN, I. I., and SHIELDS, J. (1966), 'Schizophrenia in twins: 16 years' consecutive admissions to a psychiatric clinic', *British Journal of Psychiatry*, vol. 112, pp. 809–18.

HARE, R. D. (1965a), 'A conflict and learning theory analysis of psychopathic behavior', *Journal of Research in Crime and Delinquency*, vol. 2, pp. 12–19.

HARE, R. D. (1965b), 'Acquisition and generalization of a conditioned fear response in psychopathic and non-psychopathic criminals', *Journal of Psychology*, vol. 59, pp. 367–70.

HARE, R. D. (1965c), 'Temporal gradient of fear arousal in psychopaths', *Journal of Abnormal Psychology*, vol. 70, pp. 442–5.

HARE, R. D. (1968), 'Psychopathy, autonomic functioning and the orienting response', *Journal of Abnormal Psychology*, Monograph Suppl. 73, no. 3, pt. 2, pp. 1–24.

HARE, R. D. (1970), *Psychopathy: Theory and Research*, Wiley.

HESTON, L. (1966), 'Psychiatric disorders in foster-home-reared children of schizophrenic mothers', *British Journal of Psychiatry*, vol. 112, pp. 819–25.

HOFFER, A., POLLIN, W., STABENEAU, J. R., ALLEN, M., and HRUBEC, Z. (1968), 'Schizophrenia in the National Research Council's register of 15,909 veteran twin pairs', cited by D. Rosenthal in *Genetics of Psychopathology*, McGraw-Hill, 1971.

INOUYE, E. (1961), 'Similarity and dissimilarity of schizophrenia in twins', *Proceedings of the Third World Congress of Psychiatry*, vol. 1, pp. 524–30, University of Toronto Press.

KALLMANN, F. (1946), 'The genetic theory of schizophrenia', *American Journal of Psychiatry*, vol. 103, pp. 309–22.

KRINGLEN, E. (1967), 'Hereditary and social factors in schizophrenic twins: an epidemiological study', in J. Romano (ed.), *The Origins of Schizophrenia*, Excerpta Medica, 1967.

LANYON, R. (1969), 'Behavior change in stuttering through systematic desensitization', *Journal of Speech and Hearing Disorders*, vol. 34, pp. 253–60.

LAWSON, J., MCGHIE, A., and CHAPMAN, J. (1964), 'Perception of speech in schizophrenia', *British Journal of Psychiatry*, vol. 110, pp. 375–80.

LEVY, R., and MAXWELL, A. (1968), 'The effect of verbal context on the recall of schizophrenics and other psychiatric patients', *British Journal of Psychiatry*, vol. 114, pp. 311–16.

LIPPERT, W., and SENTER, R. J. (1966), 'Electrodermal responses in the sociopath', *Psychonomic Science*, vol. 4, pp. 25–6.

MADDOCKS, P. D. (1970), 'A five-year follow-up of untreated psychopaths', *British Journal of Psychiatry*, vol. 116, pp. 511–15.

MAHER, B. (1968), 'The shattered language of schizophrenia', *Psychology Today*, vol. 2, pp. 30–32.

MAHER, B. (1972a), 'The psychology of delusions', in R. Nesbitt and J. London (eds.), *Cognitive Alteration of Feeling States*, Aldine.

MAHER, B. (1972b), 'The language of schizophrenia: a review and interpretation', *British Journal of Psychiatry*, vol. 120, pp. 3–17.

MCGHIE, A., and CHAPMAN, J. (1961), 'Disorders of attention and perception in early schizophrenia', *British Journal of Medical Psychology*, vol. 34, pp. 103–16.

MCGHIE, A., CHAPMAN, J., and LAWSON, S. (1964), 'Disturbances in selective attention in schizophrenia', *Proceedings of the Royal Society of Medicine*, vol. 57, pp. 419–22.

MEDNICK, S. (1970), 'Breakdown in individuals at high risk for schizophrenia: possible predispositional perinatal factors', *Mental Hygiene*, vol. 54, pp. 50–63.

MEDNICK, S., and SCHULSINGER, F. (1968), 'Some pre-morbid characteristics related to breakdown in children with schizophrenic mothers', in D. Rosenthal and S. S. Kety (eds.), *The Transmission of Schizophrenia*, Pergamon.

OLTMAN, J., and FRIEDMAN, S. (1967), 'Parental deprivation in psychiatric conditions', *Diseases of the Nervous System*, vol. 28, pp. 298–303.

RAEBURN, J. M., and TONG, J. E. (1968), 'Experiments on contextual constraint in schizophrenia', *British Journal of Psychiatry*, vol. 114, pp. 43–52.

ROBINS, L. N. (1966), *Deviant Children Grown Up*, Williams & Wilkins.

ROSENBERG, S., and COHEN, B. (1966), 'Referential processes of speakers and listeners', *Psychological Review*, vol. 73, pp. 208–31.

ROSENTHAL, D., WEDNER, P. H., KETY, S. S., SCHULSINGER, F., WELNER, J., and ØSTERGAARD, L. (1968), 'Schizophrenics' offspring reared in adoptive homes', in D. Rosenthal and S. S. Kety (eds.), *The Transmission of Schizophrenia*, Pergamon.

SALZINGER, K. (1972), *Schizophrenia: Behavioral Aspects*, Wiley.

SALZINGER, K., PORTNOY, S., PISONI, D. R., and FELDMAN, R. S. (1970), 'The immediacy hypothesis and response-produced stimuli in speech', *Journal of Abnormal Psychology*, vol. 76, pp. 258–64.

SCHALLING, D., and LEVANDER, S. (1967), 'Spontaneous fluctuations in EDA during anticipation of pain in two delinquent groups differing in anxiety proneness', Report no. 238, Psychological Laboratory, University of Stockholm.

SHAKOW, D. (1962), 'Segmental set', *Archives of General Psychiatry*, pp. 1–17.

SLATER, E. (1953), *Psychotic and Neurotic Illnesses in Twins*, HMSO.

SMITH, A. C. (1968), 'Notes on difficulties in the definition of delusion', *British Journal of Medical Psychology*, vol. 41, pp. 255–9.

SMITH, E. E. (1970), 'Associative and editing processes in schizophrenic communication', *Journal of Abnormal Psychology*, vol. 75, pp. 182–6.

SPOHN, H. E., THETFORD, P. E., and WOODHAM, F. L. (1970), 'Span of apprehension and arousal in schizophrenia', *Journal of Abnormal Psychology*, vol. 75, pp. 113–23.

STAMPFL, T. G., and LEWIS, D. J. (1967), 'Essentials of implosive therapy: a learning-theory-based psychodynamic behavioral therapy', *Journal of Abnormal Psychology*, vol. 72, pp. 496–503.

SUTKER, P. B. (1970), 'Vicarious conditioning and sociopathy', *Journal of Abnormal Psychology*, vol. 76, pp. 380–86.

TIENARI, P. (1963), 'Psychiatric illness in identical twins', *Acta Psychiatrica Neurologica Scandinavica*, Supplement 171.

TIENARI, P. (1968), 'Schizophrenia in monozygotic male twins', in D. Rosenthal and S. S. Kety (eds.), *The Transmission of Schizophrenia*, Pergamon.

TRUSCOTT, I. P. (1970), 'Contextual constraint and schizophrenic language', *Journal of Consulting and Clinical Psychology*, vol. 35, pp. 189–94.

VENABLES, P. (1964), 'Input dysfunction in schizophrenia', in B. Maher (ed.), *Progress in Experimental Personality Research*, vol. 1, Academic Press.

VERINIS, J. S. (1970), 'Therapeutic effectiveness of untrained volunteers with chronic patients', *Journal of Consulting and Clinical Psychology*, vol. 34, pp. 152–5.

VON DOMARUS, E. (1944), 'The specific laws of logic in schizophrenia', in J. Kasanin (ed.), *Language and Thought in Schizophrenia*, University of California Press.

YATES, A. J. (1966), 'Data-processing levels and thought disorder in schizophrenia', *Australian Journal of Psychology*, vol. 18, pp. 103–17.

YATES, A. J., and KORBOOT, P. (1970), 'Speed of perceptual functioning in chronic non-paranoid schizophrenics', *Journal of Abnormal Psychology*, vol. 76, pp. 453–61.

# Part Three
# **Developmental Psychology**

In a science, even one as young as psychology, there are seldom more than a very few really dramatic developments within the space of a decade or so. Yet two have occurred within that span in the same area of psychology – the study of children – in recent times. One was initiated by the work of a psychologist, the other by developments outside psychology, and yet both illustrate profoundly that reorientation towards the study of cognition which emerges as a major theme of this book.

The first development has to do with the work of the Swiss psychologist Jean Piaget.* Although his productive life as a scholar started many years ago, it is only recently that his work has been taken up seriously in the English-speaking world, where it is now a dominant influence in the study of cognitive development. One might almost speak of the Piagetian assault on Anglo-Saxon psychology, particularly in North America, so rapid have the growth in interest and research activity been.

The second development was initiated outside psychology, in the field of linguistics in the late 1950s, where a strong challenge to the associationist and behaviourist accounts of language acquisition was mounted, particularly by Chomsky in America. However one may view the controversies which have arisen over the nature of language acquisition between different schools of thought, the immediate impact on psychological research on language, and language learning, is beyond dispute. Along with the Piagetian tradition in cognitive development, it is now one of the major areas of research on children.

The two chapters in Part Three are devoted to these developments. In the first of them Dr Halford outlines the major features of Piaget's position, and goes on to show what sorts of attempt have been made to verify and further elucidate it by experimental analysis. The issues are not simple, and few of them have been conclusively resolved, but the search for resolution is proving fruitful and yielding important insights into children's cognition.

*Professor Piaget would himself prefer to be thought of, I understand, not as a psychologist, or not *only* as a psychologist, but as an epistemologist and logician too. However, it is his psychological contributions that we are concerned with here.

One of the enduring controversies in the Piagetian arena has been over the role of language in cognitive development. The controversy, essentially over whether language is a *product* of cognitive growth or a *tool* which helps it to occur, has no simple answer; one would expect that both points of view would have some validity. Yet if we look at the second chapter in this part, Professor Slobin's review of language development, we find there plenty of evidence to indicate that cognitive development in certain important respects *precedes* full or correct use of language, so that the former view (of language as product) should perhaps be given greater weight. At all events, this point will serve to show that the compartmentalization of a review of psychology into chapters is fairly artificial, not altogether desirable, and forced on us by the exigencies of multiple authorship.

In other respects, also, the two chapters are quite closely related. The study of language is very old, and even investigations of children's language have been going on for a long time: it is the study of language to gain insight into the *nature* of children's cognition which is new, and exciting. This is quite similar to the Piagetian strategy of attempting to gain insight into the nature of cognitive development through observation and analysis of other very specific sorts of behaviour.

# 8 The Impact of Piaget on Psychology in the Seventies*

Graeme S. Halford

## Phenomena discovered by Piaget

Piaget's studies of child behaviour have presented the science of psychology with many new phenomena which are not only intriguing, but pose a real challenge to existing conceptual systems and methods. He seems to have shown that the behaviour of children reflects thought processes which are quite different, not only from those of adults, but from any previously recognized forms of thought. In the last decade psychologists have been vigorously attempting to assess Piaget's findings and to extend them.

An indication of the extent of interest in Piaget in contemporary psychology is the large number of interpretative summaries of his work which have appeared; e.g., Baldwin (1967), Boyle (1969), Flavell (1963), Ginsburg and Opper (1969), Hunt (1961), Phillips (1969). The reader can obtain a reasonably comprehensive introduction to Piaget's work by consulting one or more of these summaries; the purpose of this chapter is to consider some of the fundamentals of current work in the field.

Although Piaget's primary purpose is to study the development of thought and knowledge, or 'genetic epistemology', his best-known contribution is his description of the *stages* of development in child behaviour. The four main stages are:

*The sensori-motor stage*, which normally lasts from birth to age two. This is a stage of 'motor actions, without thought activity ... not yet internalized in the form of representations (thought)'. Nevertheless, it displays 'some of the features of intelligence as we normally understand it' (Piaget, 1957, p. 9).

Piaget considers that the infant's conceptual development is part and parcel of his sensori-motor development during this stage. For instance, it was not until she was eighteen months old that Piaget (1953) observed his daughter Jacqueline travelling around a sofa to retrieve a ball that had rolled under it. The inference is that prior to this age the child did not have the necessary sensori-motor organization to understand that the path around the sofa was equivalent to the path beneath it, and that if the ball

* This chapter was written while the author was on sabbatical leave at Queen's University, Kingston, Ontario.

has disappeared by one path, it can be recovered by the other. As we shall see later, Piaget considers that the child cannot have the concept of the permanent object without this sensori-motor organization.

*The pre-operational stage* normally lasts from about two years until somewhere between five and eight years. The pre-operational child has gone beyond sensori-motor development in that he can represent things and events to himself, but cannot distinguish between the general and the particular, so his reasoning leads him into (sometimes quaint) fallacies. More recently Piaget (1968a, 1968b) and Mehler and Bever (1967, 1968) have found precursers to logical thought in this stage. One of these is the discovery that the pre-operational child appears to have a sort of 'function-logic', based on simple functional, but not causal, relations. For instance, if an object is attached to a string which moves around pulleys on a frame, the child can predict how far the object will move as a function of how far the string is moved. He does not however recognize that the relationship ceases to exist if the string is cut at some point.

*The concrete operational stage* usually lasts until eleven years or later, and is characterized by coordination of representations to produce genuine thought, albeit thought which is only a reflection of concrete things. The difference between the pre-operational and concrete stages can be illustrated by one of the tasks used by Piaget (see Piaget, 1950, pp. 135–6). Children are shown three coloured beads, which are threaded on a wire in the order red, blue and green, and placed in an opaque tube. At the early pre-operational stage (which Piaget calls *the pre-conceptual sub-stage*) children can predict that the beads will emerge from the opposite end of the tube in the order red, blue, green. In the later pre-operational stage (intuitive sub-stage) the children can predict that the beads will emerge in the opposite order if withdrawn from the same end as they went in. If the tube is rotated horizontally through 180 degrees, the pre-operational child may not be able to predict that the order of emergence (from either end) will be reversed. Furthermore, if he discovers the correct order after one half turn, he will have to discover anew the order which will result after two half turns, and after three, etc. The concrete operational stage begins when the child can coordinate all the relationships existing in the situation, and can assign a particular result to any circumstance in a reliable fashion.

It is the concrete operational stage which has aroused most interest amongst contemporary investigators of Piaget's work, mainly because concepts which seem basic to logical thinking, such as conservation, inclusion, seriation, etc., are acquired at this stage. The concept of conservation (Piaget, 1952) has received most attention. It can be illustrated by reference to Figure 1.

The child is shown two identical, cyclindrical containers, $A_1$ and $A_2$, and his agreement that they contain the same amount of liquid (or the same number of marbles, etc.) is obtained. Then $A_2$ is poured into B while the child watches. The child is then asked whether there is the same amount of material in B as in $A_1$. If B is taller and narrower than $A_1$, pre-operational children tend to say that B contains more. If B is shorter than $A_1$, they say it holds less. Concrete operational children are aware that if material has been merely poured from $A_2$ to B without any being added or removed, then there must still be the same amount of material. The concrete operational child is thus said to 'conserve' the 'whole' – he regards the quantity as a constant when merely transferred from one place to another, and is not misled by any one aspect of the situation, such as the height of the column of liquid.

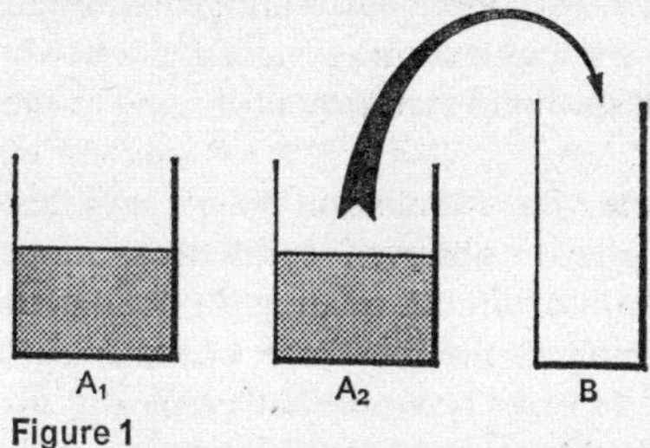

Figure 1

*The formal operational stage* is the last of the major stages of thought development, and begins at about eleven years. Inhelder and Piaget (1958) have shown that formal operational children seem to be able to relate their own thoughts to one another, and to perform operations which go beyond a reflection of experienced contingencies. This allows them to reason by hypothesis, and to explore systematically as yet unrealized possibilities.

This chapter is restricted to studies of child thought as it relates to the stages outlined above, because most recent interest has centred on this problem. Nevertheless Piaget's work on morality (Piaget, 1932) and his work on perception (Piaget, 1961) richly deserve further study. Kohlberg (1963), working with a different orientation, has outlined six stages of development of child morality which to some extent parallel those of Piaget. The perception work has recently been revised and translated (Seagrim, 1969) and it is reasonable to hope that more activity will result in this area soon. Furthermore the study of figurative perception (Elkind, 1969) promises to develop an important link between Piagetian studies of perception and cognition.

## Piaget's views on the nature of behaviour

Piaget's description of the stages of development of thought and behaviour implies a certain conception of the way organisms function. Many of his studies are designed to trace the origin and development of what he calls the 'operations' of thought. He defines operations as follows: 'Psychologically, operations are actions which are internalizable, reversible, and coordinated into systems characterized by laws which apply to the system as a whole.' (Piaget, 1957, ch. 2). All these systems are governed by the overriding principle of 'equilibration', i.e., putting things into relation with one another so as to achieve a system which is stable, consistent or non-contradictory. Such a system is often called a 'scheme' or 'schema'.

The system would deal with its environment by *assimilating* new objects to itself and then *accommodating* (or developing) its own structure so as to include the new object. Thus equilibration is achieved by balancing assimilation and accommodation so that when something new disturbs a system of behaviour, the system itself is accommodated until equilibrium is restored. Thus a disequilibrium between an existing system and a newly presented object or situation is one of the main factors contributing to the development of the system itself.

Should accommodation predominate over assimilation, Piaget says that imitation would result. Children may often be observed repeatedly to adopt actions of older persons (accommodation) without relating the actions to the situation (assimilation). An example is the repetition of statements made by adults in a way which is verbally accurate but comically inappropriate. When assimilation predominates over accommodation, play results. In play the internal organization of behaviour (scheme) is all-important, and external things are assumed or imagined to fit the scheme whether they actually do or not. Thus a child who has a passion for being a bus-driver climbs upon a garden-seat and declares 'This *must* be the bus.' The child's bus-playing scheme is not accommodated to the nature of the object as a seat. In non-play situations this failure to accommodate an internal scheme to an external object would produce substantial conflict or disequilibrium.

One of the properties which Piaget considers a system in equilibrium must have is reversibility, or the property of preserving the whole by reversing or compensating for any changes that occur. Thought is normally reversible in this sense – e.g. in thought I am aware that if A is larger than B, then B is smaller than A. However, emotional reactions and some simple learned behaviours are not automatically reversible. If we have learned to travel from point A to point B in a strange city, we do not necessarily know our way from B to A, as many a perplexed traveller has discovered.

## The significance of Piagetian phenomena

### *Methods*

Piaget's methods of studying child thought are 'clinical' rather than experimental in the sense that his testing procedures are not rigorously objective and standardized, and they depend largely on the child's verbal judgements and explanations. The experimenter asks questions while varying the situation so as to explore the child's understanding as completely as possible.

Because of these features of Piaget's methods many researchers have felt the need to replicate his studies using more exact and standardized methods. Some of the best replication studies are to be found in the excellent collection of papers edited by Sigel and Hooper (1968). In general it can be said that Piaget's findings have received a fair degree of confirmation. However, concrete operational concepts *appear* to be mastered earlier if tested by non-verbal methods rather than by Piaget's methods. For instance, Braine (1959) found transitivity of length at age five, although Smedslund (1963c) disputed that Braine's methods measured genuine transitivity. As the subsequent dialogue between Braine (1964) and Smedslund (1965, 1966) shows, it is not as easy to determine objective methods for assessing Piagetian concepts as was once hoped. Also Bruner *et al.* (1966, ch. 9, experiment by Frank) has found conservation earlier than Piaget's suggested ages. However, Piaget (1967) has argued that it may have been pseudo-conservation that the subjects learned.

Another finding from replication studies is that the correlation between various concrete operational performances is not as high as might have been hoped. For instance, Dodwell (1962) found little relationship between understanding of number and classification concepts, although Dodwell's group tests involved modifications of Piaget's procedures. Tuddenham (1970) has also found that the low inter-correlations between various Piagetian tasks makes them difficult to use in test construction. From a pragmatic point of view these results are disappointing, but it is doubtful whether they reflect on the validity of Piaget's position. Firstly, it is not clear whether Piaget necessarily implies that concrete operational performances would be closely related to one another (see Dodwell, 1962; Piaget, 1957, pp. 15–16). Secondly, correlational studies are usually based on samples with a small age range. If the age range were increased, the correlations would probably go from low positive to high positive. Thus the bearing of correlational studies on Piaget's systematic position is difficult to assess.

A new method for investigating Piagetian concepts in children is that of studying surprise reactions, a method originally developed by Charlesworth (for a summary see Charlesworth, 1969). The surprisal method should be particularly suitable for Piagetian investigations, because the question of what the child actually knows or believes is at issue in a way which is not true in more behaviouristically oriented investigations.

The problem can be illustrated this way. Suppose a child sees a clay ball rolled into a long cylinder and says there is now more clay. Does he really *believe* there is more clay? Would he be surprised if the clay was found to weigh more on a balance? This problem was studied by Miller (1971), who simulated increased weight by activating an electro-magnet placed beneath a balance pan. In general it appeared that conservers showed more surprise than non-conservers when their expectations were violated. This would suggest that they have stronger beliefs in the constancy of quantity across changes in shape than non-conservers have in their assertions that quantity changes when shape is changed.

Children's beliefs about quantity were further studied by Block (1971), who asked non-conservers to suggest a way of increasing the amount of Coca-Cola in a glass. If they suggested adding more from the can, they were asked to find another way, and some taller and narrower glasses were available near by. The children did not suggest pouring the Cola into one of the narrower glasses, and did not predict that this would be an effective way of increasing the amount when it was suggested to them. Yet when these non-conservers saw liquid poured into a taller and narrower vessel, they said it had become more. So what do they really think? Block also found that when conservers saw a small amount of liquid greatly increase in volume as it was poured into another vessel (due to the injection of some additional liquid through a hidden tube in the bottom), they showed some surprise, but not as much as might be expected. Some said it was still the same amount because nothing had been added, despite the obvious increase. However non-conservers showed no surprise at the increase in quantity, so there evidently are differences in the cognitive processes of the two groups, although the differences are not as absolute as Piaget's theory had tended to imply.

Halford (1968a, 1968b) asked children to make judgements of quantity based on a witnessed transferral from one vessel to another. Children saw material which just filled vessel A transferred to vessel B of a different shape, just filling it too. They were then asked whether a third vessel, as wide as B but shorter and also filled to the top, would overfill, underfill or just fill vessel A. In the control condition the children saw the same arrangement but did not see A poured into B. To the extent that children can draw inferences from the fact that A was transferred to B, their judgements should be more accurate in the experimental condition than in the control condition. This was so for both conservers and non-conservers at school age, but was not so for pre-schoolers, although the absolute magnitudes of the effects were small. Thus the work of Block and of Halford would both suggest that transferrals or transformations of material gain increasing significance with age, but that there is no perfect association between ability to conserve and recognition of the significance of transformations.

*Operativity*

One of the most subtle and important, but also most controversial aspects of Piaget's whole position is his contention that phenomena such as conservation actually reflect operational thinking. In the examples used here this means that when the child sees liquid poured from vessel A to vessel B he thinks the quantity has increased because he lacks the operation of logical multiplication (which is roughly equivalent to the ability to classify by two criteria simultaneously). The effect of this is that he does not think of the decrease in breadth as compensating for the increase in height. He is aware of both of these changes, but apparently fails to associate them with the maintenance of a given quantity. This can be illustrated by means of a check test described by Piaget (1967). If the child is shown some liquid in A, and asked how high it would reach if poured into B, which is narrower, he realizes it would be higher than in A. However, Piaget considers that this is merely empirical knowledge, and calls it 'co-variation'. To demonstrate an operation, the child must spontaneously think of the liquid in terms of both height and breadth simultaneously. This can be demonstrated by showing the child some liquid in A, and asking him to pour some other liquid into B so there will be the same amount in both. Children who lack the appropriate logical operation are not aware that the column of liquid in B must be higher if there is to be the same amount in both vessels. Block (1971) has conducted a most careful analytical investigation of this performance and has confirmed that non-conservers are not aware that the quantities in the two vessels cannot be equal unless a change in one dimension is compensated by a change in the other.

Nevertheless there are still very considerable difficulties with Piaget's operational view which cannot be considered in the space of this article. One important problem however is the diagnosis of operations by 'clinical' inferences drawn from observation of behaviour. It is not easy to see how to improve on this, but Peel (1967) has developed a method of testing the child's understanding of the binary logical operations (connectives) of implication, disjunction and mutual exclusion. Peel's methods may well be capable of development as a general technique of assessing operativity.

Recent work on memory (e.g. Murray, 1970; Piaget, 1968a) also promises to shed new light on the notion of operativity. It seems that recall of stimuli such as might be used in a conservation task improves with time since original exposure, and is also associated with the level of operational development of the subject. This is consistent with the view that the operational structures constitute a sort of mnemonic device, and that as the structures become more complete and equilibrated, recall will improve in accuracy.

The problem of operativity and thought will be the main underlying theme of the following sections. The problem may become clearer if we consider certain theoretical approaches next, and then go to sensori-motor and formal operational studies. This is the reason for the slightly unusual sequence of sub-headings which follows.

*Theoretical interpretations*

While Piaget would consider the concept of operational thinking to be the very core of the phenomena he has discovered, the possibility always exists that the same phenomena can be subsumed within existing psychological systems, possibly after the systems have undergone further development and modification. Berlyne (1965) attempted to reconcile Piaget's conceptions with neo-behaviourism. His purpose was in part to rectify Piaget's failure to consider the possible role of learning in producing transitions from one stage of development to the next. Berlyne's reinterpretation was based on Maltzman's (1955) 'habit family hierarchy' theory of thinking, which in turn was based on the work of Hull (1943, 1952). Berlyne postulated that a subject would have 'situational responses', which represented states of things (e.g. a given order of beads in the example used earlier), and 'transformational responses', which represented changes (such as the rotation of the tube containing the beads). Structures of thought were formed by tying these responses together in parallel chains so all responses would be subject to the same reinforcement. While Berlyne has described Piagetian systems of thought in terms familiar to learning psychologists, and although he claims that his chains of mediating responses are equivalent to operations, he does not actually demonstrate that they would function as operations.

Gagné (1968) has attempted to show that Piagetian concepts can be regarded as products of cumulative learning. He postulates a hierarchy of types of learning from S–R connections to chains, multiple discriminations, concepts and finally to rules. This is a promising approach, but Gagné unfortunately applies his theory to a hypothetical task which is only indirectly related to Piagetian concepts. Thus it is difficult to assess the likely contribution of Gagné's work to this area at the present time.

Bruner (1964) has developed an independent system of cognitive stages which in some respects parallel those of Piaget. Bruner postulates three stages, the enactive, the iconic and the symbolic. The first two correspond to Piaget's sensori-motor and pre-operational stages respectively, and provide a very clear and useful account of both Piagetian and other phenomena (see, for example, Biggs, 1968). The symbolic stage seems to be based on a conception of behaviour which is in certain respects opposed to Piaget's. Operational concepts are frequently symbolic, but are not necessarily so. Work on children's mathematical thinking by Collis (1971) indicates that children can utilize symbols of a kind normally associated with formal operational thinking without having these operations, so that formal operational thinking is evidently not simply 'symbolic' thinking.

A similar problem arises if we attempt to relate 'symbolic' thinking to concrete operational thinking. Bruner, Olver and Greenfield (1966) have argued that the acquisition of conservation results from symbolic accounts of quantity coming to dominate perceptual accounts. While this probably occurs, it does not necessarily refute Piaget's operational hypothesis, because the symbolic account could result from acquisition of operations. It is possible that three different questions should be asked here; what leads to the development of operations; what leads to the development of systems of symbols (or language); and are these two developments the same? The fact that they may not be the same is indicated by the failure of Bruner's concept of the symbolic stage to embody a distinction paralleling that between concrete and formal thinking. An important difference between Bruner's and Piaget's systems is that Bruner has a 'representational' view of cognition, whereas Piaget has a 'constructivist' view.

This difficult but important distinction has been considered in great depth by Furth (1969) who argues, following Piaget, that all knowledge has an operational component. This means that knowledge is not attained by simply internalizing experience in the form of symbols which represent external events. Rather the basis of knowing is to be found in relationships between activities of the person and sensory data. Thus knowing is an 'act' which transforms not only the sense data but the organism as well. Furth (1970) has shown that this view has important consequences for educational theory and practice, and it is hoped that more ways will be found soon to incorporate these considerations into empirical research.

Braine and Shanks (1965) have made a proposal which is related to Bruner's, and in this context would mean that non-conservers do not understand the term 'same amount' and interpret it to mean 'same height', or 'same breadth', etc. Although Braine and Shanks have shown that non-conservers probably have less verbal understanding of the relevant terms than conservers, it is doubtful whether this is responsible for their failure to conserve. No one can understand the meaning of a term if he lacks the concept to which the term relates, and Piaget (1968a) claims that there is evidence that language development depends upon cognitive development, rather than the reverse. This complex issue seems likely to remain open for some time.

The work discussed earlier indicating there are differences between the cognitions of conservers and non-conservers seems to put the positions of Bruner and of Braine and Shanks under some strain.

The concept of conservation has been given yet a further interpretation by Saltz (1971). He has shown that young children do not think a man is still a father if he is found to be a drunkard, which is not unlike their failure to recognize that a quantity is the same even if it is taller. Although Piaget has discovered phenomena resembling those of Saltz, nevertheless Saltz's work has placed Piagetian concepts in quite a new context. Thus, like Bruner, Berlyne, and Braine and Shanks, Saltz has helped to remove the aura of isolation and mystery which once surrounded Piagetian concepts.

Attempts to interpret Piaget's stages of development in terms of information-processing capabilities have been made by Halford (1968b, 1972). McLaughlin (1963), Pascual-Leone (1970), and Pascual-Leone and Smith (1969), and McLaughlin suggests that the child's digit span must be equal to the number of concepts which the child needs to consider simultaneously. He represents pre-operational performances as requiring $2^1 = 2$ concepts simultaneously, concrete operational performances as requiring $2^2 = 4$ concepts simultaneously, and formal operational concepts as requiring $2^3 = 8$ concepts. The first two stages would correspond to the memory spans of the children at the appropriate ages, but formal operations would not be acquired until much later than eleven years of age in average children if McLaughlin's views are correct, and would never be attained by adults whose memory spans did not develop beyond seven items.

Pascual-Leone has postulated that the stages of thought are related to an information-processing construct $M$, which is the maximum number of discrete 'chunks' (Miller, 1956) of information which can be utilized in a single act. $M = a+2$ at the late pre-operational stage, $a+3$ and $a+4$ at the early and later concrete operational stages respectively, and $a+5$ at the formal operational stages (where $a$ is an empirical constant). In a series of ingenious experiments, Pascual-Leone has obtained striking support for his formulations.

Halford has postulated that pre-operational concepts correspond to regularities with a minimum of one dimension or information unit, concrete operations correspond to regularities with two dimensions, and formal operations to three dimensions. A continuum is also implied between discriminations, concepts at various levels, and operations. The memory span required at each stage would be twice the number of dimensions, so that concrete operations would require a memory span of four and formal operations of six.

*Sensori-motor studies*

Piaget (1953, 1954) considers that during the sensori-motor period the child actively constructs for himself the concept of an object as a permanent, independent entity in space. He does this by constructing a coherent representation of spatial displacements or movements, and this representation has the properties of a mathematical group (see, for instance, Adler, 1958; Boyle, 1969). We can illustrate the problem by reference to one of Piaget's observations with his daughter Jacqueline at nineteen months (Piaget, 1954, p. 79). Figure 2 shows a slightly idealized version of the arrangement in which Piaget took a coin from the child and placed it under a coverlet, then took the coin in his closed hand and placed it under the cushion. The child looked first under the coverlet, then immediately looked under the cushion and found the coin.

We can consider three possible types of displacements; firstly there is the null displacement, which leaves the object where it was. We call this I. Then there are clockwise displacements from child to coverlet, coverlet to cushion, cushion to child. We will call these P. Then there are anti-clockwise displacements, from child to cushion, cushion to coverlet, coverlet to child. We will call these Q. Now the point is that any two of these

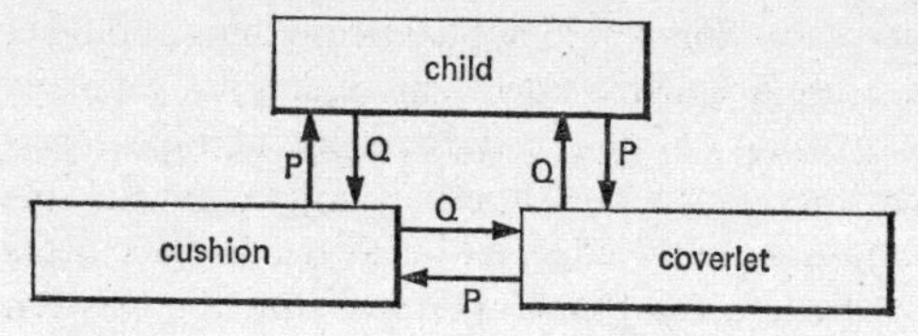


Figure 2

displacements corresponds to one specific displacement, as shown in Table 1. For instance, P followed by P is equivalent to Q (i.e. from child to coverlet, then from coverlet to cushion, is equivalent to child to cushion). The structure shown in Table 1 is a mathematical group. Now the crux of Piaget's argument seems to be that the child's ability to recognize that the coin must be under the cushion indicates that she has a representation of the situation which corresponds to this group. Furthermore, any complete set of spatial displacements of a permanent object must form a group and Piaget considers that a group-like representation is necessary for the object to be recognized as permanent.

This argument is really considerably more complex and subtle than the

Table 1

| | | Second displacement | | |
|---|---|---|---|---|
| | | I | P | Q |
| First displacement | I | I | P | Q |
| | P | P | Q | I |
| | Q | Q | I | P |

highly oversimplified version of it given above would imply, but space does not permit the matter to be considered further here. However, we can consider some interesting recent research on the problem, such as the studies by Evans and Gratch (1971), Gardner (1971); LeCompte and Gratch (1971); and Mundy-Castle and Anglin (cited by Bruner, 1969). Basically, these studies seem to show that children in their first year will show surprise when an object is hidden and reappears as a different object, as if by magic.

The question is whether these studies show that the infant has the concept of the permanent object, thereby refuting Piaget's position.

Without attempting to pre-judge a subtle and complex issue, one can point out that an expectation that an object will maintain a reasonably constant form is not necessarily the same thing as an actively constructed concept of the permanent object. We can imagine that Piaget's child, Jacqueline, might have been surprised if she had seen a coin hidden and had discovered a bank note in its place. This would not tell us anything about her representation of the spatial displacements. Furthermore, it is not yet really clear whether it tells us anything about the dependence of object permanence on these displacements. Piaget could perhaps argue that the surprise was a reflection of empirical knowledge, and that the displacements depend on an internal construction, and Furth's (1969) distinction between operative and figurative knowing would also be relevant. The research discussed above would then be viewed as asking whether the child has a concept of permanency in a sense other than Piaget's. This is perfectly legitimate, since Piaget does not have, and should not be given, a monopoly of the concept. All that can be confidently asserted at present is that this problem will be a fertile ground for both theoreticians and empiricists in the future.

*Formal operational studies*

A type of study which is particularly worthy of mention in this context is represented by the work of Wason (1966), who presented subjects with four cards with face sides similar to those in Figure 3.

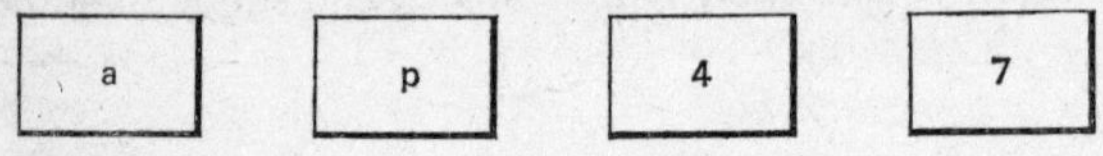


Figure 3

The subject was told to verify the rule that if there is a vowel on one side of the card, there is an even number on the other side, by examining only those cards which were necessary. The rule 'vowel implies even' can be expressed as $v \supset e$. Using $\bar{v}$ and $\bar{e}$ for 'not vowel' and 'not even' respectively, then $v \supset e$ itself implies $\bar{e} \supset \bar{v}$. Thus the subject must examine the first and fourth cards to verify the rule, and it is unnecessary to check the other two. In order to realize this the subjects must be aware of the relation between the two operations $v \supset e$ and $\bar{e} \supset \bar{v}$, which is clearly a formal operational performance in Piaget's terms, because it depends on recognition of the relations between two of the sixteen binary operations of propositional logic (Inhelder and Piaget, 1958; Lunzer, 1965; Piaget, 1957). Since few of Wason's adult subjects performed correctly, Wason's study seems to cast doubt on Piaget's position.

However, such a conclusion assumes that if subjects have a particular ability, it will be manifested under all conditions. Wason has however shown that *if* adults have what Piaget calls formal operations, then Piaget has done very little to specify the conditions under which they will be observed. His findings vindicate Bruner, Olver and Greenfield (1966), who criticize Piaget for being unduly concerned with the logical as opposed to the psychological aspects of thought.

This problem of the conditions under which formal operational thought will be exhibited has been extensively studied by Seggie (1969, 1970a, 1970b), who has also shown that Piagetian formal operational concepts can be linked to the classic study of concept attainment by Bruner, Goodnow and Austin (1956). We will consider Seggie's (1971) study of adults' understanding of the concept of correlation. Whereas Smedslund (1963d) had shown that his subjects (nurses) were unable to make an abstract judgement of the presence or absence of a correlation, Seggie found that his subjects (also nurses) were able to make a practical decision (still apparently based on formal operations) using correlational data. The same contingencies were used in both cases. Thus Seggie's results suggest that the subjects had a cognitive structure isomorphic to the concept of correlation, and it was only necessary to find the appropriate conditions for them to utilize it. This problem warrants more study at both the theoretical and empirical level.

**The origin of Piagetian phenomena**

*Training studies*

It was seen in the previous section that Piaget considers conservation and other concrete operational concepts as indices of certain kinds of logical thinking. It is therefore basic to Piaget's position that such concepts are not simply learned in the way one might learn a 'fact' of (say) geography, such as the distance from New York to Geneva, but are attained through 'equilibration' (for a lucid discussion of this issue see Smedslund, 1961, 1962, 1963a, 1963b).

In recent years some debate has occurred whether Piaget said such concepts could be learned or not. One could adduce arguments either way by selecting appropriate quotations, but it would seem more important to try to relate the essentials of Piaget's position to the evidence which has accrued.

Smedslund (1961 to 1963) began making attempts to train children in concrete operational concepts, but with limited success. Nevertheless Smedslund's work resulted in an explosion of Piagetian training studies, the number of which is so great that it will probably never be possible to write a comprehensive review of them. However a selective review by Brainerd and Allen (1971) would be a reasonable starting point for the reader who wishes to become familiar with this area, and the fine collection of papers edited by Elkind and Flavell (1969) and the review by Elkind and Sameroff (1970) would be indispensable aids to interpretation. All that can be done here is to consider certain types of training studies and to indicate general trends.

Some training studies were designed to incorporate specifically Piagetian mechanisms. Sigel, Roeper and Hooper (1966) report a pioneering study in which children were taught to give multiple descriptive labels for a variety of objects; e.g., they were shown a banana and encouraged to say it has peel, you can eat it, etc. They then progressed to multiple classification and finally to reversibility. Some subjects trained in this way attained conservation on some post-tests, whereas no control subjects did so, the difference being statistically significant.

This study suggests that it is possible to effect improvement in conservation by training in a situation which does not resemble the conservation task. Thus if this isolated result can be accepted, it suggests that conservation may be attained through reorganization of the underlying cognitive processes, rather than through specific learning. Unfortunately, relatively few studies have attempted to achieve this, so it is not possible to judge whether the findings of this study can be generalized.

One of Smedslund's early studies (Smedslund, 1961) used two training methods, both of which can be related to Piaget's notions. In Smedslund's 'deformation' method the subject was shown, for instance, two red plasticine balls of the same volume and weight (or, in some cases, of different volume and weight). One of the balls was successively deformed to a sausage, snake, cake and pancake. The two balls were placed on opposite pans of a balance before and after the deformations. The rationale of the procedure is that it induces a conflict between the appearance of inequality, and the observation of equality when the balls are seen on the balance. The subject might resolve the conflict by adopting an 'inner frame of reference', such as that the balls were the same since nothing had been added or subtracted. If this method of resolving the conflict is adopted, the subject might achieve equilibration or 'a change in the direction of increasing stability, consistency and completeness of behavioural structures' (Smedslund, 1961, p. 71). A non-equilibration resolution of the conflict might be to simply regard the appearance of the objects as unrelated to their effects on the balance. In Smedslund's 'addition–subtraction' method, small amounts were added to or subtracted from the balls instead of the deformations of shape. While the concept of equilibration can be applied to either of these methods, neither alone would be sufficient to embody the concept adequately.

Smedslund found some learning of conservation by both methods, with the deformation method being slightly but not significantly better than the addition method. Since Piaget (1968a) would argue that the addition–subtraction scheme is essential to the attainment of the concept of identity of substance or weight, Smedslund's finding that the addition–subtraction method adds nothing to the deformation method tends to refute Piaget's position. Smedslund's finding is consistent with that of Wallach, Wall and Anderson (1967) but not that of Wohlwill (1959). The best way to resolve this issue is probably indicated by Smedslund (1962), who showed that various addition and subtraction operations are differentially related to conservation. Furthermore, as we shall see later, conservation might be induced for a variety of reasons, some of which are more closely related to addition and subtraction than others.

A study which was conceived in a more pragmatic framework, largely independently of Piaget's notions, is that of Beilin (1965), who used four training methods. They were: non-verbal reinforcement (of a conservation response); verbal orientation reinforcement (to appropriate attributes); equilibration; and verbal rule instruction. The equilibration method was really Smedslund's (1961) deformation procedure. The verbal, rule instruction procedure involved giving the subject a verbal explanation of the conservation principle as it applied to each training problem on which he made an error. Beilin found that training produced significantly more improvement in conservation than was observed in the control group, but there were no significant differences among the training groups themselves. The verbal-rule instruction procedure gave the highest overall level of performance, which is interesting in that Piaget's ideas would be antithetical to the employment of such procedures. Beilin also gave subjects a test of understanding of the concept of 'same' and found that 'not understanding "same" does not preclude success (in learning to conserve), and training appears to remove all pretest differences in such comprehension'. This finding suggests that the subjects learn the meaning of the word 'same' by acquiring the concept, and not the reverse, thus supporting the positions of Piaget (1967) and Sinclair-de-Zwart (1969), and refuting that of Braine and Shanks (1965).

Beilin's conservation tests are an example of the many departures that have been made from Piagetian test procedures. While Beilin's tests are more objective (in the sense of less verbal) one cannot be certain that they measure the same thing as Piaget's conservation tests. The children had to judge which of two rows of corks was 'like' a standard row, where one row was the same length as the standard, and the other was the same number as the standard. They made this judgement both before and after seeing the standard changed in length. Nevertheless, we cannot be sure that this is the same as asking a child whether there is the same *number* before and after the transformation (see, for instance, Beilin, 1969); Mehler and Bever, 1968; Piaget, 1967, 1968b.

A study which was conceived in a non-Piagetian framework is that of Gelman (1969), who used oddity problems as shown in Figure 4. The subject was required either to say which row was different from the other two, or to say which two rows were the same, and was reinforced for a correct response.

One control group received the same oddity problems without reinforcement, and another group received oddity problems which were irrelevant to conservation. Gelman's training group not only showed substantial and significant improvement in conservation, but the improvement transferred to quite different types of conservation problems. Gelman interpreted her study as showing that children learn to conserve by being trained to recognize that quantity is the relevant dimension.

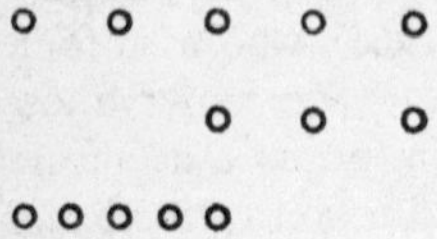

o o o o o

o o o

o o o o o

Figure 4

*Critique of training studies*

Enough examples of training studies have now been given for a discussion to be meaningful, although any conclusions of course need to be based on a much wider sample of studies. Many experiments have been based on the strategy of trying to find the best method of inducing conservation. The rationale of this strategy does not seem to have been explicitly examined, but it is possible that it is hoped thereby to find a method of facilitating the acquisition of logical thinking. The problem is that it is not at all clear what is achieved by teaching conservation. There is very scanty evidence that any training procedure devised so far has actually changed the operations of child thought. It is equally likely that the training procedure served to increase the child's knowledge of the conservation situation. The child would then be better able to see that the task was an instance of an operational concept which he had already attained, but the relevance of which he had not seen. If this is so, then we need to reassess the significance of conservation training. It may shed more light on the validity of Piaget's theories to try to teach logical operations, and in this respect the work of Furth (1970) and Peel (1967) would be more relevant.

It might be hoped that if a method was found that was superior to all others, it might serve as a model of the development of thought. On present indications it seems unlikely that this will be achieved (Gelman's 1969 study has come nearest to fulfilling this aim), but even if it was, it does not follow that that method most accurately reflects the process by which thought develops spontaneously.

The studies reported so far seem to indicate that almost any method works sometimes, and no method works for all subjects, even within a given age group. This is consistent with the view that the development of Piagetian concepts depends on internal constructions, rather than on the absorption of information (see Beilin, 1970; Halford, 1970). It does little however to explicate what these constructions are, or how they are developed. It is perhaps a little ironical that the non-Piagetian experimental literature probably sheds more light on this question than most studies under the Piagetian rubric (see Mandler, 1962).

A further problem is that all training procedures permit almost unlimited variations, many of which would be too subtle and elusive to pin down precisely by experimental analysis. Almost any method could be made either more or less successful than its competitors by employing appropriate variations.

One particularly acute problem is that of deciding why training procedures work. Although the studies considered here are probably amongst the best in the field, we can illustrate the problem with each of them. For instance, Smedslund (1961) and Wallach and Sprott (1964) both used training procedures designed to induce conflict. There is little guarantee that conflict was actually induced, or if it was, that it was the effective agent of change. Beilin's (1965) verbal rule instruction might have taught a verbal rule, or it might have enabled the subject to cognize or code what he observed in the training items. The procedure of Gelman (1969) might have taught the children to respond to the relevant 'attributes' (quantity or length), or it might have taught them that they could not succeed without employing the addition–subtraction scheme, compensation or reversibility (see Brainerd and Allen, 1971; Halford, 1970). We do not know whether the children had these schemes, and we do not know their origin, so it is impossible to judge whether this is so or not.

*Theoretical considerations related to training*

In general we cannot determine the relevance of Piaget's concepts of operational thinking to phenomena such as conservation without adequate tests of the operations themselves. The tests in turn must be based on an analysis of the 'deep structure' of the operations, and some progress has been made in this in recent years. Wallach (1969) has presented a rigorous examination of the underlying logic of the conservation problem, and has pointed out that mechanisms such as compensation and reversibility do not provide an adequate logical basis for conserving. At the same time Wallach provides a penetrating interpretation of Berlyne's (1965) learning-theory account of Piagetian concepts. In general Wallach's analysis throws considerable light on what it means to an adult to say that two quantities are equal, thus rectifying a notable error of omission in Piaget's work.

Elkind (1967) has shown that there are two logically distinct conservation problems; conservation of identity, which means that a quantity is the same before and after transformation, and conservation of equivalence, which means that if two quantities are equal initially, they are equal after one of them has been transformed. This distinction has been given empirical justification by Hooper (1969). Piaget's position might be that the underlying operations are the same in both cases (see Boyle, 1969), but even if this is so, Elkind's distinction is of considerable importance for task analysis.

Halford (1970, 1972) proposes that the addition–subtraction scheme can be conceptualized as a semi-group structure which can be externalized through certain manipulations. We can consider three types of changes which can be made to a quantity of, for instance, liquid. We can pour it from one vessel to another, we can add to it, or we can subtract some liquid from it. If a vessel of liquid is poured into another vessel, then some is added, we will find we have more when it is returned to the first vessel, just as we would if we had added some while it was in the original vessel. Similarly, if we had poured it into a second vessel and removed some, then returned it to the original vessel, we would have had less. However, if we added some while it was in the original vessel, then poured it into the second vessel, again we would find that when it was returned to the first vessel there would be more than there was in the beginning. If we merely poured it into the second vessel and then back again, we would have the same.

From the various pourings combined with additions and subtractions which can be explored in this way, important relationships can be learned; firstly, that additions and subtractions are not affected by pourings. Adding after pouring has the same effect as adding before pouring, if we use the original vessel as our criterion. Secondly, the effects of pouring can be cancelled by merely pouring back, so that pouring cancels pouring. However, addition can only be cancelled by subtraction, not by pouring or by further addition. Thus certain stable and consistent relationships can be discovered simply by exploration, without didactic help or external reinforcement. They result in pouring being differentiated from adding and subtracting, and in group-theory terms, they give pouring the status of an identity element (i.e. an element which, when combined with any other element, yields the same result as that element alone). Thus the identity element is constructed by finding relationships within the situation.

This structural differentiation of pouring from addition and subtraction clears the way for the child to learn that pouring leaves the quantity the same. Without this differentiation a statement such as 'You haven't any more, because you only poured it, you haven't added any,' would have very little meaning. This didactic information can however be linked or assimilated to the structure above, which can be accommodated to it as follows; the subject can say that pouring means (i.e. is equivalent to, or yields) 'same'. Since he probably already knows that adding yields more and subtracting yields less, he has the set of mappings shown in Table 2.

The integration of pouring into this structure gives it a meaning which is consistent with the relationships which the subject has already discovered, and gives the subject a reasonably coherent view of quantity. Further quantification can be achieved by breaking down 'more' and 'less' into units; this will eventually yield a group structure, and the remaining inconsistencies in Table 2 will be removed.

In a recent experiment by the author, children were shown pourings combined with additions and subtractions as described above, and asked to predict the result when the material was returned to the original vessel.

Table 2

| | same | more | less |
|---|---|---|---|
| same | same | more | less |
| more | more | more | same (?) |
| less | less | same (?) | less |

The results indicate that children know relationships isomorphic to those shown in Table 2 from about age five onwards. Thus after this age they have at least a crude knowledge of the 'logic of quantity', and should only require increased knowledge of the conservation situation to be able to apply this logic to it. Thus training procedures, including verbal instruction, should be successful after age five but not before, which is what the training literature seems to demonstrate.

**Educational implications**

Educators have enthusiastically accepted the challenge of working out the implications of Piaget's theory for their work, and a collection of papers edited by Athey and Rubadeau (1970) gives an overview of this field. Lunzer (1968) and Lunzer and Morris (1968) have succeeded in the very difficult task of giving Piaget's work an in-depth interpretation in the context of a wide cross-section of psychological systems, and then applying this interpretation to education. In addition, Almy (1966) and Furth (1970) have made vital contributions to this area.

The most obvious applications of Piaget's work are to the teaching of mathematics and the physical sciences, since both of these explicitly require operational thinking. Ordinary arithmetic operations of addition, subtraction, multiplication and division seem to require the concrete operational level of development. Mathematics which involves the transformation of operations, as in the solution of equations, would seem to require formal operations. Hypothesis-testing and the systematic consideration of possibilities, as required in elementary physics and chemistry, would seem to necessitate formal operations.

However, Piagetian analyses of conceptual level have also provided interesting results in the social sciences. Peel (1966, 1967) and Szeminska (1965) have conducted studies in this area. It would seem that formal operational thought is acquired later in subjects like history than in subjects like physics. More recently Elkind (1969) has found a promising link between the development of operational thought and reading.

## Conclusion

The title of this chapter should really be a question: what impact, if any, will Piaget have on psychology in the 1970s? Not since the Hullian era has so much investigation been applied to a system developed by one person, yet it would be hard to think of two conceptual systems more different than Piaget's and Hull's, notwithstanding the attempt by Berlyne (1965) to relate them.

The extent of this interest tends to disguise the fact that Piaget's conceptions are still far from being integrated into the main body of psychological thought and knowledge. For instance, many training procedures have been based on learning set or concept attainment models, thus apparently combining Piagetian and neo-behaviouristic approaches. However, it is the Piagetian concepts rather than the concept-attainment or learning-set models which have undergone most modification. This is not to support Piagetian interpretations as opposed to others; it is simply that a theory cannot be tested by an experimental programme which allows it no opportunity to be confirmed. Many contemporary experimental approaches do not impinge on the processes implied by Piaget's system, since their results could occur whether the system is valid or not.

In general it can be said that the majority of both empirical investigators and theoreticians have been more willing to embrace Piagetian phenomena than the Piagetian conceptual system. There are many possible reasons for this. The phenomena themselves are striking, easy to demonstrate and (superficially at least) easy to appreciate. The system is immensely complex and subtle, very poorly expounded, and riddled with gaps and inconsistencies, apparent or real.

It is not only appropriate but essential that Piagetian phenomena should not be uncritically accepted as support for the conception of behaviour which Piaget has promulgated. It is not appropriate, however, for the system to be by-passed, and the notion that the child constructs for himself the operations of thought is a challenging and potentially important one, as Furth (1969) has shown. The study of this process may even help to clarify some old problems. For instance, while we know how people recognize the relevance of concepts which have already been formed, we do not know how they form concepts in the first place.

Thus the future impact of Piaget's work on psychology in general will depend not only on whatever intrinsic merits the work has, but on how readily investigators come to grips with the system, difficult as it is. They will have to attempt the colossal task of rendering the system testable, which may well require sophisticated and creative reinterpretation. While monumental efforts have been made in this respect, and here the work of Bruner and Berlyne comes most readily to mind, the main task still constitutes a challenge for the future.

## Further reading

ATHEY, I. J., and RUBADEAU, D. O., *Educational Implications of Piaget's Theory*, Ginn-Blaisdell, 1970. A collection of rather brief papers, but representing many of the prominent authors in the field.

BALDWIN, A. L., *Theories of Child Development*, Wiley, 1967. The chapters on Piaget provide a very lucid introduction, particularly to the logic of concrete operational thought.

BOYLE, D. G., *A Student's Guide to Piaget*, Pergamon, 1969. This is one of the clearest but also most sophisticated of the introductory accounts.

BRAINERD, C. J., and ALLEN, T. W., 'Experimental inductions of the conservation of "first order" quantitative invariants', *Psychological Bulletin*, vol. 75, 1971, pp. 128–44. This selective review argues that 'reversibility' is the main factor influencing success in training studies. The thesis is interesting, but seems to be based on a somewhat restricted view of the problem.

BRUNER, J. S., OLVER, R. R., and GREENFIELD, P., *Studies in Cognitive Growth*, Wiley, 1966. A collection of research studies organized around a theme which is a possible alternative to Piaget's formulation.

ELKIND, D., 'Developmental studies of figurative perception', in L. P. Lipsitt and H. W. Reese (eds.), *Advances in Child Development and Behavior*, Academic Press, 1969. A very interesting article and a worthwhile extension of Piaget's work.

ELKIND, D., and FLAVELL, J. H., *Studies in Cognitive Development*, Oxford University Press, Inc., 1969. Includes a variety of important original articles.

ELKIND, D., and SAMEROFF, A., 'Developmental psychology', *Annual Review of Psychology*, vol. 21, 1970, pp. 191–238. Important for a view of Piagetian research in the context of developmental psychology.

FLAVELL, J. H., *The Developmental Psychology of Jean Piaget*, Van Nostrand, 1963. The most comprehensive interpretative summary of Piaget's work, but could well be supplemented with some of the later summaries.

FURTH, H. G., *Piaget and Knowledge: Theoretical Foundations*, Prentice-Hall, 1969. A highly sophisticated treatment, indispensable to the reader who really wants to understand the basis of Piaget's work.

FURTH, H. G., *Piaget for Teachers*, Prentice-Hall, 1970. Puts an interesting point of view and outlines techniques which are of value to psychologists as well as educators.

GINSBURG, H., and OPPER, S., *Piaget's Theory of Intellectual Development: An Introduction*, Prentice-Hall, 1969. The best summary of the logic of formal operational thinking, and good in other respects.

HUNT, J. MCV., *Intelligence and Experience*, Ronald Press, 1961. The chapters on Piaget were the first interpretative summary widely read in English, and are still one of the best.

LUNZER, E. A., and MORRIS, J. F., *Development in Human Learning*, Staples Press, 1968. Contains many important contributions, and puts the work of Piaget in a wider context.

PHILLIPS, J. L., Jr, *The Origins of Intellect: Piaget's Theory*, Freeman, 1969. A good introductory account of Piaget's work.

PIAGET, J., *The Psychology of Intelligence*, trans. M. Piercy and D. E. Berlyne, Routledge & Kegan Paul, 1950. Rather difficult reading, but is probably the best place to begin reading Piaget's own works.

PIAGET, J., *Logic and Psychology*, Basic Books, 1957. A succinct summary of Piaget's logic. Indispensable to the intending specialist.

SIGEL, I. E., and HOOPER, F. H., *Logical Thinking in Children*, Holt, Rinehart & Winston, 1968. A representative collection of important papers.

**References**

ADLER, I. (1958), *The New Mathematics*, Signet.

ALMY, M. (with E. Chittenden and P. Miller) (1966), *Young Children's Thinking: Studies of some Aspects of Piaget's Theory*, Teachers' College Press, Columbia University.

ATHEY, I. J., and RUBADEAU, D. O. (1970), *Educational Implications of Piaget's Theory*, Ginn-Blaisdell.

BALDWIN, A. L. (1967), *Theories of Child Development*, Wiley.

BEILIN, H. (1965), 'Learning and operational convergence in logical thought development', *Journal of Experimental Child Psychology*, vol. 2, pp. 317–39.

BEILIN, H. (1969), 'Stimulus and cognitive transformation in conservation', in D. Elkind and J. H. Flavell (eds.), *Studies in Cognitive Development*, Oxford University Press.

BEILIN, H. (1970), 'The training and acquisition of logical operations', paper read to Conference on Piaget-Type Research in Mathematical Education, Greyston Conference Center, Teachers' College, Columbia University, October.

BERLYNE, D. E. (1965), *Structure and Direction in Thinking*, Wiley.

BIGGS, J. B. (1968), *Information and Human Learning*, Cassell.

BLOCK, Susan (*née* Carey) (1971), personal communication.

BOYLE, D. G. (1969), *A Student's Guide to Piaget*, Pergamon.

BRAINE, M. D. S. (1959), 'The ontogeny of certain logical operations: Piaget's formulation examined by non-verbal methods', *Psychological Monographs*, whole no. 475.

BRAINE, M. D. S. (1964), 'Development of a grasp of transitivity of length: a reply to Smedslund', *Child Development*, vol. 35, pp. 799–810.

BRAINE, M. D. S., and SHANKS, B. L. (1965), 'The conservation of a shape property and a proposal about the origin of conservations', *Canadian Journal of Psychology*, vol. 19, pp. 197–207.

BRAINERD, C. J., and ALLEN, T. W. (1971), 'Experimental inductions of the conservation of "first order" quantitative invariants', *Psychological Bulletin*, vol. 75, pp. 128–44.

BRUNER, J. S. (1964), 'The course of cognitive growth', *American Psychologist*, vol. 19, pp. 1–15.

BRUNER, J. S. (1969), *Ninth Annual Report*, Harvard Center for Cognitive Studies.

BRUNER, J. S., GOODNOW, J. S., and AUSTIN, G. A. (1956), *A Study of Thinking*, Wiley.

BRUNER, J. S., OLVER, R. R., and GREENFIELD, P. (1966), *Studies in Cognitive Growth*, Wiley.

CHARLESWORTH, W. R. (1969), 'The role of surprise in cognitive development', in D. Elkind and J. H. Flavell (eds.), *Studies in Cognitive Development*, Oxford University Press, Inc.

COLLIS, K. F. (1971), 'A study of concrete and formal reasoning in school mathematics', *Australian Journal of Psychology*, vol. 23, pp. 289–96.

DODWELL, P. C. (1962), 'Relations between the understanding of the logic of classes and of cardinal number in children', *Canadian Journal of Psychology*, vol. 16, pp. 152–60.

ELKIND, D. (1967), 'Piaget's conservation problems', *Child Development*, vol. 38, pp. 15–27.

ELKIND, D. (1969), 'Developmental studies of figurative perception', in L. P. Lipsitt and H. W. Reese (eds.), *Advances in Child Development and Behavior*, Academic Press.

ELKIND, D., and FLAVELL, J. H. (1969), *Studies in Cognitive Development*, Oxford University Press, Inc.

ELKIND, D., and SAMEROFF, A. (1970), 'Developmental psychology', *Annual Review of Psychology*, vol. 21, pp. 191–238.

EVANS, W. F., and GRATCH, G. (1971), 'The stage-four error in Piaget's theory of object concept development: difficulties in object conceptualization or spatial localization?', paper read to Society for Research in Child Development, Minneapolis.

FLAVELL, J. H. (1963), *The Developmental Psychology of Jean Piaget*, Van Nostrand.

FURTH, H. G. (1969), *Piaget and Knowledge: Theoretical Foundations*, Prentice-Hall.

FURTH, H. G. (1970), *Piaget for Teachers*, Prentice-Hall.

GAGNÉ, R. M. (1968), 'Contributions of learning to human development', *Psychological Review*, vol. 75, pp. 177–91.

GARDNER, J. (1971), 'Development of object identity in the first six months', paper read to Society for Research in Child Development, Minneapolis.

GELMAN, R. (1969), 'Conservation acquisition: a problem of learning to attend to relevant attributes', *Journal of Experimental Child Psychology*, vol. 7, pp. 167–87.

GINSBURG, H., and OPPER, S. (1969), *Piaget's Theory of Intellectual Development: An Introduction*, Prentice-Hall.

HALFORD, G. S. (1968a), 'An experimental test of Piaget's notions concerning the conservation of quantity in children', *Journal of Experimental Child Psychology*, vol. 6, pp. 33–43.

HALFORD, G. S. (1968b), 'An investigation of concept learning: a study of conservation of quantity in children', Ph.D. dissertation, University of Newcastle, New South Wales, Australia.

HALFORD, G. S. (1969), 'An experimental analysis of the criteria used by children to judge quantities', *Journal of Experimental Child Psychology*, vol. 8, pp. 314–27.

HALFORD, G. S. (1970), 'A theory of the acquisition of conservation', *Psychological Review*, vol. 77, pp. 302–16.

HALFORD, G. S. (1972), 'Learning and conceptual development', in preparation.

HOOPER, F. H. (1969), 'Piaget's conservation tasks: the logical and developmental priority of identity conservation', *Journal of Experimental Child Psychology*, vol. 8, pp. 234–49.

HULL, C. L. (1943), *Principles of Behavior*, Appleton-Century-Crofts.

HULL, C. L. (1952), *A Behavior System*, Yale University Press.

HUNT, J. McV. (1961), *Intelligence and Experience*, Ronald Press.

INHELDER, B., and PIAGET, J. (1958), *The Growth of Logical Thinking from Childhood to Adolescence*, Basic Books.

KOHLBERG, L. (1963), 'The development of children's orientations toward a moral order: 1. Sequence in the development of moral thought', *Vita Humana*, vol. 6, pp. 11–33.

LECOMPTE, G. K., and GRATCH, G. (1971), 'Violation of infants' expectations as a method of diagnosing levels of object concept', paper read to Society for Research in Child Development, Minneapolis.

LUNZER, E. A. (1965), 'Problems of formal reasoning in test situations', in P. H. Mussen (ed.), 'European research in cognitive development', *Monographs of the Society for Research in Child Development*, vol. 30, whole no. 100.

LUNZER, E. A. (1968), *The Regulation of Behaviour*, Staples Press.

LUNZER, E. A., and MORRIS, J. F. (1968), *Development in Human Learning*, Staples Press.

MCLAUGHLIN, G. H. (1963), 'Psycho-logic: a possible alternative to Piaget's formulation', *British Journal of Educational Psychology*, vol. 33, pp. 61–7.

MALTZMAN, I. (1955), 'Thinking from a behavioristic point of view', *Psychological Review*, vol. 62, pp. 275–86.

MANDLER, G. (1962), 'From association to structure', *Psychological Review*, vol. 69, pp. 415–27.

MEHLER, J., and BEVER, T. G. (1967), 'Cognitive capacity of very young children', *Science*, vol. 158, pp. 141–2.

MEHLER, J., and BEVER, T. G. (1968), reply (to J. Piaget, same journal, same issue), *Science*, vol. 162, pp. 979–81.

MILLER, G. A. (1956), 'The magical number seven, plus or minus two: some limits on our capacity for processing information', *Psychological Review*, vol. 63, pp. 81–97.

MILLER, S. A. (1971), 'Contradiction, surprise and cognitive change', paper read to Society for Research in Child Development, Minneapolis.

MURRAY, F. B. (1970), 'Memory and conservation', *Psychonomic Science*, vol. 21, pp. 334–5.

PASCUAL-LEONE, J. (1970), 'A mathematical model for the transition rule in Piaget's developmental stages', *Acta Psychologica*, vol. 32, pp. 301–45.

PASCUAL-LEONE, J., and SMITH, J. (1969), 'The encoding and decoding of symbols by children: a new experimental paradigm and a neo-Piagetian model', *Journal of Experimental Child Psychology*, vol. 8, pp. 328–55.

PEEL, E. A. (1966), 'A study of differences in the judgements of adolescent pupils', *British Journal of Educational Psychology*, vol. 36, pp. 77–86.

PEEL, E. A. (1967), 'A method for investigating children's understanding of certain logical connectives used in binary propositional thinking', *British Journal of Mathematical and Statistical Psychology*, vol. 20, pp. 81–92.

PHILLIPS, J. L., Jr (1969), *The Origins of Intellect: Piaget's Theory*, Freeman.

PIAGET, J. (1932), *The Moral Judgment of the Child*, Routledge.

PIAGET, J. (1950), *The Psychology of Intelligence*, Routledge.

PIAGET, J. (1952), *The Child's Conception of Number*, Routledge.

PIAGET, J. (1953), *The Origin of Intelligence in the Child*, Routledge.

PIAGET, J. (1954), *The Construction of Reality in the Child*, 2 vols., Basic Books.

PIAGET, J. (1957), *Logic and Psychology*, Basic Books.

PIAGET, J. (1961), *Les mécanismes perceptifs*, Presses Universitaires de France.

PIAGET, J. (1967), 'Cognitions and conservations: two views' (review of Bruner *et al.*, with D. McNeill as other reviewer), *Contemporary Psychology*, vol. 12, pp. 530–33.

PIAGET, J. (1968a), *On the Development of Memory and Identity*, Clark UP.

PIAGET, J. (1968b), 'Quantification, conservation and nativism', *Science*, vol. 162, pp. 976–9.

SALTZ, E. (1971), *The Cognitive Bases of Human Learning*, Irwin-Dorsey, 1971.

SEAGRIM, G. N. (1969), translation of J. Piaget, *The Mechanisms of Perception*, Routledge & Kegan Paul.

SEGGIE, J. L. (1969), 'Levels of learning involved in conjunctive and disjunctive concepts', *Australian Journal of Psychology*, vol. 21, pp. 325–33.

SEGGIE, J. L. (1970a), 'The utilization by children and adults of binary propositional thinking in concept learning', *Journal of Experimental Child Psychology*, vol. 10, pp. 235–47.

SEGGIE, J. L. (1970b), 'Variables involved in confirming the consistency of a learned concept', *Australian Journal of Psychology*, vol. 22, pp. 225–35.

SEGGIE, J. L. (1971), 'An investigation of formal operational thought', Ph.D. dissertation, University of Newcastle, New South Wales, Australia.

SIGEL, I. E., and HOOPER, F. H. (1968), *Logical Thinking in Children*, Holt, Rinehart & Winston.

SIGEL, I. E., ROEPER, A., and HOOPER, F. H. (1966), 'A training procedure for acquisition of Piaget's conservation of quantity: a pilot study and its replication', *British Journal of Educational Psychology*, vol. 36, pp. 301–11.

SINCLAIR-DE-ZWART, H. (1969), 'Developmental psycholinguistics', in D. Elkind and J. H. Flavell (eds.), *Studies in Cognitive Development*, OUP Inc.

SMEDSLUND, J. (1961), 'The acquisition of conservation of substance and weight in children: I–VI', *Scandinavian Journal of Psychology*, vol. 2, *passim*.

SMEDSLUND, J. (1962), 'The acquisition of conservation of substance and weight in children: VII', *Scandinavian Journal of Psychology*, vol. 3, pp. 69–77.

SMEDSLUND, J. (1963a), 'Patterns of experience and the acquisition of concrete transitivity of weight in eight-year-old children', *Scandinavian Journal of Psychology*, vol. 4, pp. 151–6.

SMEDSLUND, J. (1963b), 'Patterns of experience and the acquisition of conservation of length', *Scandinavian Journal of Psychology*, vol. 4, pp. 257–64.

SMEDSLUND, J. (1963c), 'The development of concrete transitivity of length in children', *Child Development*, vol. 34, pp. 389–405.

SMEDSLUND, J. (1963d), 'The concept of correlation in adults', *Scandinavian Journal of Psychology*, vol. 4, pp. 165–73.

SMEDSLUND, J. (1965), 'The development of transitivity of length: a comment on Braine's reply', *Child Development*, vol. 36, pp. 577–80.

SMEDSLUND, J. (1966), 'Performance on measurement and pseudo-measurement tasks by five to seven year old children', *Scandinavian Journal of Psychology*, vol. 7, pp. 81–92.

SZEMINSKA, A. (1965), 'The evolution of thought: some applications of research findings to educational practice', *Monographs of Society for Research in Child Development*, vol. 30, whole no. 100, pp. 47–57.

TUDDENHAM, R. D. (1970), 'Psychometricizing Piaget's *méthode clinique*', in I. J. Athey and D. O. Rubadeau (eds.), *Educational Implications of Piaget's Theory*, Ginn-Blaisdell.

WALLACH, L. (1969), 'On the bases of conservation', in D. Elkind and J. H. Flavell (eds.), *Studies in Cognitive Development*, OUP Inc.

WALLACH, L., and SPROTT, R. L. (1964), 'Inducing number conservation in children', *Child Development*, vol. 35, pp. 1057–71.

WALLACH, L., WALL, A. J., and ANDERSON, L. (1967), 'Number conservation: the roles of reversibility, addition–substraction, and misleading perceptual cues', *Child Development*, vol. 38, pp. 425–42.

WASON, P. C. (1966), 'Reasoning', in B. Foss (ed.), *New Horizons in Psychology*, Penguin.

WOHLWILL, J. (1959), 'Un essai d'apprentissage dans le domaine de la conservation du nombre', *Études d'epistémologie génétique*, vol. 9, pp. 125–35.

# 9 Seven Questions about Language Development
Dan I. Slobin

The study of language development in children has a rich historical tradition in both psychology and linguistics; in its modern form as 'developmental psycholinguistics' this study is deeply involved in current issues of psychological and linguistic theory. Beginning with an SSRC conference held at the Massachusetts Institute of Technology just a decade ago (1961 – reported in Bellugi and Brown, 1964), psychologists and linguists have met in the domain of child language to work together and to argue with one another. (The reader can sample the fruits of such meetings in recent anthologies edited by Ferguson and Slobin, 1972; Hayes, 1970; Huxley and Ingram, 1971; Slobin, 1971; and Smith and Miller, 1966). The decade has seen a rapid development in subtlety of research methods, depth of theoretical issues, and complexity of problems facing the psycholinguist who wishes to account for the ontogenesis of language. In this brief review some promising new directions are sampled in the light of seven enduring questions of language development. (Recent comprehensive reviews of the field have been offered by Braine, 1971b; McNeill, 1970; and Menyuk, 1971.)

The development of transformational generative grammar in the late 1950s stimulated psychologists to study the *structure* of child language from a new point of view (see Lyons, 1970, for an introduction to current trends in linguistics). Rather than classifying child utterances in terms of the parts-of-speech and sentence types of formal adult grammar, attempts were made to characterize the systematicity of child speech in its own terms. Large samples of child speech were recorded and subjected to distributional analyses. Three independent research projects arrived at strikingly similar results: Braine at Walter Reed (1963), Brown and Fraser at Harvard (1963), and Miller and Ervin (now Ervin-Tripp) at Berkeley (1964).

By the end of the decade, however, there was a general feeling that some important things had been missed in these early studies. There has been increasing concern with the *content* of child speech as well as its form. This concern reflects a growing sense of the child as an active participant in the process of language acquisition. Recent work concerns itself with the child's semantic intentions and with the means by which he deciphers the speech of others. There has been a flowering of interest in sentence-interpretation strategies, and there have been initial attempts to specify some of the components of the 'language-acquisition device' in detail. Our perspective on child language development has been broadened by cross-linguistic comparisons and by attempts to relate more closely the study of linguistic development with the study of cognitive development. Some of these current trends are examined below.

**What does the child mean to say?**

The first phase of the Harvard, Walter Reed and Berkeley studies dealt with the structure of two-word utterances. All three studies divided the child's vocabulary at the two-word stage into a large class of content words (words which make reference) and a small class of function words (words which operate on the content words in fixed grammatical frames). The most widely quoted analysis has been Braine's (1963) description of 'pivotal constructions', in which there is a small class of 'pivot words', occupying either first or second position in a two-word utterance, in combination with a large class of content words which can freely occur in either position. For example, in the following set of utterances, *all gone* would be classed as a first-position pivot word and *on* as a second-position pivot word: *allgone shoe, allgone milk, allgone outside, allgone cookie; shoe on, hat on, fix on.* The early studies sought to write rules for the combinations of gross word classes along lines such as these (Braine's 'structural formulae', Miller and Ervin's 'relatively systematic arrangement of classes', etc.).

Grammar is a system for relating sounds and meanings. Distributional analyses describe the sounds produced by young children – suitably organized into words and word classes – but shed no light on questions of meaning. As numerous psycholinguists have pointed out recently, the meanings which a child expresses by means of two-word utterances are more various than the surface forms of such utterances. For example, Brown (1972) notes at least four basic functions of simple combinations of 'pivot' and 'content' words, which he calls 'basic operations of reference':

1. Pointing and naming ('*that* —').
2. Commenting on or requesting recurrence of a referent ('*more* —').
3. Commenting on or requesting the disappearance of a referent ('*all-gone* —').
4. Noticing or attracting the notice of a referent already present ('*hi* —').

Bloom (1970), who has done the most intensive analysis of semantic intent in early speech, has clearly demonstrated that combinations of two content words are surface manifestations of a large range of deeper semantic structures. Bloom carried out a detailed longitudinal study of three children, with full notation of the contexts in which utterances were spoken. She noted that formally identical structures occurred in varying contexts. Sometimes the identical utterance form turned out to be a structural homonym, having more than one meaning. For example, one of the children she studied said *Mommy sock* on two distinct occasions – when picking up her mother's sock, and while being dressed by her mother. It is clear that the first utterance expresses a relationship of possession, while the second expresses an agent–object relationship. Bloom notes that noun–noun combinations express at least five different underlying semantic relations: conjunction (*umbrella, boot*), attribution (*party hat*), genitive (*daddy hat*), subject–locative (*sweater chair*), and subject–object (*mommy book*). In the grammars which she has written for the speech of the three children, Bloom uses a system of transformations to describe the relationship between semantically rich deep structures and sparsely elaborated surface structures.

Studies of a number of children acquiring English and several other native languages have revealed considerable individual differences in the formal characteristics of early stages of grammar. Not all children make use of positionally defined words as 'pivots'. In addition, highly inflected languages such as Slavic languages, Finnish and Hungarian seem to facilitate the early acquisition of inflections to encode semantic relations which are expressed by word order in English child-speech (Slobin, 1972). But there is striking uniformity across children and across languages in the kinds of meanings expressed in simple two-word utterances, suggesting that semantic development is closely tied to general cognitive development. The following range of semantic relations is typical of early child speech:

| | |
|---|---|
| Identification | *see doggie* |
| Location | *book there* |
| Repetition | *more milk* |
| Non-existence | *allgone thing* |
| Negation | *not wolf* |
| Possession | *my sweets* |
| Attribution | *big car* |
| Agent–Action | *mama walk* |
| Action–Object | *hit you* |
| Agent–Object | *mama book* |
| Action–Location | *sit chair* |
| Action–Recipient | *give papa* |
| Action–Instrument | *cut knife* |
| Question | *where ball?* |

The universality of such a list is impressive. The above examples are drawn from child speech in English, German, Russian, Finnish, Turkish, Samoan and Luo. The entire list could probably be made up of examples from two-year-old speech in any language.

It is evident that the child intends a range of semantic relations before he commands the full means for expressing these relations. In fact, Bloom cites an example from the one-word stage in which it is clear that the child is attempting to go beyond a severe output limitation: the child is struggling to put a button into her pocket, which is inaccessible because she is sitting on it; she repeats the word *button* several times, and then the word *pocket*, but is unable to join the two in a single utterance. The acquisition of a two-word object–location utterance such as *button pocket*, therefore, is a linguistic achievement, but not a cognitive achievement. What has grown is some sort of sentence-programming span – a matter which is considered in more detail below.

It seems to be a general rule that a new linguistic form emerging in child speech first expresses a semantic function which was already explicit in the speech of the preceding period. Brown (1972) has noted this clearly in his detailed longitudinal study of three English-speaking children. The first use of verbs was in their bare, uninflected form – *come*, *fall*, *break*, *drink* and so on. Brown examined the contexts in which these verbs were used and found that four kinds of meanings were expressed: 'naming an action or stage ... of temporary duration and true at the time of the utterance'; referring to the immediate past; stating the child's immediate wish or intention; and imperative. He then noted the emergence of verb markings in the children's speech and discovered that the first formal verbal elements to emerge marked just these four functions which were already implicit in verb use during the unmarked stage. The first verb markings to be used by the children were the progressive *-ing* in the sense of ongoing action or state; the past tense in reference to the immediate past; and 'catenative verbs' (*gonna*, *wanna*, *hafta*) expressing the child's immediate wish or intention. The last function, the imperative, continues, of course, to be expressed by an uninflected verb in English, but Brown notes that *please*, as an imperative marker, entered at about the same time as these other verb markings.

Observations such as these – and they are frequent in child-language studies – suggest the following principle (Slobin, 1972): *new forms first express old functions, and new functions are first expressed by old forms.* Brown's example demonstrates the first half of the proposition: the verbal inflections and catenative verbs at first expressed meanings which were not new to the child. The other half of the proposition is demonstrated when children seem to be groping for means to express new and complex thoughts. It has been noted that children's temporary, idiosyncratic linguistic forms are often a clue to the fact that the development of a new notion has engendered a search for new means of expression. In a detailed analysis of their longitudinal studies, Miller and Ervin-Tripp (1972) observe: 'In all cases [of idiosyncratic rules], it appears that the non-standard rules developed because the child's semantic development had outstripped his formal grammatical development.' Acquisition of the complexities of English auxiliaries and negatives provides many familiar examples of this phenomenon, as when my three-year-old daughter said such things as 'Anything is not to break – just glasses and plates' (meaning 'Nothing is breakable except glasses and plates'), or, when recovering from an illness, 'I must have getting weller and weller.'

As Cromer (1968, p. 219) has noted, in an analysis of the development of temporal expressions in Brown's longitudinal data: '... once certain cognitive abilities have developed, we also find an active search for acquisition of new forms. Suddenly forms (and words!) which the child has been exposed to for years become a part of his own speech.' It is clear that cognitive development, and the intimately related development of semantic intentions, will be of central importance in the current decade of developmental psycholinguistics.

**How does the child understand speech?**

Interest in semantics has brought with it attention to the problem of how the child derives meaning from the speech which he hears. Numerous ingenious research techniques have been devised for the study of comprehension. It has become clear that children do not attend to all aspects of speech input; rather, they appear to sample speech selectively, making use of various short-range strategies for sentence interpretation. Bever (1970) and others have begun to trace out the ontogenetic course of such strategies and have found, paradoxically, that performance does not always improve with age. In fact, three and four year olds seem to often rely on quick and easy strategies, which work in many cases but lead them astray in others, sometimes resulting in an actual decrement in performance in relation to younger children. The following portion of one of Bever's studies exemplifies the approach. Children are given a toy horse and a toy cow and are asked to act out sentences such as the following:

1. The *horse kisses* the cow.
2. It's the *horse kisses* the cow.
3. It's the cow the *horse kisses*.
4. The cow is kissed by the horse.

Two year olds perform appropriately on the first three sentences but are correct only half of the time on the fourth sentence. It seems as if they have a simple sentence interpretation rule to the effect that noun–verb means 'actor–action'. The first three sentences, as indicated by the italicized portions, have an uninterrupted noun–verb sequence. Bever suggests that such a sequence is treated as 'a kind of primitive *Gestalt*' wherever it occurs in a sentence – even if it does not occur at the beginning of the sentence, as in (3). In the fourth sentence the noun–verb sequence is apparently disrupted by the intervening *is*, and the response of two year olds is random. (If the strategy were not blocked, the passive sentence should be significantly *mis*-interpreted.)

Four year olds seem to use a strategy in which the first noun is the actor, which leads them astray on sentences like (3) and produces reversed interpretation of passives like (4), but which insures good performance on sentences like (1) and (2). Thus, comprehension does not uniformly improve with age as different strategies are brought to bear.

Other studies of comprehension have demonstrated the role of task variables in children's sentence-interpretation strategies. Instructions which are congruent with the way in which a child conceives of a task are easier to carry out promptly and correctly than instructions which are at variance with his conception. For example, Huttenlocher and Strauss (1968) presented children with a ladder on which coloured blocks could be placed. A block of a given colour was placed on the middle shelf of the ladder, and the child was given a block of another colour to place on the ladder, above or below the block placed by the experimenter. The instructions were of the form: 'Make it so that the — block is on top of/under the — block.' It was much easier for the child to perform correctly if the block he held in his hand corresponded to the subject of the relational term. There is apparently a connection in the child's mind between the subject of the locative and the block which is under his control. Huttenlocher, Eisenberg and Strauss (1968) report related findings when active and passive sentences are used, and all of the findings of these two studies were replicated by Bem (1970). When the child is given a movable truck to place relative to a fixed truck, with instructions that one 'is pushing' the other or 'is pushed by' the other, he again finds it easiest to perform if the truck he is to place corresponds to the subject of the sentence. The use of passive sentences, however, makes it clear that the child's definition of 'subject' is that of 'logical' or 'underlying subject', for he performs better when the fixed truck 'is pushed by' his truck than when his truck 'is pushed by' the fixed truck. These studies, and others like them, are important in that they go beyond formal description of the linguistic system itself to relate it to meaningful use of speech in context. As Huttenlocher and Strauss (1968, p. 300) put it, 'one's understanding of a statement may depend upon the relation between that statement and the extra-linguistic situation it describes'.

Clark (1972) has developed a detailed psycholinguistic theory of the relations in comprehension between statements and the situations they describe. One aspect of his theory (which is too complex to summarize here) involves the congruence between an instruction form and the manner in which the subject conceptualizes the task. Bem (1970), in a careful series of studies, showed that children can be trained to comprehend the tasks of Huttenlocher, Eisenberg and Strauss. The training consisted of showing the child, on another ladder, what the correct block placement for a given instruction would be, and then removing the model ladder from sight. With training of this sort, the difference between carrying out subject instructions and object instructions disappeared. In addition, training on block placement transferred to truck placement with instructions involving *push* and *pull*, as well as *in front of* and *in back of*. Bem concludes (pp. 354–5): 'Providing the child with end state representations apparently enabled him to discover what to produce, that is, to initiate a strategy for problem solving.' Bem's findings are important for comprehension theories such as Clark's. At the same time, her study is an important caveat: in order to interpret a child's performance on a task, one must be reasonably sure of how the child comprehends the task; and, what is more, one should determine the extent to which that comprehension can be altered by training.

**How does the child organize meanings?**

Very little is known about the structure of children's lexicons, and linguists disagree sharply on the characterization of lexical structures in adult language. But the rapid ferment in linguistic semantics has its counterpart in developmental psycholinguistics. A prominent and controversial approach is being taken by Clark and Clark, on the basis of the semantic-feature approach in linguistics (see also Bierwisch, 1970). Clark (1970, 1972) has offered solutions to some puzzling questions of semantic development in terms of semantic features – underlying components of meaning which are held to determine word meanings in combinatorial fashion. Clark considers some puzzling findings reported by Donaldson and Balfour (1968) and by Donaldson and Wales (1970) in regard to children's apparent understanding of English comparatives. Donaldson and Balfour, in an article appropriately entitled 'Less is more', report a study in which children were given two toy trees with hooks on them and various quantities of apples to hang upon the trees. When given two blank trees and asked to put either *more* or *less* on one of the two trees, the children either put the same number of apples on both trees or interpreted both *more* and *less* as meaning 'more'. In numerous other tasks it was clear that 'less is more'. Given two trees with equal numbers of apples, some children agreed that they were the *same* but also stated that one or both had *more*.

Donaldson and Wales investigated comprehension of a number of polar adjectives and found earlier comprehension of the positive poles (e.g., *more*, *bigger*, *longer*, *thicker*) than of the negative poles (*less*, *smaller*, *shorter*, *thinner*).

Clark presents a general analysis of the underlying meaning of polar adjectives, noting that the positive pole is 'unmarked' and also serves as a neutral name for the entire dimension (e.g., something has *length* whether it is long or short, and, in a neutral way, one asks, 'How long is it?'). Reviewing a large body of research, Clark argues that children first learn that both members of a pair of polar adjectives refer to the general dimension (e.g., both *less* and *more* mean *some*, i.e., 'having extent'). So, for example, when children are shown two trees with equal numbers of apples and are asked, 'Does one tree have more/less apples on it than the other?', Donaldson and Wales report answers like 'Both of them.' Such a reply must mean something like 'That one has many (or some) and that one has many (or some).' At the next stage they learn that there is a dimension involved, and they identify both terms with the positive pole (*less* = *more*). It is apparently the larger or longer or more extended object which draws children's attention at this stage. Finally, children learn that the dimension has two ends, and that the polar terms can be used contrastingly. As Clark points out, this developmental scheme is hypothetical and needs further support, but it indicates a direction in which research on semantic development is moving.

**When does language learning end?**

Until recently students of child language stopped their research at the age of five or so, satisfied that they had investigated the major aspects of language development. It is probably true that all of the basic linguistic apparatus is acquired by this age – in fact, most of the types of underlying rules and structures are present by about age three and a half. But it is evident that the learning of details, exceptions, special cases, nuances and niceties goes on for much longer – even in adulthood. Carol Chomsky (1969) has extended the range of attention in her book, *The Acquisition of Syntax in Children from Five to Ten.* This age range promises to become increasingly well studied. Chomsky has demonstrated that there are interesting problems in late acquisition (see also Cromer, 1970; Kessel, 1970; Olds, 1968).

In one part of her study Chomsky found late acquisition of the special rules involved in the use of the verbs *promise* and *ask* in English. *Promise* is a special case in that it violates the 'Minimal Distance Principle' (Rosenbaum, 1967) generally used to decide on the subject of an infinitival complement verb. For example, in (1) the subject of the complement verb *to leave* is *Bill*, but in (2), where *promise* appears, the subject is *John*:

1. John wanted Bill to leave.
2. John promised Bill to leave.

*Promise*, being exceptional, was mastered at a later age than 'normal' verbs. However, *promise*, although exceptional, is *consistently* exceptional: it always violates the Minimal Distance Principle. *Ask*, on the other hand, is inconsistent. Compare (3), where *Bill* is the subject of the verb in the complement, with (4), where *John* is the subject:

3. John asked Bill to leave.
4. John asked Bill what to do.

Chomsky found that full comprehension of *promise* came at an earlier age than full comprehension of *ask*, suggesting that it is easier to learn a consistent exception than an inconsistent exception.

Another aspect of later linguistic development is the ability to interpret sentences with minimal surface cues to meaning. Older children are better able to interpret sentences in which aspects of underlying meaning are only implicitly signalled. For example, Chomsky (1969) and Olds (1968) found that many seven year olds and some nine year olds were confused by *ask* and *tell*. For example, in Olds' study children often failed to carry out correctly the instruction 'Ask/Tell your opponent which piece to move one space.' This sentence is apparently difficult because a clause has been deleted. Children's performance was improved when the missing material was provided – e.g., 'Ask your opponent which piece you should move one space.' Chomsky also found that children were less likely to misinterpret *ask* and *tell* when a pronoun indicated the underlying subject of an embedded sentence. For example, in her study (1) and (2) were more difficult for children to interpret than (3) and (4):

1. Ask Laura what to feed the doll.
2. Tell Laura what to feed the doll.
3. Ask Laura what you should feed the doll.
4. Tell Laura what she should feed the doll.

Thus, throughout childhood children develop both in their ability to process language more efficiently and in their mastery of complex details of the language.

**What difference does parental speech make?**

A good deal of recent attention has been paid to parental speech, and the general answer to the question – at least as far as grammatical development is concerned – is that parental speech doesn't seem to make much difference at all. The matter has been approached from several different directions.

In the longitudinal studies of Brown and his co-workers (e.g., Brown, Cazden and Bellugi, 1968), there is no marked relation between the frequency of a form in parental speech and its time of acquisition in the child. This is, of course, what one would expect from the discussion of semantic development at the beginning of the chapter. The child cannot attend to a given element in parental speech until he can make some guess as to its meaning. Thus, the child hears huge numbers of words referring to time yet does not begin to use them himself until he is able to begin thinking about time. The longitudinal studies show that parental frequency of use of given grammatical forms remains constant across the course of development. For example, Cromer (1968) notes that there is no change in parental use of the present perfect tense, yet it develops late (at about four). The child has heard the present perfect frequently and even commands the relevant formal components of the tense, having used past participles and auxiliary *have* (in *have to*) since about the age of two and a half. He does not begin to make use of this aspect of his speech input, however, until a certain level of cognitive development is reached: 'the ability to properly use the perfect tense rests on a late-developing ability to consider the relevance of another time to the time of the utterance' (Cromer, 1968, p. 122).

Several studies have also asked whether parental speech provides an especially good data source for the child. Drach *et al.* (1969) found that a mother's speech to her two-year-old child was drastically different from her speech to another adult: the latter was full of false starts, hesitations and errors; but the speech to the child consisted of short, simple, grammatical sentences, with much repetition. Compared to speech to an adult, speech to the child included few passives, more simple affirmative declarative sentences, and fewer conjoined phrases or subordinate clauses.

It is clear, then, that children receive a special form of input from mothers. But is this input unique to mother–child interaction? In many speech communities, the major source of speech input to two and three year olds is from slightly older children who are their caretakers. Slobin (1969) made a direct comparison of mother-to-child and child-to-child speech in English, comparing the speech of the mothers in Brown's Harvard sample with the speech of four and five-year-old black children in Kernan's study of language development in an urban ghetto. The children in the ghetto situation spent much of their time playing with their younger siblings, thus providing a major portion of the speech input to two and three year olds. On all grammatical measures reported for mothers' speech by Brown, Cazden and Bellugi (1968), the relative-frequency profiles for the Oakland children were the same as those for the Cambridge mothers. Apparently, little children receive the same kind of grammatically simplified input, whether it be from mothers who tailor their speech to children or from other children whose grammar is relatively less developed.

Parental speech, apparently, has no special status as a data base for grammatical induction. (Undoubtedly, of course, it plays an important role in transmitting information and values, but our concern here is with the acquisition of the grammatical system.) Are there any aspects of parental interaction with children which may facilitate grammatical development? Brown and his co-workers (Brown, 1972; Brown and Hanlon, 1970; Brown, Cazden and Bellugi, 1968; Cazden, 1968) have exhaustively considered two such aspects and have come to a negative conclusion.

One form of parental feedback to the child is in the form of expansions of the child's own speech. The child makes a statement and the mother repeats it, filling it in or questioning the child's meaning. Expansions seem like a good training device, but there is no evidence of their effectiveness. Of the three children studied longitudinally by Brown, the one who received the lowest rate of expansions from her mother was the first to develop inflections – and inflections are just those utterance elements which are filled in by expansions. Cazden (1965), in a training study offering a high saturation of expansions, found no evidence of accelerated grammatical development as a consequence.

Another form of parental feedback, of course, is approval or disapproval of the form of utterances. Brown carefully checked all cases of approval and disapproval in his extensive corpora and found that parents generally listen to *what* their child is saying, rather than to *how* he is saying it. Parents approved if what the child said was true or clever or appropriate, and disapproved if it was false or silly or inappropriate – regardless of the grammaticality of the utterance. Brown, Cazden and Bellugi (1968, p. 71) conclude:

It seems, then, to be truth value rather than syntactic well-formedness that chiefly governs explicit verbal reinforcement by parents – which renders mildly paradoxical the fact that the usual product of such a training schedule is an adult whose speech is highly grammatical but not notably truthful.

**What does the child pay attention to?**

An important component in any model of the language-acquisition process is what Braine, in his recently proposed 'Discovery—Procedures Acquisition Model' (1971a), has called the 'scanner'. Recent work has begun to reveal what aspects of speech input actually get into the child.

Shipley, Smith and Gleitman (1969) experimentally presented little children with different sorts of utterances in an attempt to answer part of this question. The utterances were either telegraphic (e.g., *throw ball*) or well-formed (e.g., *throw me the ball*), and some of the utterances of both types had nonsense words inserted in various positions. The children ranged from eighteen to thirty months in age. Their attentional strategies were closely related to level of linguistic development. The youngest children responded best to telegraphic commands – which matched their own level of speech production. They ignored utterances with nonsense words. In short, they heard in terms of their own level of production, carrying out a highly selective sampling of speech input. The children with more mature speech responded better to well-formed than to telegraphic utterances and tended to repeat nonsense words as if they were trying to understand them. They were at a stage at which they could assimilate more complex input and even try to accommodate to it. This study casts important new light on the child's language-acquisition strategies at a very early stage of linguistic development. Smith (1970, p. 18) suggests

we doubt that their primary linguistic input is as rich or as confusing as has sometimes been suggested. For whatever complex of linguistic, conceptual and perceptual reasons, children at this stage . . . can apparently handle only the high-stress content words that they utter themselves. Perhaps their listening is mainly an attempt to 'find' words they know; too many other words, even familiar ones, may make it difficult to do this, and unfamiliar words may make it impossible.

Slobin (1972), in comparing data on the acquisition of some fifteen different languages of different structural types, makes a number of proposals in regard to children's initial linguistic-attention patterns. Whereas English-speaking children have difficulty acquiring prepositions and articles, children learning highly inflected languages rapidly master rudimentary inflections, as pointed out above. One reason may be that attention seems to be readily deployed to the ends of words. Word-endings are generally stressed and tend to be imitated by children. (Furthermore, even in languages like Czech, where all words are stressed on the first syllable, children still tend to imitate the ends of words.) Thus one finds, for example, that Finnish and Hungarian children express a wide range of locative relationships by means of inflections long before English-speaking children express similar relationships by means of prepositions. One finds that children acquiring Slavic languages are quick to master genitive, dative and accusative inflections, which are noun suffixes, while German children take far longer to master the same inflections, which occur on pre-nominal articles in German. (This is not due to semantic difficulty in acquiring the notion of articles, because Bulgarian articles, which are suffixed to nouns, are mastered quickly and easily.) If it is indeed true that word-endings attract children's attention, then one can propose that for any given semantic notion, grammatical realizations in the form of suffixes or postpositions will be acquired earlier than realizations in the form of prefixes or prepositions. This is one example of the contribution of the cross-linguistic method to developmental psycholinguistics (for a review of recent work on the acquisition of languages other than English, see Slobin, 1972).

A number of recent studies suggest that children pay attention to word order in adult utterances. Bever's sentence-perception strategies are an important reflection of this tendency. Various studies have found a stage at which passive sentences are interpreted as if they were active, reversing subject and object. Bever (1970, p. 298) has proposed as a general strategy of English sentence interpretation: 'Any *Noun–Verb–Noun* (N V N) sequence within a potential internal unit in the surface structure corresponds to *actor–action–object*.' Other studies have shown that conjoined sentences referring to two temporally ordered events are first given the interpretation that order of mention matches order of occurrence, even if the conjunction indicates otherwise (Clark, 1971; Cromer, 1968; Hatch, 1969). For example, it is relatively more difficult for children to understand sentences of the form 'Event 2 *after* Event 1' and '*Before* Event 2, Event 1' than sentences of the form 'Event 1 *before* Event 2' and '*After* Event 1, Event 2'. English-speaking children clearly pay attention to the order of words in attempting to interpret sentences.

There have been, as yet, few detailed studies of attention to word order in other languages, but it may well be a general principle of child language that sentences deviating from standard word order are interpreted at early stages of development as if they were examples of standard word order. Important cross-linguistic evidence comes from a study by Roeper (1972) of German acquisition. The standard word order for German imperatives is verb–indirect object–direct object (V–IO–DO), with inflected articles indicating which noun is direct object and which indirect. The inflections make it possible for adults to vary the order of the two nouns without losing meaning or grammaticality. German thus allows more flexible word order than English. When Roeper offered children V–DO–IO sentences for imitation, some of them tended to switch articles, placing the dative article on the first noun and the accusative on the second, and retaining word order. That is, these children showed their command of the inflections *and* their reliance on word order: they interpreted the first noun after the verb as the indirect object and inflected the article preceding that noun accordingly. Similarly, in a comprehension task Roeper found that V–DO–IO sentences were frequently comprehended as if they were V–IO–DO. Thus, in both imitation and comprehension many children tended to rely on word order over inflections as a guide to grammatical relations, even though their native language does not rely as heavily upon word order as English. More work of this sort is needed in other sorts of languages before universal conclusions can be drawn as to children's attention to word order and to other sorts of linguistic features.

**How does biological growth affect language development?**

A final word should be said about the role of physiological maturation in the ontogenesis of language. This question has been explored in detail by Lenneberg (1967) – resulting in the strong suggestion of a biological pre-adaptation to language acquisition in man. However, not all aspects of the language-acquisition device are unique to man, as recent attempts to teach chimpanzees language-like systems have shown (Gardner and Gardner, 1969; Premack, 1971).

Within the human context, however, it is clear that a gradual maturation in short-term operative capacity or sentence programming span is an important variable in the growth of syntactic complexity. Recall Bloom's child at the one-word stage, who simply could not combine *button* and *pocket* into a single utterance, though she could utter the two words separately. Processing span at first seems to be limited to the number of terms which can occur in an utterance. A two-word stage seems to be universal. During this period the child can typically express a variety of relations, as listed above, but cannot unite three terms in a single utterance. For example, he can say *mama read* and *read book*, but not *mama read book*, even though it is apparent that he understands the underlying relationship of the three terms. A growth in sentence-production span to three words is often evident in the child's successive attempts to form an utterance. Braine (1971b) has noted many examples of such sequences as *Want that . . . Andrew want that; Change pants . . . Papa change pants.* At this stage the three-word limit is quite severe. If a child chooses to modify a noun with an adjective in a three-word sentence, one of the main terms must be dropped. Thus, the child can say, for example, *Mama drink coffee* and *Drink hot coffee*, but not *Mama drink hot coffee*. (Bowerman, 1970, has noted the same phenomenon in the acquisition of Finnish.)

At this early stage output-length limitations are quite severe and seem to be limited to words rather than to structures or to linguistic operations. Such limitations do not occur in adult speech, and this aspect of development seems to be based on maturation of a very simple sort of short-term processing capacity. At later stages, however, one finds that the processing limitations have to do with structural complexity – as in adult psycholinguistic performance, but cut down to child scale. For example, Bloom (1970) has found that negation constitutes linguistic complexity for the child, in that the presence of a negative element requires that the remainder of the sentence be simplified in some way. That is, the syntactic complexity engendered by negation brings about deletion or simplification in sentence structure. For example, at an early stage, subject deletion is common in negative sentences: while the child can produce subject–verb strings like *this turn*, such strings are negated as *no turn* rather than *no this turn* or *this no turn*. One of Bloom's children, when barefoot, could describe her situation with a lengthy affirmative sentence – *Kathryn have a socks on*, but only with a cut-down negative sentence – *Kathryn no shoe*.

Bellugi (1968) has demonstrated that there are mechanical limits to the number of syntactic operations which a child can perform on a single sentence at given stages of development. For example, one child was able to invert subject and auxiliary to form yes–no questions (e.g., *Can he ride in a truck?*) and was able to propose *wh*-question words, but he could not perform both operations on one sentence and so produced *wh*-questions such as *What he can ride in?* At a later stage, with an increase in sentence-programming span, the child was able to perform both of these operations on a single sentence but failed to invert subject and auxiliary when a third operation – negation – was involved, and so he produced sentences like *Why can he go out?* at the same time as sentences like *Why he can't go out?* Bellugi demonstrated this span limitation graphically in a sentence-elicitation game in which the child was to ask questions of a puppet shaped like an old lady:

ADULT: Adam, ask the Old Lady where she can find some toys.
CHILD: Old Lady, where can you find some toys?
ADULT: Adam, ask the Old Lady why she can't run.
CHILD: Old Lady, why you can't run?

Bellugi concludes (p. 40): 'In his responses, all affirmatives were inverted, all negatives were not. The interpretation . . . fits with the notion of a limit on the permitted complexity at one stage.'

**Summary**

This has been a quick overview of seven current questions about language development. From our present historical vantage point, it seems that some of the answers will move in the following directions:

*What does the child mean to say?* The interface between linguistic semantics and the psychology of cognitive development will continue to develop actively. The debate between 'generative' and 'interpretative semantics' in linguistic theory will stimulate new psycholinguistic approaches to meaning. At the same time, more detailed study of the communicative functions of child speech – aided by videotape – will continue to move developmental psycholinguistics away from its earlier overemphasis on syntactic development, leading to a more comprehensive account of the development of communicative competence.

*How does the child understand speech?* The study of sentence-processing strategies will flourish, and a number of psycholinguistic performance models will be elaborated – both for child and adult speech processing. The study of comprehension will also be tied to new developments in semantics and in the study of speech perception.

*How does the child organize meanings?* A 'developmental ethnographic semantics' will be developed, tied closely to models of cognitive development on the one hand, and models of semantic structure on the other.

*When does language learning end?* Increasing attention will be paid to later achievements in language acquisition, blurring the distinction between child and adult as language users.

*What difference does parental speech make?* Sociolinguistics, ethnomethodology and cross-cultural research will make important contributions to the study of speech input and social setting in development. A general sociolinguistic approach to the study of the acquisition of communicative competence will be elaborated.

*What does the child pay attention to?* Studies of attention, perception and memory will greatly increase our characterization of the child's linguistic scanning and storage mechanisms. Cross-linguistic studies will clarify the issue of universal processes versus the influence of particular linguistic structures in the ontogenesis of linguistic attention.

*How does biological growth affect language development?* Understanding of the neurological mechanisms underlying linguistic performance promises to increase greatly in the coming years. The biological and maturational mechanisms underlying language development will continue to be illuminated by research in such areas as aphasia, split-brain operations, neuroanatomy and comparative psychology.

These suggested directions may reflect the biases and interests of the author, but they are certainly more than wishful thinking. Research is already moving in all of these directions, and more. These seven questions promise to be with us for a long time, and the answers promise to become more interesting as work progresses.

**Further reading**

BROWN, R., *A First Language*, Harvard University Press, 1972, in press. A superb overview of data and theory on the early stages of language development, with important new syntheses and theoretical formulations.

HAYES, J. R. (ed.), *Cognition and the Development of Language*, Wiley, 1970. Contains a number of important papers on theory, method and findings of the late 1960s, attempting to relate linguistic and cognitive development. Contributions by Thomas G. Bever, Roger Brown, Herbert H. Clark, Margaret Donaldson, Susan Ervin-Tripp, Camille Hanlon, John R. Hayes, Carlota S. Smith, Roger J. Wales and William C. Watt.

LENNEBERG, E. H., *Biological Foundations of Language*, Wiley, 1967. The major book on neurological, anatomical and evolutionary aspects of language development.

MCNEILL, D., *The Acquisition of Language: The Study of Developmental Psycholinguistics*, Harper & Row, 1970. A valuable introduction to the field, summarizing current research and theory and presenting McNeill's own influential theoretical positions.

SLOBIN, D. I. (ed.), *The Ontogenesis of Grammar: A Theoretical Symposium*, Academic Press, 1971. A collection of original papers and discussions setting forth the principal theoretical positions on language acquisition. Contributions by Martin D. S. Braine, Susan Ervin-Tripp, David McNeill, David Palermo, I. M. Schlesinger, Dan I. Slobin and Arthur W. Staats.

SLOBIN, D. I., and FERGUSON, C. A. (eds.), *Studies of Child Language Development*, Holt, Rinehart & Winston, 1972. A collection of major research papers from the United States and Europe, presenting data on phonological, syntactic and semantic development in a number of different languages.

**References**

BELLUGI, U. (1968), 'Linguistic mechanisms underlying child speech', in H. Zale (ed.), *Proceedings of the Conference on Language and Language Behavior*, Appleton-Century-Crofts.

BELLUGI, U., and BROWN, R. (eds.) (1964), 'The acquisition of language', *Monographs of the Society for Research in Child Development*, vol. 29, no. 1.

BEM, S. L. (1970), 'The role of comprehension in children's problem solving', *Developmental Psychology*, vol. 2, pp. 351–8.

BEVER, T. G. (1970), 'The cognitive basis for linguistic structures', in J. R. Hayes (ed.), *Cognition and the Development of Language*, Wiley, pp. 279–362.

BIERWISCH, M. (1970), 'Semantics', in J. Lyons (ed.), *New Horizons in Linguistics*, Penguin Books Inc., pp. 166–84.

BLOOM, L. M. (1970), *Language Development: Form and Function in Emerging Grammars*, MIT Press.

BOWERMAN, M. F. (1970), 'Learning to talk: a cross-linguistic study of early syntactic development, with special reference to Finnish', unpublished doctoral dissertation, Harvard University.

BRAINE, M. D. S. (1963), 'The ontogeny of English phrase structure: the first phase', *Language*, vol. 39, pp. 1–13.

BRAINE, M. D. S. (1971a), 'On two types of models of the internalization of grammars', in D. I. Slobin (ed.), *The Ontogenesis of Grammar: A Theoretical Symposium*, Academic Press, pp. 153–86.

BRAINE, M. D. S. (1971b), 'The acquisition of language in infant and child', in C. Reed (ed.), *The Learning of Language*, Appleton-Century-Crofts, pp. 7–95.

BROWN, R. (1971), *A First Language*, Harvard University Press, in press.

BROWN, R., CAZDEN, C., and BELLUGI, U. (1968), 'The child's grammar from one to three', in J. P. Hill (ed.), *Minnesota Symposia on Child Psychology*, vol. 2, University of Minneapolis Press, pp. 28–73.

BROWN, R., and FRASER, C. (1963), 'The acquisition of syntax', in C. N. Cofer and B. S. Musgrave (eds.), *Verbal Behavior and Learning: Problems and Processes*, McGraw-Hill, pp. 158–97.

BROWN, R., and HANLON, C. (1970), 'Derivational complexity and order of acquisition in child speech', in J. R. Hayes (ed.), *Cognition and the Development of Language*, Wiley, pp. 11–53.

CAZDEN, C. (1965), 'Environmental assistance to the child's acquisition of grammar', unpublished doctoral dissertation, Harvard University.

CAZDEN, C. (1968), 'The acquisition of noun and verb inflections', *Child Development*, vol. 39, pp. 433–48.

CHOMSKY, C. (1969), *The Acquisition of Syntax in Children from Five to Ten*, MIT Press.

CLARK, E. V. (1971), 'On the acquisition of the meaning of *before* and *after*', *Journal of Verbal Learning and Verbal Behavior*, vol. 10, pp. 266–75.

CLARK, H. H. (1970), 'The primitive nature of children's relational concepts', in J. R. Hayes (ed.), *Cognition and the Development of Language*, Wiley, pp. 269–78.

CLARK, H. H. (1972), 'Semantics and comprehension', in T. A. Sebeok (ed.), *Current Trends in Linguistics*, vol. 12, *Linguistics and Adjacent Arts and Sciences*, Mouton, in press.

CROMER, R. F. (1968), 'The development of temporal reference during the acquisition of language', unpublished doctoral dissertation, Harvard University.

CROMER, R. F. (1970), ' "Children are nice to understand": surface structure cues for the recovery of a deep structure', *British Journal of Psychology*, vol. 61, pp. 397–408,

DONALDSON, M., and BALFOUR, G. (1968), 'Less is more: a study of language comprehension in children', *British Journal of Psychology*, vol. 59, pp. 461–71.

DONALDSON, M., and WALES, R. J. (1970), 'On the acquisition of some relational terms', in J. R. Hayes (ed.), *Cognition and the Development of Language*, Wiley, pp. 235–68.

DRACH, K., KOBASHIGAWA, B., PFUDERER, C., and SLOBIN, D. (1969), 'The structure of linguistic input to children', Language Behavior Research Laboratory, University of California, Berkeley, Working Paper no. 14.

FERGUSON, C. A., and SLOBIN, D. I. (eds.) (1972), *Studies of Child Language Development*, Holt, Rinehart & Winston.

GARDNER, R. A., and GARDNER, B. T. (1969), 'Teaching sign language to a chimpanzee', *Science*, vol. 165, pp. 664–72.

HATCH, E. (1969), 'Four experimental studies in syntax of young children', *Technical Reports*, no. 11, Southwest Regional Laboratory for Educational Research and Development, Inglewood, California.

HAYES, J. R. (ed.) (1970), *Cognition and the Development of Language*, Wiley.

HUTTENLOCHER, J., EISENBERG, K., and STRAUSS, S. (1968), 'Comprehension: relation between perceived actor and logical subject', *Journal of Verbal Learning and Verbal Behavior*, vol. 7, pp. 527–30.

HUTTENLOCHER, J., and STRAUSS, S. (1968), 'Comprehension and a statement's relation to the situation it describes', *Journal of Verbal Learning and Verbal Behavior*, vol. 7, pp. 300–304.

HUXLEY, R., and INGRAM, E. (eds.) (1971), *Language Acquisition: Models and Methods*, Academic Press.

KESSEL, F. S. (1970), 'The role of syntax in children's comprehension from ages six to twelve', *Monographs of the Society for Research in Child Development*, vol. 35, no. 6.

LENNEBERG, E. H. (1967), *Biological Foundations of Language*, Wiley.

LYONS, J. (ed.) (1970), *New Horizons in Linguistics*, Penguin Books Inc.

MCNEILL, D. (1970), *The Acquisition of Language: The Study of Developmental Psycholinguistics*, Harper & Row.

MENYUK, P. (1971), *The Acquisition and Development of Language*, Prentice-Hall.

MILLER, W. R., and ERVIN, S. M. (1964), 'The development of grammar in child language', in U. Bellugi and R. Brown (eds.), 'The acquisition of language', *Monographs of the Society for Research in Child Development*, vol. 29, no. 1, pp. 9–33.

MILLER, W. R., and ERVIN-TRIPP, S. M. (1972), *Development of Grammar in Child Language*, Holt, Rinehart & Winston in press.

OLDS, H. F. (1968), 'An experimental study of syntactical factors influencing children's comprehension of certain complex relationships', *Report no. 4*, Harvard Center for Research and Development on Educational Differences.

PREMACK, D. (1971), 'Language in chimpanzee?', *Science*, vol. 172, pp. 808–22.

ROEPER, T. (1972), 'Theoretical implications of word order, topicalization and inflections in German language acquisition', in C. A. Ferguson and D. I. Slobin (eds.), *Studies of Child Language Development*, Holt, Rinehart & Winston.

ROSENBAUM, P. S. (1967), *The Grammar of English Predicate Complement Constructions*, MIT Press.

SHIPLEY, E., SMITH, C. S., and GLEITMAN, L. (1969), 'A study in the acquisition of language: free response to commands', *Language*, vol. 45, pp. 322–42.

SLOBIN, D. I. (1969), 'Questions of language development in cross-cultural perspective', in K. Drach *et al.*, 'The structure of linguistic input to children', Language Behavior Research Laboratory, University of California, Berkeley, Working Paper no. 14.

SLOBIN, D. I. (ed.) (1971), *The Ontogenesis of Grammar: A Theoretical Symposium*, Academic Press.

SLOBIN, D. I. (1972), 'Cognitive prerequisites for the development of grammar', in D. I. Slobin and C. A. Ferguson (eds.), *Studies of Child Language Development*, Holt, Rinehart & Winston.

SMITH, C. S. (1970), 'An experimental approach to children's linguistic competence', in J. R. Hayes (ed.), *Cognition and the Development of Language*, Wiley, pp. 109–35.

SMITH, F., and MILLER, G. A. (eds.) (1966), *The Genesis of Language: A Psycholinguistic Approach*, MIT Press.

# Part Four
# Social Behaviour

The three chapters in this last part are about social behaviour. The first of them, by Professor McGuire, is a review of the current situation and probable future trends in the field traditionally known as social psychology. Here, as in several previous cases, we find that changes of interest and emphasis are quite rapid and marked at the present time. Social psychologists, perhaps more than any others, are addressing themselves to questions about the relevance of their research, the ethical and political aspects of engaging in investigations which could have real consequences both for individuals and societies, and the pressures which are thereby brought to bear on them. Traditional forms of investigation seem to be cracking under the strain, and it looks as if a whole new era of social psychological research effort is getting under way.

Dr Smith's chapter, the second in this part, is devoted to questions of individual effectiveness in social interactions, a distinct area of social research, as he clearly shows, although closely related to the general field of social psychology. Here again the question of relevance and the ethics of research are of importance, because the more one learns about how behaviour can be manipulated in social contexts, the more potential one must have for affecting the lives of others. Such questions are likely to be raised increasingly by those to whom psychologists apply their skills, as well as by professional psychologists themselves.

Finally, we come to the chapter by Professor Latané and Dr Hothersall, on social attraction in animals. This delightful exposition of a rather new field of research serves to remind us that we as human beings do not by any means have an exclusive right to the title 'social organisms'. Also, although the behaviour discussed is not exactly cognitive, in the usual sense of the term, it does reinforce the refrain which runs through nearly all of this review: mice and men are not machines. We are not even quasi-mechanisms to be explained in terms of the push and pull of basic biological drives like hunger, thirst and sex. The thirst for knowledge – a revealing phrase – for social recognition, for understanding of the world, seem to be basic to the nature of man. Our final chapter suggests that, contrary to a theory once popular amongst psychologists, the origins of social interaction may be biological, but not tied to specific primary needs. This too opens up a new perspective on the nature of social behaviour in general.

# 10 Social Psychology

William J. McGuire

The energetic reader wishing to familiarize himself with recent developments in social psychology is fortunate in having a royal (though lengthy) road to this end in the new edition of the *Handbook of Social Psychology* edited by Lindzey and Aronson (1969). The five volumes of this Handbook require forty-five chapters totalling four thousand pages to summarize the more important theories, methods and empirical evidence of social psychology. The Handbook's formidable size reveals the large output of social psychological research in recent years. In 1954 when Lindzey edited the first edition of this Handbook only two volumes were required; and back in 1935, Murchison needed only a single volume. Moreover, the bibliographies in the present edition show that most of the work now deemed worth reporting was carried out during the past decade.

Some feel that the new edition of the Handbook, while undeniably a milestone, is also a tombstone. Not that the dead weight of this massive tome itself killed social psychology (albeit its sixteen pounds could constitute a lethal weapon in the wrong hands) but rather that it marks the end of an era, appearing at a moment when social psychology is branching out in new directions. Hence it enshrines the remains of a body of work which no longer constitute the growing points of the field. A great deal of the research that fills the journals continues to reflect past interests, including heavily worked areas that have been mined out. We shall try to indicate the immediate future by selecting areas of research which, besides being heavily investigated recently, also serve to map out new directions in which social psychology is embarking.

## Current conventions and future trends

Most of the research reported in the new Handbook has been guided by a widely shared paradigm as to how the social psychologist should proceed in both the creative (or hypothesis-generation) phase of his work and its critical, hypothesis-testing phase. We shall describe each of these aspects of the current paradigm before describing the new directions that the field is beginning to take.

*Recent paradigm guiding hypothesis generation*

The bright young people and their still vigorous elders who constitute the establishment of social psychology have, during recent years, pretty much agreed on how one ought to generate hypotheses, however much they disagreed on what the correct hypotheses were. The standard creative paradigm was to derive one's hypotheses from theories that typically came from other areas of psychology, such as cognition, animal behaviour, psychopathology or verbal learning. (For example, most current research on attitude-change tests hypotheses derived either from learning theory, perceptual theory, functional theory or consistency theory.)

But the refined and quantitative statements often attained by these theories in their original areas have been largely ignored when they are applied to social phenomena. (For example, social psychologists have predicted how the amount of incentive used to induce a person to defend a point of view discrepant from his own affects the amount of internalized opinion change that he exhibits as a result of this forced overt compliance. But they have used only the most qualitative aspects of the elegant incentive theories of the animal behaviourists.) In general, social psychological hypotheses tended to be selected for their relevance to theories originating in other areas of psychology, and treated somewhat more superficially and programmatically than warranted by the current levels of development within the original field.

*Recent paradigm guiding hypothesis testing*

As regards hypothesis testing, the general paradigm of recent social psychological research has been the manipulational experiment carried out in the laboratory. The researcher attempts to improvise within the laboratory certain situations in which the social behaviour under investigation has a reasonable probability of occurring, and attempts to vary the situation to manipulate levels at which the hypothesized independent variable is set, while keeping constant other variables that might affect the social behaviour under study. Typical elaborations of this scheme involve a factorial design in which several independent variables are manipulated orthogonally, and where not only the ultimate social behaviour under investigation is measured but also hypothesized intervening processes.

*Deviations from the paradigm*

While most recent social psychological research has followed this paradigm of selecting hypotheses for their relevance to some general psychological theory and testing them by means of manipulational laboratory experiments, a few researchers have violated one or more aspects of the paradigm. For example, Milgram has persistently selected problems because of their relevance to social problems or their *ad hoc* interest, as in his research on obedience, on the lost-letter technique, and the small-world problem; and Milgram has often tested hypotheses in field situations.

Sherif, while inclined toward deriving hypotheses from theory, has shown an abiding willingness to test them in field situations as well as the laboratory. But while such work has been done, it constitutes a very small segment of the total research effort and has been recognized as lying outside the main stream.

*Some developing new directions*

*The concern with social relevance.* While these past departures were idiosyncratic, there are stirrings that give promise of a new paradigm. The growing desire to do research with more immediate social relevance is leading to selecting hypotheses for their direct bearing on the human condition rather than their relevance to the growing points of psychological theory. Thus, the dependent variables for study are chosen for their obvious social importance (such as violent behaviour, or coming to the aid of a victim in distress); and the preferred independent variables are those which, if the research shows them to be important, could subsequently be adjusted by economic or political intervention (such as contents of the mass media or crowding). As regards the hypothesis-testing phase of research, this social-relevance-inspired new direction involves a shift from the laboratory into the natural environment.

*More sophisticated conceptualization.* A second, quite different recent development is the more powerful use of conceptual analysis than the rather oversimplified and qualitative application of obvious theories that characterized the recent paradigm. This improved conceptualization is shown in more subtle, non-obvious theories (such as Bem's self-observation notions); in more elegant mathematical models (for example, Anderson's work on social judgement 1971); or in the utilization of more refined and imaginative variables (such as measuring physiological responses in conformity behaviour); or in a more inclusive range and precise definition of dependent variables (typified in the attitude area, for example, by Cook's multi-indicator approach, Webb's non-reactive measures, or Fishbein's distinctions among attitude components).

*Schisms within social psychology.* These two innovative styles seem to be leading the more creative social psychologists in two opposite directions. There may result a split within the field between one group who will continue to deal with qualitative hypotheses, but select them for social rather than theoretical relevance, and test them in field situations rather than the laboratory; while the other group will move increasingly towards less obvious and more elegant theories, continuing to test them in laboratory situations, but employing increasingly intricate designs, more demanding measurement procedures and mathematical analyses. (At the same time, there are signs of a third innovative approach employing correlational designs with multi-variate and time-series analysis of masses of social data, typified by the work of Coleman and Blalock. This third new departure is being pursued by psychologists such as Campbell – who indeed should be mentioned in connection with several of the previously described innovative approaches. However, perhaps due to historical accident rather than intrinsic logic, the bulk of this work is being done by sociologists and so we shall not be concerned with it in the present chapter.)

The existence of these rather conflicting new tendencies will undoubtedly cause crises in the foreseeable future within social psychology training programmes, since the old and the two new directions involve very different styles of thinking and mastery of specific techniques so demanding that few researchers would be able and willing to master the several sets. Such tensions are not new to social psychologists as the field has traditionally included a number of rather diverse problem areas and procedures. But the present divergent trends are sufficiently novel, exciting and demanding for it to seem likely that some pedagogic reorganization of the field will become necessary, considering most students' need for self-identification in terms of rubrics with recognizable meaning.

One likely resolution is that the new atheoretical direction characterized by field testing of hypotheses involving intrinsically interesting dependent variables will become the new establishment paradigm for social psychology during the 1970s, in place of the current style of theoretically derived, laboratory-tested hypotheses. The second innovative group, who are developing more refined approaches to attitudes, psychological implication, judgemental processes, and psycholinguistics, may on the other hand cease to be regarded as 'social psychologists' and be grouped as 'cognitive psychologists' along with a number of the researchers now regarded as the innovative students of human learning, memory and perception.

*Overview.* We shall review the recent progress in four broad areas that indicate these new trends within social psychology without ignoring the old. First we shall consider current work on information processing within belief structures, which best illustrates the more elegant theorizing about social cognition that has evolved out of the older simplistic and qualitative notions that had guided the field. A second area to be reviewed is that of attitudes and their relation to action, which serves to illustrate the heightened aspiration regarding measurement of social variables, the linking of the popular laboratory variables of attitudes to socially significant overt behaviour, and the development of more subtle conceptualizations like some of the attribution theories. The third section will describe recent work on interpersonal affect, both attraction and hostility, with respect to the impact of social factors on these personally significant variables. Finally, a fourth section will be devoted to current work on ethics and psychology, including both social psychological research on morality and the morality of social psychology research, an issue whose relation to developing concerns with social relevance is obvious.

## Information processing and social cognition

How a person processes new information within his belief system has been a topic of intense study in recent years. More than most of the other topics we shall discuss in this chapter, it has attracted attention for its theoretical relevance rather than for any immediate practical applicability. Despite the abstractness and difficulty of the area, interest in it is inevitable since it focuses on such basic and pervasive psychological processes. The work reported in this section appears in the psychological literature under many different rubrics, including impression formation, social judgement, person perception, attitude structure, belief systems, information processing, subjective probability, psychological implication and information integration.

This short chapter offers no opportunity to discuss each of these topics in any detail. Rather, we shall review selected findings regarding each of the three successive steps a person can take when confronted with new information about some significant object of judgement. First, his old beliefs regarding that object of judgement may affect how he encodes the new information. Secondly, this encoded new information may be integrated with his previous concept regarding the object, resulting in a new belief. Third, since objects of judgement are psychologically linked to one another, this new belief may have repercussions in changing the person's beliefs on related objects of psychological significance to him. We will consider some recent work under each of these three headings.

### *Effects of prior belief on information processing*

*Selective-avoidance hypothesis.* It is generally assumed that people find it painful to have their beliefs disconfirmed and hence that they avoid new, belief-discrepant information. However, the accumulating empirical data do not confirm the selective-avoidance assumption, and often indicate that people have an opposite tendency to seek out the novel belief-discrepant material. On reflection, this outcome is not so surprising. A tendency to avoid all new information might offer some momentary psychological comfort, but in the long run it would be maladaptive and interfering with one's ability to cope with the environment and to adjust one's behaviour to the changing situation.

*Perceptual distortion.* There is more empirical support for the notion that, while the person does not try to avoid all belief-discrepant information, he does tend to distort it at least slightly towards his preconception. For example, when we hold a certain belief on an issue and are confronted by the information that an attractive person holds a very different belief, we tend to narrow the gap not only by changing our own belief, but also by distorting the other person's position so that it is somewhat closer to our own initial stand. One of the most elegant theories regarding such distortion in social judgement, put forward by Sherif and Hovland, predicts that slightly discrepant new information is assimilated towards one's own initial stand while highly discrepant information is contrasted, that is, perceived as even more discrepant from one's own position than it really is. Recent evidence has been stronger for assimilation than contrast effects.

Besides the tendency to see others as more in agreement with oneself than they really are is the tendency to perceive one's social world as balanced; that is, to exaggerate the extent to which people one likes agree with oneself and disliked people oppose one's own position. It would follow that there would be both a reversal and an asymmetry in the perceptual distortion of other people's beliefs, depending on whether we like or dislike the other. Information about someone we like is subject to a double assimilation distortion, both from the tendency to exaggerate agreement and to exaggerate balance. On the other hand, one should perceive information about people one dislikes more accurately, since the tendency to exaggerate agreement would result in an assimilation distortion, while the tendency to exaggerate balance would tend to produce contrast distortion, and the two erroneous tendencies would tend to cancel each other out. The prediction still needs adequate empirical testing.

### *Information integration*

After new information has been encoded, the person must combine it with what they already knew about the object, to arrive at an integrated judgement about it. Information integration has been heavily studied during the past several years, usually under the rubrics of 'impression formation' and 'person perception', since the method involves studying how our evaluation of another person changes when we receive the new information that he has additional pleasant or unpleasant traits.

*Order effects.* Interest in impression formation first centered on sequence effects, namely, the extent to which our first impression of another person is dominant, so that a given piece of information regarding him changes our impression less, the later it comes in the series of things we learned about him. Subsequent research has shown that there is by no means a universal 'law of primacy'. Sometimes one's first impressions are the most powerful ones; but under a quite wide range of conditions there is actually an opposed 'recency effect' such that our final evaluation of a person is most influenced by what we have learned about him lately. Later in this chapter we shall discuss one such case, namely, that our liking for a person is greatest when he first makes negative judgements regarding us and then begins to evaluate us positively.

*Additive versus averaging models.* The most heavily studied impression-formation issue in recent years has been on the averaging-versus-additive controversy. The issue here is whether one's general evaluation of a person is determined by the average attractiveness of the items of information that we know about him or by their total attractiveness. For example, if we know a half-dozen very attractive things about a person and then find that he has another trait that is attractive but only moderately so, then averaging theory predicts a lowered, and additive theory a heightened, attractiveness. Again, if we know a half-dozen very attractive things about the person and then learn a seventh equally attractive thing about him, the averaging theorists would predict no change, and the additive theorists an increase in net attractiveness. Elegant models of these two views of information integration (and variants of each) have been devised and tested recently, with some support and some disconfirmation of each model.

Refinements have been introduced to take into account such factors as trait redundancy, the distinction between evaluative and descriptive aspects of traits, differential weightings of various traits, context effect, and modes of handling widely inconsistent information. This research has led to more sophisticated theoretical models, particularly impressive among which is Anderson's theory of information integration (1971), which de-emphasizes the distinction between the additive and averaging approaches, by showing that seeming additive effects can be explained as averaging effects when one takes into account the subject's initial attitude and gives appropriate weight to the subsequent items of information.

*Remote psychological repercussions of new information*

Once new information is integrated with what the individual already knew about the specific object of judgement, allowing him to arrive at a new judgement about that object, the resultant belief change will tend to have ramifications on other beliefs within the person's cognitive system. Studying these remote changes allows testing, altering and elaborating theories regarding the structure of the conscious and unconscious mind.

*McGuire's (1968) probabilogic model.* This formulation assumes that the cognitive field can be mapped by putting its content into propositional statements and its structure into the axioms of formal logic (with the modification that, rather than being seen simply as true or false, the propositions are accepted by the person as having varying degrees of subjective probability). Hence, when new information affects the subjective probability of a given proposition, this change is communicated to other propositions in accord with the rules of probability theory and formal logic. However, in this formulation the logical man model is modified, taking into account other postulated factors, such as additional assumptions of a wishful-thinking tendency and a temporal and spatial inertia, such that the logically required ramifications on remote beliefs are effected only gradually and incompletely.

*Recent modification.* This intricate line of theorizing was neglected for a decade or so, but with the recent willingness to formulate complex models, it has received some notable advances in the work of Watts and Holt, and especially Wyer (see Wyer and Goldberg, 1970). The recent experiments confirm that a combination of formal logic and probability theory is quite powerful in accurate prediction of how new information affects remote areas of the cognitive system (even without taking into account the additional, non-rational processes postulated by McGuire). We think further progress can be made in this interesting and important – if rather complex and demanding – line of research by use of Bayesian models, more complicated cognitive structures, and by distinguishing between immediate and delayed ramifications. The current trend toward applying these formulations to several different areas of empirical investigation (for example, by Wyer and by Anderson) promises to facilitate cross-fertilization of the findings and conceptualizations from one area to another.

A still more adventurous approach to all three of the steps in the social information-processing models is found in the work on computer simulation of cognition (Abelson and Reich, 1969). This technique is even more demanding, as regards both conceptualization and data collection, than the approaches discussed in this section. Its success is by no means assured but its promise is high.

**Attitudes and actions**

The relation between attitudes and action (that is, between the person's conscious beliefs and experiences and his overt behaviour), and how each is affected by third factors, has been of perennial interest to psychologists. As questions relevant to many aspects of theory and practice, this interest is readily understood. We shall describe three general lines of recent work in this area. First, there have been advances in several directions regarding measuring attitudes and their relations to beliefs, intentions and overt behaviour. A second line of work has focused on the causal direction involved by any attitudinal–behavioural relationship, usually guided by a viewpoint that might be termed 'attribution' theory after Kelley or 'self-observation' theory following Bem. A third area of research focuses more narrowly but deeply on the effectiveness of threats in producing changes in attitude and actions.

*Construct validations of attitudes*

The person's attitude regarding an object has typically been measured by presenting him with an 'opinionnaire', a series of statements (usually evaluative) regarding the object, and asking him to indicate the extent of his agreement with each statement. Because such verbal reports are valid only to the extent that the person is fully aware of his own attitudes and willing to report them honestly, researchers have recently been investigating additional indices of attitudes, such as physiological, unobtrusive and composite measures.

*Physiological indices.* The renewed interest in physiological measures of attitudes probably reflects the increasing availability of biological monitoring devices rather than any great leap forward in theory. The basic assumption underlying the use of such measures is that when the individual is presented with some attitudinal object or a symbolic representation of it, the strength of the feelings it evokes is revealed by the amount of physiological activation it produces. Galvanic skin resistance continues to be a popular measure of such autonomic responsiveness, but the use of various more direct circulatory measures has been growing even faster. Interest in pupil dilation as an autonomic index of attitude, the popular 'growth industry' in this market a few years back, has not lived up to its early promise and will probably receive relatively less attention in coming years in view of its difficulty of measurement.

A limitation of all these autonomic measures is that they indicate the strength of the person's attitude without much information regarding its content. That is, they do provide a moderately reliable and valid measure of how aroused the person is, but they do not pinpoint very well what aspect of the object arouses him, the nature of his arousal (e.g., whether fear or anger), or even whether he is aroused in a positive or negative direction. Despite the disappointments to date, the plausibility and potential importance of autonomic patterns that provide more specific information about subjective states seem sufficient to justify continued research.

*Unobtrusive indices.* In contrast to the internality of physiological measures are the non-reactive measures of attitudes which involve the passive external observation of the person's ordinary behaviour. Webb and others have attempted to outline a variety of ways in which people's attitudes might be inferred from their behaviour and even from the rather tenuous traces that remain of their past behaviour. For example, one might make inferences regarding the comparative popularity of various kinds of art work by consulting museum records to find out the relative frequency with which the floor covering has to be replaced in the several galleries of the museum devoted to these different art forms. Or the researcher might intervene to provide opportunities for the non-obtrusive measures, as in Milgram's 'lost letter' procedure, where letters addressed to various organizations (whose respective attitudes on an issue are notorious) are discarded in a certain area and the sympathies of the passers-by are estimated from the proportion of 'found' letters to these various organizations that are posted. While these procedures are often highly ingenious, the overt behaviour tends to be related to the attitudes so circuitously and to be affected by so many other factors that they probably provide a rather noisy index of the attitudes. Also, some ethical questions have been raised (as discussed in the final section of this chapter) as to whether such indices may invade the privacy of others or engineer their participation in experiments without informed consent.

Another procedure popular in recent years is inferring a person's attitude from his non-verbal behaviour. It is reported that standing closer to an object, maintaining more eye contact with it, adopting certain postures and tones of voice, etc., indicate a more positive feeling towards the object (though it seems to this writer that ultimately it may turn out that intermediate levels of distance, eye contact, etc., indicate the most positive aspect, rather than there being a simple rectilinear relationship).

*Composite indices.* Cook has adopted a multi-method approach to attitude measurement which includes the above procedures, various forms of traditional verbal report measures, and additional indices such as several 'error' procedures. For example, the person might be asked to memorize a series of statements about an object and his attitude towards it estimated from the relative proportion of information favourable versus non-favourable to the object that he learns and retains.

Other researchers, most notably Fishbein (1972) and Triandis, have devised composite measures of the person's attitude towards an object that include not only his evaluation of the object but also how he perceives the consequence of his acts, other people's expectations regarding his behaviour, etc. Some high correlations have been obtained, but typically only at the cost of collecting a large amount of information, focusing on very narrow attitudes and actions, and using verbal statements about intended actions rather than actions *per se*.

The relationships between beliefs and behaviour have also been in-investigated in more dynamic situations, comparing the attitude change versus action change produced by a persuasive communication. Below, when we discuss the efficacy of threats for changing beliefs and behaviours we shall see that there is surprisingly little relationship between these two.

*Evaluation.* In sum, these recent studies reveal disappointingly small interrelations among various attitudinal indices and between them and actual behaviour. Perhaps these negative results indicate nothing more serious than the complexity and inclusiveness of most attitudes, so that we must use a broad composite index to measure them. Or perhaps the more radical conclusion is warranted that attitudes do not really represent a meaningful psychological entity; or that they are so specific as regards object and manifestation that they are of very little use in testing general theory or in predicting general behaviour. But while these recent attempts to entrap attitudes within a broader net of measures have so far failed to ensnare their quarry, and have led some to doubt whether this snark exists at all, we keep the faith that this broad array of measures will eventually yield interesting positive results when the data are obtained within more elegant experimental designs and are reduced and combined by more powerful modes of analysis (e.g., the new multi-dimensional techniques and more sophisticated mathematical models).

*Attribution (and self-observation) theories*

*Basic assumptions.* The most popular new theoretical fashion within social psychology is the 'attribution' approach. It has proved particularly attractive to many adherents of the previously fashionable orientation, dissonance theory and, like it, represents Heider's commonsense approach to psychology and a focusing on perceived causation. Such theorists try to understand how a person behaves by considering how the person perceives his circumstances, particularly the causation to which he attributes his own and other people's behaviour. A basic assumption of attribution theories is that the person is able and motivated to make inferences regarding such causation, at least when he is pressured for an explanation or needs one in order to decide how he himself should react.

*Uses of attribution theory.* An interesting example of this approach is the work by Schachter (1971) and his colleagues regarding the person's interpretation of his own emotional and motivational states (with the consequent behavioural manifestations of laughing, eating, feeling afraid, etc.) on the basis of his general physiological activation and critical aspects of the situation to which he can attribute this arousal. A quite different example is the research by Jones and others on the ingratiation phenomenon, involving predictions that the person responds to another's positive behaviour very differentially, depending on the motivation he attributes to the other person for that behaviour.

The most stimulating use of the attribution approach is Bem's theory that self-observation of our own behaviour is the basis on which we infer our own attitudes. Starting with the general notion that we judge other people's beliefs and feelings regarding an object by how they behave towards it,

Bem conjectures that we come to know our own attitudes and feelings in a very similar way, from observing our own behaviour. If someone asks us whether we like coffee, we cannot answer him until we first review our own drinking behaviour so that we can reply perhaps, 'I guess so, I'm always drinking the stuff.'

The conventional assumption regarding attitude–behaviour congruity is that attitudes cause behaviour; that is, because a person feels a certain way he behaves accordingly. But Bem's theory and related formulations argue that the causal direction might flow in the opposite direction, with actions leading to attitudes. That is, we may have no attitudes toward a particular object until somebody asks us how we feel about it; then we observe how we behave in order to infer how we feel. This recent theorizing that there is a causality going in both directions between attitudes and behaviour is a somewhat paradoxical case of over-explanation since, as we have described in the previous section, there is disappointingly little positive correlation between the two. Still, attribution explanations like Bem's have been generating a great deal of interesting research. While the empirical results bearing on the non-obvious predictions are mixed, there have been enough confirmations to assure that the approaches will remain popular for the near future.

*Behavioural and attitude change under threat*

For the past twenty years and particularly recently there has been much conceptual and empirical work on how the amount of attitudinal and behavioural change produced by a persuasive communication is affected by the extent to which it arouses fear about the consequences of one's failure to change. The popularity of this topic derives from its having both theoretical and practical relevance. As regards theory, it bears upon critical questions regarding the nature of motivation and emotion such as the two-factor theory of anxiety and the interrelations among conscious, physiological and gross behavioural reactions. On the practical side, this topic has significant implications for public-health campaigns to induce the public to obtain X-rays and other medical check-ups, to get preventive inoculations, and to avoid or give up cigarettes and other habit-forming drugs.

*Two-factor theory.* Janis reported in the early 1950s that high-school students are less likely to adopt urged health practices when the dangerous consequences of neglect are pointed out to them with very high, rather than mild vividness. Subsequent research in the area has often been guided by a two-factor theory which depicts anxiety and other motivational states as having both energizing and cue aspects. As an energizer it multiplies response tendencies; hence, assuming that a communication urging certain health practices elicits some tendency to adopt them, then the higher the fear arousal, the greater should be the attitudinal and behavioural change towards the urged practice. In its cue aspect, on the other hand, anxiety would tend to reduce compliance since, as a distinctive signal, it would tend to elicit learned responses which in previous frightening situations produced a rewarding reduction in this unpleasant anxiety. The types of responses likely to be evoked by anxiety in a communication situation (e.g., avoidance or repression of the topic, hostility to the source, etc.) would tend to interfere with the comprehension of and compliance with the message.

McGuire has described the mathematical properties of this class of two-factor theories which predict that the persuasive impact of a communication variable depends on two mediating tendencies, one of which has a positive and one a negative effect. There would tend to result an overall non-monotonic relationship between the dependent and independent variables, in the form of an inverted U with maximum persuasibility occurring at intermediate levels of fear arousal.

The two-factor theory has an attractive richness in predicting this overall non-monotonic effect and numerous interaction effects dealing with how personal and environmental variables affect the threat level at which maximum attitude and behavioural change will occur. These implications have been heavily researched in the past several years by Leventhal (1970), Janis, Mann, Mausner and others, in laboratory and field experiments involving public-health practices having to do with tooth brushing, inoculations, smoking, medical check-ups, etc., or undergoing diagnostic procedures.

*Empirical results.* For all that it deserves to be true because of its heuristic provocativeness, its plausibility, and its relevance to theory and practice, the weight of empirical results seems to bring down rather than shore up the two-factor theory, though the evidence is still too mixed to render a final judgement.

The prediction of an overall inverted-U relationship with maximum persuasive impact at intermediate levels of fear arousal has received occasional, indirect support. For example, Mausner and Platt report that role-playing experiences more effectively reduce smoking if the smoker plays the role of physician telling a patient he has lung cancer (a moderately anxiety-arousing part) than if he role-plays the patient (very anxiety arousing) or takes an observer's role (low anxiety arousal). But more results lend themselves to the simpler empirical generalization that the higher the threat level the greater the attitude change.

A devoted and obstinate two-factor theorist could argue that most experimental situations have been such that the level of fear arousal achieved falls short of the inflection point at which further arousal would be detrimental to impact. But while such a claim might allow the theory to elude disconfirmation, it would at the same time cast doubt on the practical utility of the theory since many of the experiments actually aroused a level of fear higher than would be practical in most preventive-medicine situations.

The two-factor theory receives mixed support also for its predicted interaction effects. The predicted interactions of level of fear with immediate versus delayed impact and with clarity of coping instructions have typically not been found. On the other hand, there is a fair amount of support for the predicted interactions that increasing fear arousal is more effective in getting people to make illness-detecting rather than illness-avoiding acts, with higher rather than low self-esteem respondents, and with those unconcerned about illness.

Empirical support has been sufficiently spotty so that alternatives or elaborations of the two-factor theory have been proposed in recent years. McGuire's (1972) model predicts how increased fear arousal in a communication can have a positive or negative effect of persuasive impact, depending on such factors as message complexity, the chronic and acutely induced anxiety levels of the recipient, his habitual coping mechanisms, etc. Janis has described qualitatively different mechanisms which may be set into play as progressively higher levels of anxiety are aroused. And Leventhal has proposed a 'parallel' theory which postulates that fear arousal and danger arousal are two separate and parallel effects of a threatening communication and that the behavioural and attitudinal impact of the message will vary greatly depending on which is dominant. He contrasts this to a simplified 'series' theory (under which he seems to force all two-factor theories) which represents fear as an intervening process.

The rich theoretical relevance, the large body of interesting empirical relationships, and the high degree of practical importance of this research on fear-arousing aspects of persuasive messages, and the many issues still in doubt, assure that the area will continue to be a heavily studied one for the next several years.

## Interpersonal attraction and hostility

Why people feel and behave positively or negatively towards one another continues to be a focus of social psychological research. We shall first report some of the recent findings regarding conditions which lead to interpersonal attraction and then some results on the origins of hostile behaviour.

### *Interpersonal liking*

*Similarity and attraction.* Byrne and his colleagues have frequently demonstrated that one person likes another to the extent that he perceives the other as being similar to himself. The Byrne (1972) studies include both well-controlled if somewhat artificial laboratory situations and naturalistic, though hard to control, field situations involving, for example, 'computer dating' in which couples are matched to produce varying degrees of belief congruity. Ideological similarity proves to be particularly important, even more than demographic, so that, for example, White segregationists like Black separatists better than they do White pro-integrationists.

The psychological processes underlying this positive relationship between similarity and liking remain in question. Byrne has suggested that perception of similarity in another person is itself reinforcing and hence leads to increased liking of him. A problem with this reinforcement interpretation is that even if one admits that perception of similarity is rewarding, such reinforcement should increase the probability of the response being made at the time, which would seem to be in this case reading about the other person rather than liking him. This objection is a bit forced, however, since it could be argued that people do in general like one another and one is inclined to give even a stranger the benefit of the doubt, so that some initial liking would likely be experienced; also, even if the response that is reinforced is simply learning about the subject, there is evidence that increased familiarity brings about increased liking.

An alternative interpretation is that perception of the other person's similarity may operate not so much as a reinforcement, but as a cue allowing the inference of other characteristics in the person that would lead to liking him. Some support was given to this interpretation by the failure of Byrne's earlier work to show an interaction between trait importance and similarity, though more recent experiments have been more successful in showing that trait importance does have some effect on the level of attraction, in conjunction with other variables.

A number of recent studies have attempted to show that the similarity–attraction relationship is due to another mechanism, namely, one's general tendencies to ascribe to oneself positively evaluated characteristics and to admire others who have positively evaluated characteristics. Hence, discovering that another person has characteristics similar to one's own would in effect indicate that he has positively evaluated traits, and it might be for the latter reason that he is liked. It should be recognized, of course, that even if this latter mechanism is operative, it does not rule out the possibility that the reinforcement mechanism also operates. Suitably designed research could unconfound the two possible explanations and perhaps show that each is valid.

Aronson and his co-workers have conducted a rather different line of research bearing on this similarity–attraction relationship. They find that when a superior person takes a pratfall (making him less admirable but more similar to the ordinary respondent) this *faux pas* under certain conditions makes him more rather than less attractive. This outcome, however, needs further empirical clarification.

*What has he said about me lately?* Aronson (1970) and his colleagues have also carried out another line of interesting studies on the possibility that we come to like another person in the course of a series of interactions to the extent that his evaluation of us becomes progessively more positive. What is important in producing liking is not the other person's average evaluation of the subject but the direction of change in his evaluation. Aronson found some support for the basic prediction (though the relationship has eluded some other investigators) but he points out that the relationship, even if confirmed, might derive from a variety of factors as varied as anxiety effects on generalization, inference that the other person has good discernment, a linear-operator contrast effect, etc. He has conducted some work, suggestive but not yet conclusive, on the relative importance of these possible underlying mechanisms.

*Interpersonal hostility*

*Example as an instigator to violence.* Complementing the research just discussed on antecedents to interpersonal liking is the study of the opposite interpersonal effect, namely, dislike for others, especially as manifested in aggressive behaviour. A wide variety of psychologists have studied aggression for its *ad hoc* interest and its relevance to diverse theoretical issues. There has been a marked increase in aggression research recently, probably because of the apparent growth of overt social violence as manifested in political confrontations, crimes of violence, and assassinations of prominent figures.

The hypothetical antecedent that has received the most intense study recently is the effect of witnessing violent behaviour (for example, on the mass media) in instigating subsequent violent behaviour by the viewer. Interest in mass-media effects derives from both theoretical and policy concerns. On the theoretical side, there has been the long controversy regarding possible 'cathartic' versus 'modelling' effects of witnessing events that arouse strong emotional states such as hostility. According to catharsis theory, by expressing his pent-up hostilities vicariously while watching violent scenes the person tends to purge himself of aggressive tendencies so that he subsequently responds with less overt hostility to other people. But while the psychodynamic therapist posits a beneficial cathartic effect from witnessing violence, the behavioural therapist predicts the opposite effect, namely, that witnessing aggressive behaviour serves as a model that under appropriate conditions instigates and perhaps vicariously reinforces such behaviours in the viewer, making him more hostile in his subsequent interactions with people. On the policy side, interest in the issue derives from the conjecture that the apparently rising level of violence in society might reflect increasing exposure to the depiction of violence in the media. A decade earlier it was violence in 'comic' books that aroused concern; now criticism has focused on the appallingly high level of violence in entertainment and news programmes on television. Symptomatic of the concern is that the US Congress has taken the unusual step of explicitly directing the National Institutes of Mental Health to support a large-scale evaluation of this conjecture (Surgeon-General, 1972).

All of the evidence is not yet in on this issue; indeed, one hopes that the books will never be closed on so important and complex an issue while relevant social conditions continue to change. Hence, definitive recommendations cannot be made with certainty at this point. But uncertainty is endemic to scientific information and by no means makes it useless for improving decision making. What makes one particularly hesitant to make recommendations in this case is that a serious conflict is involved. On the one hand, if television programmes are to some extent responsible for violence in society and one does not assert this strongly enough, then one's negligence involves one with responsibility for this violence. On the other hand, if one asserts more emphatically than is justified that television plays a role in inciting social violence, then one risks being responsible for inappropriate censorship of the mass media.

On the basis of years of accumulated evidence it seems only fair to draw the interim conclusion that there is very little evidence that witnessing violent depictions has a cathartic effect, such that the person's subsequent behaviour shows less overt violence. (However, the possibility that under certain circumstances the depiction of violence on television might indeed have the healthy effect of releasing violence in fantasy rather than actuality cannot be completely ruled out because of occasional studies with positive results. For example, Feshback and others recently found that adolescent boys who were given a six-week heavy diet of television violence programmes showed more aggressiveness in the stories they produced, but less actual aggressiveness to their peers, than did a control group who for the six weeks were shown non-violent television programmes. Overlooking some methodological flaws almost inevitable in field research of this type, it could be inferred that depiction of violence channels one's aggressive tendencies into fantasy rather than the actual world. However, such studies supporting the healthy cathartic reaction are decidedly in the minority.)

Rather than its having a beneficial cathartic effect, the weight of evidence suggests the worrisome conclusion that depictions of violence increase the subsequent level of overt violence by the witness. A wide variety of studies show that exposing children and adults to aggressive models (e.g., being shown a film of a vicious prizefight, witnessing someone kicking a plaything, etc.) tends to result in the witness increasing his own level of violence (e.g., punishing other people more painfully in a pedagogic situation, destroying toys oneself, etc.). The extent to which such modelling occurs seems to depend on many factors, such as the extent to which additional anger is aroused by extraneous factors, the witness's previous and current rewards for being aggressive, the similarity of the witness or his potential target to the persons in the depiction, etc. Admittedly the relationship is conditional, the experimental conditions often artificial, and the outcomes somewhat mixed, but this writer is led by the evidence available to an interim conclusion that the depiction of violence in the mass media is far more likely to increase than reduce the level of violence in society. The question must be asked therefore whether there are other benefits from such depictions of violence (e.g., its entertainment value, accurate reporting of the news, channelling of hostility towards deserving parties, protecting freedom of information, etc.) which justify the possible dangers involved.

## Ethics and psychology

Feelings of moral unease have been sharply on the rise in the past several years. Moreover, it has become the style within the house of intellect to express so stridently this disquiet regarding other people's ethics that the uneasiness has become hard to ignore even for those who had long been accustomed and quite reconciled to living the unexamined life. This concern has found two expressions within psychology, a preoccupation with the morality of psychological research and an interest in the psychology of morality. In this section we shall describe each of these lines of inquiry in turn.

### *The ethics of psychology*

*Treatment of research participants.* The aspect of psychological research that has been most widely criticized lately is the treatment of 'subjects', that is, the people studied. One complaint is that informed consent is not always obtained from the subject. Sometimes he is unduly pressured to participate and often he is informed insufficiently or misinformed regarding the nature of the research. Still another criticism is that some research involves an invasion of the subject's privacy. More serious still, it is argued that some psychological research exposes the subject to an appreciable amount of threat, danger, or psychological or physical stress. While some critics may exaggerate the amount of psychological research flawed by these faults, an appreciable portion can be validly criticized on one or more of the above points.

What is to be done? If in a research project the subject is exposed to an element of coercion, deception, invasion of privacy, or stress, must it on that account not be conducted, at least until the offending member is exorcised? The psychological researcher is obligated to do good and ethical research. Hence, it is morally reprehensible to do unethical research; but it is also morally reprehensible to do bad research or no research. (Of course everyone is not morally obligated to do research. But any person whose role in society is adding to our knowledge through research, either should do research or follow another calling.)

An ethical premise of Western thought during the past century, movingly expressed by writers such as Kierkegaard, Sartre and de Beauvoir, is that the decision not to act is an act that may itself be morally reprehensible. Probably any piece of research has morally reprehensible aspects and not doing it would have the moral gain of avoiding these undesirable consequences. But not doing research also has its moral costs as well as gains, and doing the work also has moral gains as well as costs. Having detected the morally reprehensible aspects of the work, the researcher should evaluate the costs and gains of doing the research versus not doing it, or of continuing to do it with the reprehensible aspect versus some substitute procedure.

Provoking a search for procedures alternative to the ethically worrisome ones has been one of the most valuable impacts of the recent wave of criticism, likely to improve the field methodologically as well as morally. But the substitutes must themselves be critically scrutinized. For example, many social researchers deceive their subjects lest their awareness of the purpose of the experiment might affect their behaviour and yield spurious results that would deceive the reader as to the implications of the study. Alternative procedures like the role-played simulated experiment or observation of naturally occurring phenomena have been suggested. But should it prove, say, that relationships revealed in role-played experiments are more misleading than those revealed in deception experiments, we must decide whether deceiving the relatively few subjects with whom one comes into a close personal relationship is excusable in order to avoid the deception involved if a much greater number of people are misled in generalizing the findings. Or if observation of natural occurrences avoids the subject deceptions needed in laboratory research, but at the cost of greater invasion of privacy, the researcher must weigh the gains and losses of each.

While the researcher ought not to abdicate his own final responsibility for deciding whether to continue or quit the research or to pursue it along one line or another, whenever the issues seem even marginally worrisome he should come to the decision only after consultation with others in two ways. First, he should discuss with others the permissibility of his procedures after describing the morally questionable aspects as well as the likelihood of possible gains from the experiment, including among the discussants those primarily concerned with the welfare of the subjects or the public welfare, as well as those identifying with the advancement of psychological knowledge. Secondly, he should give thoughtful consideration to the codes of ethics developed for the guidance of behavioural researchers.

*A proposed code.* In this last area, a significant advance has been taking place recently in the code being developed by Cook and his committee, a preliminary draft of which is now available. A quite extensive code of ethics for psychologists had been published in 1953 by the American Psychological Association, providing guidance regarding the treatment of subjects in research, as well as other moral issues likely to arise in the pursuit of a psychological vocation. A few years ago (as one manifestation of the growing moral sensitivity regarding treatment of subjects in research) the Association instructed the Cook committee to develop the section of this code dealing with the researcher's obligations to his human subjects. The Cook committee collected from many thousand APA members and others over five thousand ethically critical incidents, so as to provide an empirically realistic starting point and to achieve maximum feasible participation on the part of the membership in the development of the code. Using these incidents in conjunction with generally accepted moral principles, a preliminary series of guidelines for the ethical treatment of subjects in research were induced. The guidelines were subjected to a great deal of discussion within the committee and in consultation with people concerned about research ethics, including psychologists, scientists from other fields, and non-scientists. A preliminary version of a possible code is now available for discussion and revision (Cook, 1971). It suggests guidelines on such difficult topics as requiring students to participate in research as a condition for admittance to the course, using money payment to induce participation, doing secondary analyses of archival social data when obtaining informed consent from the original respondents is impractical, investigating therapeutic procedures that expose patients or others to possibly harmful treatments or, in control conditions, withholding from them treatments which are thought to be beneficial.

No amount of consultation with others or consideration of ethical codes releases the individual researcher from responsibility for deciding what is the most permissible course to take in his concrete situation, but these outside resources might serve to deepen the level at which he will face the moral issues and at which he will reach a least unsatisfactory resolution.

*Political aspects.* The foregoing discussion of research ethics has focused on the treatment of the people who serve as subjects in research because this has been the main moral preoccupation of the field during the past few years. More recently, there are signs that this concern may be eclipsed by ethical questions of a more political nature regarding, not how the research is done, but the purposes it serves. Criticisms have been expressed that the social psychologist must take more seriously his responsibility for the uses and misuses to which the research might be put, or its possible effect on the balance of interests in the body politic. Some have argued that social research has been trivial or irrelevant and served no useful purposes, while others argue that it is all too relevant and serves the evil purposes of one or another special interest group. The discussion of these issues is still so recent, and viewpoints so divergent, that it would be inappropriate to try to resolve them here.

*Artifacts in social research.* Contemporaneously with recent ethical criticism of laboratory social research has been criticism on methodological grounds. It has been argued that artifacts (introduced by such factors as the use of volunteer subjects, demand character, experimenter bias, evaluation apprehension, subjects' suspiciousness of experimenters' purposes, etc.) make it hazardous to generalize from the results of laboratory experiments to the behaviour and experience of ordinary people in the natural environment.

The question of artifacts is related to ethical concern because the conduct of misleading research raises moral questions and because the artifacts sometimes arise from an attempt to avoid unethical procedures (as in the use of volunteer subjects to avoid coercion). The ethical problems, in turn, sometimes arise from an attempt to avoid artifacts (as when the researcher deceives subjects to avoid demand character). The methodological aspects of artifacts have received much research attention (Rosenthal and Rosnow, 1969) and yet are regarded by the 'in' group in the field as rather dull and pursued by those more remarkable for their tenacity than their imagination. On occasion, however, methodological research on artifacts has evolved into interesting substantive investigations. For example, the work on experimenter bias, after a phase of rather repetitious methodological demonstrations, has developed into substantive investigations of the non-verbal forms of communication by which the experimenter unintentionally transmits his expectations to the subject; and the methodological studies of deception and suspiciousness of the experimenter's intent has instigated substantive thinking on how warnings of an impending persuasive attack can itself be persuasive. Yesterday's artifact occasionally becomes tomorrow's theoretical focus.

*Psychology of ethics*

*The study of morality.* Further evidence of enhanced moral sensitivity is found in the serious research attention given recently to the psychological processes involved in phenomena with a moral dimension, such as political activism, alienation, social responsibility, etc. One positive moral response that has been heavily investigated lately is the Good Samaritan phenomenon (also called 'pro-social behaviour' and 'spontaneous altruism') involving the study of how variables like empathy or diffusion of responsibility affect the likelihood that a person will come to the aid of someone else who needs his help (Latané and Darley, 1970). A morally negative response that has received equally heavy research attention recently is human violence and aggression, particularly the role played by the mass media in instigating it, a topic discussed above.

The recent upsurge of work on each of these topics derives both from issues in psychological theory (for example, the controversies regarding the nature of de-individuation or catharsis) and also from notorious events in the natural environment (such as the failure of large numbers of people to help others in acute distress and the increase in violent crimes). Similar convergence of motives has led other researchers to tease out the stages of moral development, their antecedents and consequents. Of like origin is the current focus on attribution of responsibility for harm that befalls another person.

*Relevant psychology.* A number of taboo topics, suppressed inequities, and invisible groups have recently begun to receive a sizeable amount of attention from both society and psychological research. Several factors are behind this awakening of interest: some problems have become too severe to be ignored; some victims are no longer willing to be silent; or they have been brought to our attention by improvement of communication or enhanced moral sensitivity. We have in mind such issues as death, drug abuse, homosexuality, the legal system (including police practices, courts and prisons), alternatives to the monogamous family, racial antipathies and identities, social injustices to women, etc. Once suppressed, it now seems as if the sin that yesterday dare not speak its name, today refuses to say anything else. But the raucous outcry, which at times threatens to distract hearers from the injustice being voiced, is less frightening than the former silence, there being a natural tendency to blame the silent victim for his misfortune. Bloy said that in this world fraught with misery and injustice, the only honourable sounds are cries of pain and cries of rage. It may be that they are also the most effective sounds.

The demand that topics for psychological research be chosen more for their immediate relevance to social problems than their relevance to psychological theory began with agitation by innovators and anti-Establishment minorities, but is now becoming the establishment consensus and a criterion used by governments and foundations in awarding research funds. While there is a clear trend towards problem-relevant research, its contributions remain promises rather than accomplishments. The reader who wishes to keep abreast of the work might consult the *Journal of Social Issues*, which has scheduled between 1971 and 1973 whole quarterly issues devoted to such topics as drug use, the role of women, Black consciousness, the legal system, etc.

Social psychology has been going through an exciting and disturbing time during the period reviewed. Old assumptions are being questioned to the extent that a growing number of social psychologists feel unable or unwilling to pursue research along the former lines; indeed some seem to find it increasingly difficult to pursue research at all. This mood of profound doubt and absence of a working consensus is likely to continue into the near future at least. At times the contentiousness grates and it seems that, 'The best lack all conviction, while the worst are full of passionate intensity'. But intermittently the excitement and freshness catch one, and one realizes that it is occasionally at times like these that 'A shape with lion body and the head of a man slouches towards Bethlehem to be born'.

## References


ABELSON, R. P., and REICH, C. (1969), 'Implication modules: a method for extracting meaning from input sentences', *Proceedings of the International Joint Conference on Artificial Intelligence*, pp. 641–48.

ANDERSON, N. H. (1971), 'Integration theory and attitude change', *Psychological Review*, vol. 78, pp. 171–206.

ARONSON, E. (1970), 'Some antecedents of interpersonal attraction', in W. J. Arnold and D. Levine (eds.), *Nebraska Symposium on Motivation*, University of Nebraska Press, pp. 143–73.

BYRNE, D. (1972), *The Attraction Paradigm*, Academic Press, in press.

COOK, S. W. (ed.) (1971), 'Ethical standards for psychological research – a preliminary draft', *American Psychological Association Monitor*, vol. 2, no. 5, pp. 9–28.

FISHBEIN, M. (1972), 'Attitudes and opinions', in P. H. Mussen and M. R. Rosenzweig (eds.), *Annual Review of Psychology*, Palo Alto, California, *Annual Reviews*, vol. 23, pp. 487–544.

LATANÉ, B., and DARLEY, J. M. (1970), *The Unresponsive Bystander: Why Doesn't He Help?*, Appleton-Century-Crofts.

LEVENTHAL, H. (1970), 'Findings and theory in the study of fear communication', in L. Berkowitz (ed.), *Advances in Experimental Social Psychology*, Academic Press, vol. 5.

LINDZEY, G., and ARONSON, E. (1969), *Handbook of Social Psychology*, Addison Wesley, 2nd edn, 5 vols.

MCGUIRE, W. J. (1968), 'Theory of the structure of human thought', in R. P. Abelson, E. Aronson, W. J. McGuire, T. Newcombe, M. J. Rosenberg and P. Tannenbaum (eds.), *Theories of Cognitive Consistency: A Sourcebook*, Rand McNally, pp. 140–62.

MCGUIRE, W. J. (1972), 'Attitude change: the information-processing paradigm', in C. G. McClintock (ed.), *Experimental Social Psychology*, Holt, Rinehart & Winston, in press.

ROSENTHAL, R., and ROSNOW, R. (eds.) (1969), *Artifact in Behavioral Research*, Academic Press.

SCHACHTER, S. (1971), *Emotion, Obesity and Crime*, Academic Press.

SURGEON GENERAL'S SCIENTIFIC ADVISORY COMMITTEE (1972), *Television and Growing Up: The Impact of Televised Violence*, US Government Printing Office.

WYER, R. S., and GOLDBERG, L. (1970), 'A probabilistic analysis of the relationships among beliefs and attitudes', *Psychological Review*, vol. 77, pp. 100–120.

# 11 The Skills of Social Interaction

Peter B. Smith

The classic studies in social psychology have mostly been concerned with the description and attempted explanation of social phenomena. Researchers have had increasing success in isolating within the laboratory such phenomena as conformity, attitude change, social facilitation and the emergence of leadership. A natural second stage has arrived during which hypotheses are formulated and tested which attempt to specify the determinants of these phenomena. Work based on the testing of various modifications of consistency theories and of exchange theory has become increasingly frequent in recent years.

This chapter is oriented towards a different level of analysis, focusing on a variety of recent findings relevant to social interaction skills. These studies are oriented not towards the explanation of a given behaviour, but towards the question of whether the behaviour achieves its intended purpose. It is argued that the implications for practice of currently developed theories in social psychology are somewhat meagre. For example, if one can show that conformity in a certain situation is a consequence of a person's need to evaluate his abilities with reference to the performance of others, the most that this finding provides for the person in question is a new set of concepts for discussing his behaviour. If on the other hand one could determine whether in the given situation conformity behaviour achieved the person's goals or defeated them, the finding would be of more immediate utility. To adopt such an approach is not to forswear any form of theorizing, but rather to aspire towards formulating hypotheses which predict the outcomes of a behaviour rather than the occurrence of that behaviour.

The reason why such studies have not been more frequent is not hard to find. If one wishes to evaluate the effectiveness of a behaviour in achieving a goal, one must specify that goal. Yet if one interviews the subject of one's research it usually turns out that he has multiple goals, some of which are mutually incompatible. Furthermore, some of his goals are ones which he is unlikely to tell you about and there are others of which he himself is unaware. It is evident that studies in this area will have to make many simplifying assumptions before any work at all is possible. The most radical simplification possible is that it is useful to postulate a unitary trait of 'social skill' of which some people have more than others, and which enables them to achieve their goals more than others do. Many of the writers whose work is to be examined in this chapter do indeed write as though it were possible to sustain this assumption, but their prescriptions for social skill are diametrically opposed. The prescriptions range from the Machiavellian (Christie and Geis, 1970) to the humanistic (Likert, 1961, 1967; Truax and Carkhuff, 1967). It will be argued here that this contradiction is more apparent than real in so far as different researchers focus on different types of goals.

Any analysis of social skills will need to make at least one further distinction, namely that between behaviour and attitudes. Many studies have shown that those who most fervently hold a particular attitude are not necessarily those who will take the strongest action. For example, in an American study De Fleur and Westie (1958) were able to show that students who showed least prejudice against black people were not necessarily the most willing to sign 'releases' of photographs showing them with a black person. The releases were graded from relatively small-scale anonymous usage to a large-scale national publicity campaign. More generally there is no reason to expect that those who perceive the social environment with the greatest accuracy will also be those most able to translate their knowledge into effective action. Accordingly this review will focus first on studies of perceptual accuracy and later turn to studies of behavioural skills, which here fall under six headings: Machiavellianism, Ingratiation, Therapist Effectiveness, Industrial Supervision, Studies with Children, and Training in Social Skill.

## Perceptual accuracy

Numerous studies have been completed indicating that there are significant differences in the degree to which different people perceive others accurately. The usual format of such studies has been to expose the subjects to some stimulus material concerning one or more persons and then ask the subjects to make predictions as to how the stimulus person actually behaved subsequently, or how he filled in a particular questionnaire. In either case the stimulus person is a real person and the accuracy of predictions can therefore be checked against what actually did occur. Weiss (1963) conducted such a study, comparing the perceptual accuracy of sixty physical scientists with that of sixty clinical psychologists. The subjects were asked to make predictions as to the behaviour of three different undergraduates. For each undergraduate twenty-eight questions were constructed referring to episodes which had occurred during their life history. There were two conditions in the experiment: half the judges were given information only as to the age, sex, occupation and education of each undergraduate, but the other half of the judges were given also a transcript of a half-hour interview with each undergraduate. The interviews did not refer directly to the episodes the judges were asked to make predictions about. The findings were that under the minimal-information condition, the clinical psychologists were more accurate, but where greater information was available, the physical scientists were significantly better predictors. One might have expected that with greater information the psychologists would be progressively more accurate than those with no training in the field. However, a number of other studies have also shown that those trained in psychology are either no better than or else worse than other judges (Crow, 1957; Taft, 1955; Trumbo, 1955).

Such findings may not contradict the common sense of the man in the street, who may have no high opinion of psychologists, but psychologists at least will feel that the findings demand some explanation. Most recent studies of perceptual accuracy have been much influenced by the work of Cronbach (1955), who argues that perceptual accuracy must be looked at in terms of a number of quite separate components. A number of the components Cronbach distinguished were relevant only to studies current at that time which used rating scales upon which to measure predictive accuracy. The more enduring distinctions are those which Cronbach makes between accuracy of assumed similarity, stereotype accuracy and differential accuracy. Accuracy of assumed similarity arises where the judge assumes that everyone is like himself. If a university professor assumes that everyone is as intelligent as himself, he will probably be more accurate when talking with students than when he goes shopping. Stereotype accuracy arises where the judge assumes that everyone is similar in some respect. If a clinical psychologist assumes that everyone is neurotic, he is more likely to be accurate when relating to his clients than when meeting people in some other capacity. Differential accuracy accords most closely with the layman's understanding of predictive accuracy; it consists of the ability to rank order a number of people accurately on a particular attribute. Someone high on differential accuracy could correctly infer that A was more intelligent than B or that C was more neurotic than D. Assumed similarity and stereotype accuracy have often been looked on as sources of error affecting differential accuracy; Cronbach's importance was in establishing them as equally important aspects of accuracy. Returning to the Weiss study, we may now consider possible explanations of the findings.

In the Weiss study the judges were not asked to compare different stimuli, but rather to predict the consequences of a specific action. We may therefore expect that this study was concerned not with differential accuracy but with either stereotype accuracy or else the accuracy of assumed similarity. For example, if the stereotypes which physical scientists hold about students are more accurate than those which clinical psychologists hold, this might account for the finding. It might still be true that clinical psychologists were more skilled in differential accuracy tasks.

The research studies in this field do not at present generate measures of the incidence of each type of accuracy in various populations. There is, however, some evidence that judges who perform well on one task also do well on other tasks of a similar nature (Cline and Richards, 1960). Those who showed differential accuracy with regard to one class of stimuli showed it with regard to others also.

The field of perceptual accuracy has received relatively little attention in recent years. All that can be concluded is that the impressions we form of others will differ in accuracy along a number of independent dimensions. We turn now to more recent studies which have attempted to examine the actions people take in attemping to relate to others.

## Machiavellianism

The name of Machiavelli is linked with a manipulative approach towards interpersonal relationships. Machiavelli argued that one is more likely to achieve one's goals by concealing one's own feelings and opportunistically exploiting others, using whatever strategies the situation dictates. Christie and Geis (1970) have summarized a substantial body of research investigating the truth of Machiavelli's precepts. Their basic research tool is a questionnaire referred to as the Mach scale. Subjects are asked to agree or disagree with such items as 'The best way to handle people is to tell them what they want to hear', and 'It is hard to get ahead without cutting corners here and there'. In either case agreement implies a high Mach score. In a series of ingeniously designed experiments Christie and Geis attempted to determine whether or not high Mach scorers were indeed more effective in achieving their goals. In one experiment groups of three subjects were seated around a table on which was placed ten dollars. Their instructions were that any two of the subjects were at liberty to take the ten dollars provided that they could agree how it should be divided among them. They were not permitted to share the money between all three subjects. Each triad contained one person high on Mach, one who was median and one who was low. Seven triads did the task and the high Mach was included in the winning pair on every single occasion. On five occasions he made an agreement with the median and on two occasions with the low. This distribution is highly significant.

In another study, triads played a board game in which they were free to make coalitions with either of the others. Sixty-six subjects played in six games each. The highs were far more successful than the medians and the lows were far less so. This effect was even more marked when the situation was made more ambiguous by permitting the players to conceal the strength of their hands from one another. A study was made of the tactics employed by the high Machs in the course of their success. It was found that they did not differ significantly in the incidence of proposing, accepting or breaking coalitions. Instead they were thought to have a more acute sense of timing in these activities.

Christie and Geis argue that the reason for the superiority on these tasks of high Machs was that they remained more dispassionate while low Machs permitted themselves to become emotionally involved. To test this interpretation, Geis *et al.* (1970) designed a complex role-playing experiment entitled 'Legislature', in which subjects were briefed to act as congressmen. Each was given a variety of issues on which he had either a strong or a weak need to obtain a favourable vote. In one condition of the experiment all the issues before congress were those on which subjects themselves had strong views, such as civil rights and disarmament; in the other condition issues were trivial, such as specifications for sewage pipes and the issue of a new postage stamp. It was predicted and found that the superior performance of the high Machs obtained only in the hot-issues games and not in the neutral-issues games.

The Geis *et al.* study lasted about two hours, which gave the seven subjects in each game time for considerable interaction. Geis and Levy (1970) capitalized on this to test whether high and low Machs differed in perceptual accuracy. Subjects were asked to select one other subject who they felt they now understood and predict what his responses to the Mach scale must have been. High Machs were found to have more accurate stereotypes. They expected those they described to be somewhat Machiavellian and they were, while low Machs did not expect those they described to be Machiavellian. On the other hand comparison of low Machs' judgements indicated that they showed differential accuracy. The high Machs gave no indication of any differential accuracy.

Other findings reported indicated that high Machs are better able to look one in the eye while telling a lie (Exline *et al.*, 1970) and that they are less likely to be persuaded to change their attitudes in a dissonance experiment (Bogart *et al.*, 1970). In summarizing their work Christie and Geis conclude that high Machs perform in a superior manner to low Machs where interaction is face to face, where there is some possibility for improvisation, and where the task arouses irrelevant affect. The Machiavellianism studies are cogently argued and vigorously researched and their findings show an impressive consistency. Is the Machiavellian then a possessor of superior social skills?

Such a conclusion would not at present be justified by the empirical findings. It should be quickly noted that all the studies completed by Christie and Geis were in experimentally contrived situations where strangers interacted with one another for periods from a few minutes up to a maximum of two hours. Secondly the tasks performed in these experiments were mostly concerned with bargaining or the allocation of some scarce resource between a number of people who were in conflict. The fact that the high Machs were successful in outmanoeuvring the low Machs under these circumstances is relatively poor evidence as to whether they would achieve similar results under the more sustained and varied conditions of non-experimental settings. It may be that the high Mach relies for his effectiveness on the possibility of a 'rapid' getaway. In this way he continues to maintain social distance from his peers, thereby effectively concealing from them his true goals. Some clues as to the limitations of the situations to which the findings might be extrapolated are indicated by further findings reported by Christie and Geis. They indicate that a study at Pennsylvania State University showed a significant correlation between grades obtained and Mach scores of students. However, in a separate study of a private school with an enrolment of a few hundred, no significant relationship was found between grades and Mach scores. The authors suggest that in the school, grades correlate highly with ability because the teachers are well acquainted with all the students; whereas in a large state university students can acquire favourable grades by Machiavellian strategies for drawing attention to themselves when they would not otherwise be noticed by the instructor. Thus in a situation where sustained interaction is found Mach scores do not predict achievement, whereas in a situation where transient relations obtain Mach scores do predict achievement.

Some comment is also called for on Christie and Geis' definition of 'irrelevant' affect. For example, in the legislature study irrelevant affect is affect oriented towards feelings of rightness or wrongness about the issues for which one was negotiating support; the only relevant issue was actually getting votes in support of policies one was committed to push for. In the legislature study expression of irrelevant affect reduced the amount of time available for bargaining with others to obtain their support. However, in naturalistic situations it is not so clear that to spend time expressing one's feelings about an issue necessarily curtails the possibility of persuading others. One could only be sure that this was so under situations of severe time pressure.

It is clear that Christie and Geis reached the conclusion both that high Machs are more effective in their social behaviour, and also that the kind of situations in which that effectiveness is demonstrated are the kind that increasingly characterize a more and more rapidly changing society.

## Ingratiation

Jones (1964) has provided further data relevant to Machiavellian behaviour in his studies of ingratiation. The behaviour of subjects asked to give a good impression of themselves was compared with that of subjects asked to give an accurate impression of themselves. After an interview, subjects were then given some favourable or else unfavourable feedback. It was found that subjects judged the favourable feedback as more accurate regardless of whether they had been trying to give an accurate or a favourable impression of themselves. Since the feedback given was not based on actual performance, but was randomly assigned, no such difference should have arisen (Jones *et al.*, 1962). Those who received favourable feedback also showed improved self-esteem (Gergen, 1965). Jones interprets these data as indicating that those subjects who were asked to ingratiate themselves were deceived by their own deceptions. Having been asked to give a falsely favourable picture of themselves, they then accepted it as accurate.

In another study discussed by Jones (1964), Dickoff (1961) showed that the ingratiator's success with others is contingent on keeping his goals concealed. Using a format similar to that described in the Jones studies, after the subject had received feedback from her interviewer, she was asked to describe the interviewer. In one condition the interviewer had been straightforwardly described as a graduate student in training who needed interviewing practice. Here the interviewer was seen more favourably, the more favourably she had seen the subject. In the other condition, the interviewer had been described as someone interested in recruiting the subject for further experiments. In this second condition, if the interviewer gave favourable feedback to the subject, the subject did not reciprocate but saw the interviewer as weak and afraid. In other words, where the experimenter deliberately revealed the ingratiating interviewer's hidden goals, the interviewer was no longer able to ingratiate herself.

In the light of these findings one might expect high Machs to be ineffective in situations where their goals are likely to be uncovered. We turn therefore to an apparently unrelated field, that of investigations into the effectiveness of psychotherapy. Psychotherapy satisfies the three conditions laid down by Christie and Geis for situations in which high Machs should be more effective than low Machs. In therapy, interaction is customarily face to face, there is some possibility for improvisation, and the task certainly arouses a great deal of irrelevant affect. A therapist might argue that the affect was relevant rather than irrelevant, but in so far as the goal of therapy is to eliminate or reduce the crippling effect of affect on the client's everyday behaviour, it must be counted as irrelevant in terms of the definition of irrelevance implied by Christie and Geis' approach.

### Therapist effectiveness

Controversy as to the effectiveness of psychotherapy has been longstanding. Critics (e.g. Eysenck, 1966) have maintained that improvement in therapy occurs as frequently among controls as it does among treated patients. Bergin (1971) argues, as have many others, that overall percentage recovery rates are very misleading. The relevant point for the present discussion is that Bergin illustrates that psychotherapy success varies widely amongst different therapists and amongst different therapeutic institutes. He also reviews the evidence that psychotherapy may lead to deterioration as well as to improvement.

A good deal of research into the qualities of the effective therapist has been conducted by workers in the Rogerian tradition. Truax and Mitchell (1971) summarize the present position. Therapists with the highest success rates are those who score high on three attributes: 'accurate empathic understanding', 'non-possessive warmth' and 'genuineness'. Scores on these attributes are arrived at by coding excerpts from tape recordings. Coders are not aware of the identity of therapists or of the client and also do not know the research hypotheses. It is not possible to define accurate empathic understanding in terms of the distinctions made by Cronbach. The concept represents a more global judgement by the coder as to the degree to which the therapist is 'in touch' with the client's feelings. The coder bases his judgement of genuineness on whether or not the therapist openly expresses his own feelings and reactions. Truax and Mitchell review fourteen studies conducted between 1963 and 1969 covering 992 subjects. Pooling all these studies, sixty-six outcome measures significantly supported the hypotheses and one measure significantly rejected the hypotheses. Four of the studies concerned individual therapy and the remaining ten concerned group therapy or counselling.

The clients who deteriorated after therapy, or who remained institutionalized longer, were those whose therapists scored low on the three attributes, while those who improved most had high-scoring therapists. Correlational findings such as these need cautious interpretation: maybe clients who are improving cause changes in the therapists' behaviour, rather than the reverse. Truax (1963) showed that this was unlikely to be the case. Twenty-four hospitalized patients were given therapy concurrently by eight therapists. It was found that scores on the three measures for each therapist were consistent across patients, whereas patients encountered different levels in their sessions with different therapists.

Not surprisingly no Mach scores are available on therapists, although Christie and Geis do report that medical students wishing to enter psychiatry have higher Mach scores than any other group of medical students. The behaviour of effective therapists turns out to be most unMachiavellian. One might perhaps argue that the effective therapist gives an *impression* of empathy, warmth and genuineness even when he does not feel these things. Such an interpretation overly flatters the Machiavellian's powers of deception. After all, Mach scores are based on the subject's willingness to admit to a somewhat cynical view of human nature on a written questionnaire; how then is he to conceal such views in a therapeutic encounter?

Truax and Carkhuff (1967) have also shown that the therapeutic skills outlined can be increased substantially by training. They found that in some situations aides with relatively little training were more effective than highly experienced therapists. This is perhaps because they were more highly motivated.

One reason why this review has so far focused principally on bargaining and on therapy is that in either case the goals of interaction are relatively clear. In bargaining one wishes to win; in therapy one looks for improvement, though there is scope for controversy as to how to measure it. In many other situations in which one might like to measure the effectiveness of behaviour the goals are less clear cut. The goals of education are a complex blend of intellectual, vocational and humanistic. Those of industrial enterprise customarily reflect a conflict between short-term and long-term perspectives, and between optimizing the part and optimizing the whole. It is consequently no surprise to find that research in these fields has been less conclusive.

**Industrial supervision**

Likert (1961, 1967) has summarized the results of a great deal of work at the Institute for Social Research, University of Michigan. During the 1950s research was focused on the attributes of the effective supervisor, as determined by the productivity of his subordinates. Supervisor behaviour was measured in terms of the perceptions by the subordinate of his superior. The findings which derived from a number of industries indicated that effective supervisors had a more clearly differentiated role from their men, not often working with them, but spending time instead on planning and training; exercised distant rather than close supervision, i.e. spent less time actually checking up on their subordinates; and were seen as employee-oriented rather than production-oriented, i.e. they sided with their subordinates in defending them from pressure from senior management.

These findings are more reminiscent of the therapy studies than of the bargaining studies. They constitute one of the firmer bases of the 'human relations' school of thought in organizational psychology. As with the therapy studies, the findings are correlational and in consequence here too it might be that lenient supervisor behaviour is a consequence rather than a cause of high subordinate productivity. The evidence that this is not so rests on a few experimental studies (e.g. Morse and Reimer, 1956) and some large-scale attempts to change the whole style of supervision in an entire company (Marrow, Bowers and Seashore, 1967).

Fiedler (1967) surveys further industrial studies, whose findings appear to contradict those of the Michigan group. He found that on certain tasks (open-hearth steel mills, agricultural cooperatives, basketball teams) leaders who were more 'psychologically distant' achieved the better results. A psychologically distant leader is one who describes poor co-workers he has had in the past in a relatively punitive manner; a psychologically close leader sees less difference between good and poor past co-workers. Here perhaps is a parallel to the Machiavellianism findings. A leader who is emotionally distant from his followers and concentrates on the task in hand sounds a good deal more like a high Mach than a low one. A leader who has a trusting approach to his co-workers and takes more note of affective matters sounds more like a low Mach.

Fiedler has proposed a complex 'contingency' model which attempts to predict under which circumstances his earlier findings favouring the psychologically distant leader would be replicated, and under which circumstances findings more like Likert's would emerge. He predicts that the distant leader will do best under two circumstances, when the environment is extremely favourable and when the environment is extremely unfavourable; in intermediate circumstances the close leader will do better. Fiedler's reasoning is that in highly favourable circumstances the quickest, most directive leadership will be best and the emotional needs of the followers will be 'irrelevant affect'. In less favoured circumstances the leader will obtain a more motivated response from his followers by attending to their emotional needs. In very unfavourable circumstances, the only possible influence modes remaining to the leader are coercion and manipulation. In his 1967 book, Fiedler argued that the determinants of environmental favourability were three: the warmth of leader–follower relations, the open or closed ended nature of the task, and the amount of power inherent in the leader's position. More recently (Fiedler *et al.*, 1969), in a study of Peace Corps teams in Latin America, he added a measure of stress.

Graen *et al.* (1970) review experimental tests of the Fiedler model. They find that although the model fits well enough to studies completed before the model was developed, it does not account for the findings of subsequent experiments. While disappointing, this is not surprising. Fiedler's complex model necessarily makes a considerable number of rather arbitrary assumptions. It would be surprising if at least some of these assumptions were not invalid. The strength of the Fiedler approach is that rather than clinging to the notion that a particular behaviour pattern is most effective in *all* settings, it attempts to theorize about the conditions of its own applicability. Much more work in this style will be required in the future in order to determine the boundaries for the effectiveness of any particular social skill.

**Studies with children**

The problem of determining the direction of causality in studies both of schools and of families is acute. Teacher behaviour has generally been shown to achieve high performance where the teacher is warmer (Christenson, 1960). Pre-school children showed better adjustment where playgroup leaders were judged warm and empathic (Truax and Tatum, 1966). Experimental studies are not so frequent. Johanneson (1967) reviews a number of experiments comparing the use of praise and blame by teachers. His own study, conducted in Swedish schools, confirmed the findings of earlier studies: praise enhanced performance and blame reduced performance on a variety of classroom tasks.

Waxler and Mishler (1970) report some progress in resolving practical problems of conducting experiments within intact families, but to date the experimental findings do not bear on the crucial issues of the family's impact on the child. In more artificially contrived settings, considerable attention has been paid to the socialization of aggression (e.g. Bandura *et al.*, 1963), and of altruistic behaviour (e.g. Bryan, 1970). In either case the child learns by imitating a model, but whether this truly constitutes learning or is merely a reactivation of behaviour patterns previously acquired remains a moot point.

The recent development of interest in altruistic behaviour shows some interesting emphases. Some of the work focuses on the acquisition of altruistic behaviour by children (Aronfreed, 1970; Bryan, 1970), while a second focus is on why adults frequently do *not* come to the aid of those in distress (Latané and Darley, 1970). Seemingly researchers, like the rest of mankind, hope for better things from their children than from themselves. Perhaps we need more studies of the acquisition of Machiavellianism.

Christie and Geis report studies by Nachamie and by Braginsky, who developed modified Mach scales for ten and eleven year olds. The children scoring higher on 'Kiddimach' were more successful in persuading other children to eat unpleasantly flavoured biscuits, and also in a bluffing game. Other studies showed that Mach scores of children in their teens increased year by year; Mach scores of adults do not show such changes.

The evidence then is sparse. We know very little about how adult social skills are acquired. Speculating, one suspects that young children are encouraged in altruistic behaviours, whereas the later pressures of life in school place a higher value on Machiavellian strategies. Further advances in this field will need to take account of our understanding of the acquisition of adult morality (Kohlberg, 1969).

**Training in social skill**

The comments above have probably conveyed the writer's belief that contemporary society trains people in Machiavellian skills. Success in educational institutions is frequently defined in terms of success on precisely the kind of competitive tasks on which high Machs have been shown to do well. Large-scale organizations provide the ideal stage for their operations: a continuing need for interpersonal relationships coupled with sufficient interpersonal distance to ensure that the high Mach has some hope of keeping his secrets intact. At the same time studies have shown that Machiavellian behaviour is by no means always the behaviour which achieves optimal results. At least for some tasks – in therapy, in management and in education – a more warm, open approach is indicated.

The developing technology of training in interpersonal behaviour is usually referred to as sensitivity training. The basic procedure consists of a group of people talking to one another about their relationships, for periods of up to ten days. T-groups and encounter groups (two allied forms of sensitivity training) have become widespread in recent years, particularly in North America. Its proponents argue that the immediacy and personal relevance of what is discussed make it far more likely to enhance social skill than other methods rooted in abstraction or detached intellectual insight. One of the leading publications describing the method (Bradford, Benne and Gibb, 1964) is subtitled 'Innovation in Education'. The contemporary educational system detracts from rather than enhances interpersonal skills, the authors would argue. T-groups are to redress the balance. The literature of sensitivity training (Schein and Bennis, 1965; Smith, 1969) is rather strongly opposed to Machiavellian approaches to social skill. Furthermore the close interpersonal contact of the T-group is a poor setting for the Machiavellian to exercise his skills. Under these circumstances his stratagems are all too transparent.

Studies of sensitivity training (Campbell and Dunnette, 1968; Cooper and Mangham, 1971) indicate that training has a durable effect on around two-thirds of trainees. In their subsequent behaviour those who work with them see them as more perceptive, more cooperative, and more willing to take interpersonal risks. The three changes listed represent three of the most important differences between high Machs and low Machs. Although no researcher has studied the effect of T-groups on Mach scores, it is very probable that T-group experience reduces Machiavellianism. T-group trainees compared to controls have been shown to become more 'human-hearted' (Rubin, 1967), less authoritarian (Nadler and Fink, 1970), less concerned with control behaviour, and more with affection behaviour (Smith, 1964).

Campbell and Dunnette conclude from their review that while the evidence is quite strong that T-groups generate subsequent behavioural change, there is little or no evidence as to whether the new behaviours are more effective. The context of the present review should make it possible to discern in which type of situations the new behaviours will generate enhanced effectiveness and in what type of situations they will reduce effectiveness. T-groups will decrease the effectiveness of bargainers who rely on threat and bluff; they will increase the effectiveness of those whose task it is to handle conflict situations by developing collaborative negotiation. T-groups may decrease the effectiveness of those for whom it is vital to keep secrets; they will increase the effectiveness of those for whom improved communication is a goal. T-groups will decrease perceptual stereotype accuracy; they will increase differential accuracy. A study relevant to this last point is that by Crow and Farson (1961), who found stereotype accuracy to be reduced in soldiers after T-group training.

## Summary

This review of investigations into the effectiveness of different behaviours turns out to be anything but value free. Much of the developing field of experimental social psychology has evaded the problem of values by focusing on descriptive theories whose implications for practice are only vague. This evasion becomes impossible as soon as one starts to look at the results that different behaviours achieve. The positions taken up by many of the reviewers whose work is discussed are normative ones and the author's own preferences are no doubt also apparent. Such value preferences should enhance rather than inhibit the development of work in the field. For example the development of sensitivity training methods clearly lies with those who are sympathetic to its values; the development of methods of increasing Machiavellian skills rests with those who value the achievements to be had from Machiavellian behaviour. And there will be increasing need for dialogue as to the appropriate settings for the use of either set of methods.

## Further reading

BERGIN, A. E., and GARFIELD, S. L., *Handbook of Psychotherapy and Behavior Change: An Empirical Analysis*, Wiley, 1971.

CHRISTIE, R., and GEIS, F., *Studies in Machiavellianism*, Academic Press, 1970.

COOK, M., *Interpersonal Perception*, Penguin, 1971.

COOPER, C. L., and MANGHAM, I. L., *T-Groups: A Survey of Research*, Wiley, 1971.

FIEDLER, F. E., 'Validation and extension of the contingency model of leadership effectiveness: a review of empirical findings', *Psychological Bulletin*, vol. 76, 1971, pp. 128–48.

## References

ARONFREED, J. (1970), 'The socialization of altruistic and sympathetic behavior', in J. R. Macaulay and L. Berkowitz (eds.), *Altruism and Helping Behavior*, Academic Press.

BANDURA, A., ROSS, D., and ROSS, S. A. (1963), 'Imitation of film-mediated aggressive models', *Journal of Abnormal and Social Psychology*, vol. 66, pp. 3–11.

BERGIN, A. E. (1971), 'The evaluation of therapeutic outcomes', in A. E. Bergin and S. L. Garfield (eds.), *Handbook of Psychotherapy and Behavior Change: An Empirical Analysis*, Wiley.

BOGART, K., GEIS, F., LEVY, M., and ZIMBARDO, P. (1970), 'No dissonance for Machiavellians', in CHRISTIE and GEIS.

BRADFORD, L. P., BENNE, K. D., and GIBB, J. R. (1964), *T-group Theory and Laboratory Method: Innovation in Education*, Wiley.

BRYAN, J. H. (1970), 'Children's reactions to helpers', in J. R. Macaulay and L. Berkowitz (eds.), *Altruism and Helping Behavior*, Academic Press.

CAMPBELL, J. P., and DUNNETTE, M. D. (1968), 'Effectiveness of T-group experience in managerial training and development', *Psychological Bulletin*, vol. 70, pp. 73–104.

CHRISTENSON, C. M. (1960), 'Relationships between pupil achievement, pupil affect-need, teacher warmth and teacher permissiveness', *Journal of Educational Psychology*, vol. 51, pp. 169–74.

CHRISTIE, R., and GEIS, F. (1970), *Studies in Machiavellianism*, Academic Press.

CLINE, V. B., and RICHARDS, J. H. (1960), 'Accuracy of interpersonal perception: a general trait?', *Journal of Abnormal and Social Psychology*, vol. 60, pp. 1–7.

COOPER, C. L., and MANGHAM, I. L. (1971), *T-Groups: A Survey of Research*, Wiley.

CRONBACH, L. J. (1955), 'Processes affecting scores on "understanding of others" and "assumed similarity"', *Psychological Bulletin*, vol. 52, pp. 177–93.

CROW, W. J. (1957), 'The effect of training upon accuracy and variability in interpersonal perception', *Journal of Abnormal and Social Psychology*, vol. 55, pp. 355–9.

CROW, W. J., and FARSON, R. E. (1961), unpublished paper, described in H. C. Smith, *Sensitivity to People*, McGraw-Hill, 1966.

DE FLEUR, M. L., and WESTIE, F. R. (1958), 'Verbal attitudes and overt acts: an experiment on the salience of attitudes', *American Sociological Review*, vol. 23, pp. 667–73.

DICKOFF, H. (1961), unpublished dissertation, described in JONES.

EXLINE, R., THIBAUT, J., HICKEY, C. B., and GUMPERT, P. (1970), 'Visual interaction in relation to Machiavellianism and an unethical act', in CHRISTIE and GEIS.

EYSENCK, H. J. (1966), *The Effects of Psychotherapy*, International Science Press.

FIEDLER, F. E. (1967), *A Theory of Leadership Effectiveness*, McGraw-Hill.

FIEDLER, F. E., O'BRIEN, G., and ILGEN, D. R. (1969), 'The effect of leadership style upon the performance and adjustment of volunteer teams operating in a stressful foreign environment', *Human Relations*, vol. 22, pp. 503–14.

GEIS, F., and LEVY, M., (1970), 'The eye of the beholder', in CHRISTIE and GEIS.

GEIS, F., WEINHEIMER, S., and BERGER, D. (1970), 'Playing legislature: hot heads and cool issues', in CHRISTIE and GEIS.

GERGEN, K. J. (1965), 'Effects of interaction goals and personal feedback on the presentation of self', *Journal of Personality and Social Psychology*, vol. 1, pp. 413–24.

GRAEN, G., ALVARES, K., ORRIS, J. B., and MARTELLA, J. A. (1970), 'Contingency model of leadership effectiveness: antecedent and evidential results', *Psychological Bulletin*, vol. 74, pp. 285–94.

JOHANNESON, I. (1967), *Effects of Praise and Blame*, Almqvist & Wiksell, Stockholm.

JONES, E. E. (1964), *Ingratiation: A Social Psychological Analysis*, Appleton-Century-Crofts.

JONES, E. E., GERGEN, K. J., and DAVIS, K. E. (1962), 'Some determinants of reactions to being approved or disapproved as a person', *Psychological Monographs*, vol. 76, whole no. 521.

KOHLBERG, L. (1969), 'Stage and sequence: the cognitive developmental approach to socialization', in D. A. Goslin (ed.), *Handbook of Socialisation Theory and Research*, Rand McNally.

LATANÉ, B., and DARLEY, J. M. (1970), *The Unresponsive Bystander: Why Doesn't he Help?*, Appleton-Century-Crofts.

LIKERT, R. (1961), *New Patterns of Management*, McGraw-Hill.

LIKERT, R. (1967), *The Human Organisation*, McGraw-Hill.

MARROW, A. J., BOWERS, D. G., and SEASHORE, S. E. (1967), *Management by Participation*, Harper.

MORSE, N., and REIMER, E. (1956), 'The experimental change of a major organizational variable', *Journal of Abnormal and Social Psychology*, vol. 52, pp. 120–29.

NADLER, E. B., and FINK, S. L. (1970), 'Impact of laboratory training on socio-political ideology', *Journal of Applied Behavioural Science*, vol. 6, pp. 79–92.

RUBIN, I. (1967), 'The reduction of prejudice through laboratory training', *Journal of Applied Behavioural Science*, vol. 3, pp. 19–50.

SCHEIN, E. H., and BENNIS, W. G. (1965), *Personal and Organizational Change through Group Methods: The Laboratory Approach*, Wiley.

SMITH, P. B. (1964), 'Attitude changes associated with training in human relations', *British Journal of Social and Clinical Psychology*, vol. 3, pp. 104–12.

SMITH, P. B. (1969), *Improving Skills in Working with People: The T-Group*, HMSO.

TAFT, R. (1955), 'The ability to judge people', *Psychological Bulletin*, vol. 52, pp. 1–23.

TRUAX, C. B. (1963), 'Effective ingredients in psychotherapy: an approach to unravelling the patient–therapist interaction', *Journal of Counseling Psychology*, vol. 10, pp. 256–63.

TRUAX, C. B., and CARKHUFF, R. (1967), *Towards Effective Counseling and Psychotherapy: Training and Practice*, Aldine.

TRUAX, C. B., and MITCHELL, K. M. (1971), 'Research on certain therapist interpersonal skills in relation to process and outcome', in A. E. Bergin and S. L. Garfield (eds.), *Handbook of Psychotherapy and Behavior Change: An Empirical Analysis*, Wiley.

TRUAX, C. B., and TATUM, C. R. (1966), 'An extension from the effective psychotherapeutic model to constructive personality change in pre-school children', *Childhood Education*, vol. 42, pp. 456–62.

TRUMBO, D. A. (1955), unpublished thesis, described in H. C. Smith, *Sensitivity to People*, McGraw-Hill, 1966.

WAXLER, N. E., and MISHLER, E. G. (1970), 'Experimental studies of families', in L. Berkowitz (ed.), *Advances in Experimental Social Psychology*, vol. 5, Academic Press.

WEISS, J. H. (1963), 'Effect of professional training and amount and accuracy of information on behavioral predictions', *Journal of Consulting Psychology*, vol. 27, pp. 257–62.

# 12 Social Attraction in Animals[*]

Bibb Latané and David Hothersall

The earth is over 4·5 billion years old.† Until about two billion years ago, its surface was barren. Today it is covered with life. From its mysterious beginnings, living matter has spread itself into almost every conceivable location; from the oceans to the deserts, to the mountains, to the arctic. In doing so, it has transformed itself into a variety of plant and animal forms, and it has transformed its environment in ways ranging from the creation of an atmosphere by blue-green algae, the creation of soil by plants and worms, and the creation of cities by man.

Life has assumed many different forms. In the history of life well over one hundred million different species have inhabited the face of the earth. Of these species 98 per cent are now extinct, and the process of extinction continues. At present more than five hundred species are in danger of extinction, including the American alligator, the Eastern timberwolf and the Southern bald eagle. And yet the earth still has a magnificent diversity and multitude of life: one and a half million different species‡ of organisms are alive today of which about 75 per cent represent animals. The number of species has increased exponentially throughout the history of the earth until it has reached an all-time high. Never before have so many different species been living at one time.

## Evolutionary considerations

In 1859 Darwin, in his book *On the Origin of Species by Means of Natural Selection*, provided the basic framework for understanding the multitude and diversity of life. Darwin claimed that all living things are related and that more complex forms of life are derived from the forms that preceded

* Preparation of this chapter was supported by NSF grants GS 2292 and GS 27340 to the senior author. We thank Howard Cappell, Virginia Joy, Lloyd Sloan, David Walton and Carol Werner, who contributed immeasurably to the research and to the ideas described in this chapter.

† We are using the American billion, $10^9$, rather than the billion of the British numeration system, $10^{12}$.

‡ These estimates are conservative since many species, especially among the insects, have yet to be discovered and described. For example, the number of living species of insects may be as high as 3·75 million.

them by a process of adaptation through natural selection, called evolution.

The earliest of earth's life-forms were single celled, asexual micro-organisms – the products of spontaneous chemical reactions in pools of water. As the evolutionary time-course continued, the process of sexual reproduction appeared, primitive invertebrate creatures such as sponges developed, and later, about six-hundred million years ago, similar creatures with protective shells evolved. Some four hundred and twenty-five million years ago, a crudely formed fish with an internal skeleton, the ostracoderm, appeared. Another sixty million years produced the ancestor of the amphibians, a remarkable fish-like animal called the crossopterygian, which had both gills and lungs, allowing it to move both in the earth's waters and on the land. From later amphibians the reptiles evolved and still later, one hundred and eighty million years ago, the mammals, of which man is one, and the birds.

*Sex*

One of the fundamental inventions which allowed organic life so successfully to adapt itself to such a variety of environments was the process of diploid reproduction, or sex. The simplest of early life-forms, like blue-green algae today, reproduced simply by asexual cell division, so that offspring were genetically identical to parents. Thus there was no genetic variability and little room for adaptive selection. A maladaptive mutation could lead to the extinction of a whole line.

Amoebas at the start were not complex;
They tore themselves apart and started sex.
(Guiterman)

In sexual, biparental reproduction, on the other hand, offspring can be genetically quite different from either parent or from other offspring because they have a different *combination* of genes. This greater variability allows more efficient selection, especially since selection can take place at the level of the individual gene, rather than at the species level. Sexual reproduction allows species to adapt themselves genetically to new or changed environmental conditions.

*Mobility*

A second fundamental invention, which has allowed many forms of animate life to adapt themselves more precisely to their environments, has been the development of individual mobility. Animals crawl, slither, burrow, swim, hop, walk and fly from one place to another. This enables them to cope with the daily cycles of sun, tide and darkness, to protect themselves against seasonal changes by migrating, to seek out new sources of food and shelter, and to colonize new territory. Non-random mobility allows individuals to find the environment to which they are best adapted.

*Social attraction*

In order for these two inventions to be simultaneously successful, nature has had to invent a third – social attraction. Mobility means that animals are free to move apart, to scatter themselves across the surface of the earth. Biparental reproduction requires that they come together, at least temporarily, to recombine their genetic materials.* The two together require that animals permanently or periodically give up the life of the lonely wanderer in order to be with others of their own kind. Thus social attraction, like attraction to food for the individual, is fundamental to the success of a species.

In fact, the evidence shows that although animals may differ greatly in the type and intensity of social behaviour, they are rarely completely solitary. Animals come together in flocks, herds, schools, swarms, packs, crowds and cocktail parties. They come together in order to eat, sleep, fight and play as well as to copulate. No individual animal is believed to be independent of all other animals at all times in its history. Even the Wandering Albatross, which spends most of its lonely life far out at sea, returns to land every two years to breed.

Animals do not scatter themselves randomly over space; they tend to distribute themselves in clusters. In part, this is because the resources they need are not randomly distributed over space, but rather are concentrated in specific locations. Animals may cluster around a water hole, in a tidal pool, or a protected valley because it is a good place to be, not because other animals are there. Groups of animals that are brought together only because each individual is independently attracted to a source of food, water or protection and not because of attraction to conspecifics are called *aggregations*. In other social groupings, individuals are attracted to the presence of their species mates.

Within a cluster, animals do not distribute themselves randomly. Many animals, members of non-contact species, prefer to maintain a specific distance from each other. Fish in a school space themselves regularly. Birds on a telephone wire maintain a specific distance between themselves, closing the gap if one bird leaves and moving away if a neighbour comes too close. Other animals, such as the laboratory rat, seem to enjoy physical contact and regulate their social interaction by the amount of time they spend in contact rather than the distance they keep apart. Scientists have intensively studied the threat displays and aggressive behaviours which serve to keep animals spaced apart; they have paid little attention to the forces which bring them together.

One of the advantages to a species of social attraction is that it simplifies

* Some species of marine animals discharge their sexual products into the water and depend on currents to bring them together.

the problem of genetic recombination. However, social attraction serves other functions for animal species besides sexual reproduction. Animals living together in groups are frequently better protected against hunger, cold and predation than are solitary animals. They may even aid other members of the group. Porpoises have been observed to circle parturient females to protect them against sharks and to give sick schoolmates physical support. Researchers have photographed the death throes of an African elephant cow who, contrary to popular tales of a lonely 'elephant graveyard', died in the midst of her herd. Her fellows responded actively to her distress; one bull, for example, vigorously attempted to lift her to her feet when she collapsed, forced grass and herbs into her mouth, and finally tried to arouse the stricken female by mounting her!

Social attraction serves many functions for the species. It is tempting to imagine that these functions can explain why individuals come together. If natural selection favours sociable animals because they have more opportunity to engage in sex, one might assume that individual animals are sociable because of an underlying sexual motivation. If sociable animals have a selective protection against predation and other natural hazards, one might believe that animals are motivated to approach each other to avoid danger or reduce fear. However, just because an adaptation serves an identifiable function does not mean that it evolved in response to selection pressures related to that particular function. Even if it did, the evolutionary function of an adaptation tells us little about the individual or psychological mechanisms of how it operates. The adaptive function of an act for a species does not necessarily correspond to the psychological motivation for that act to an individual. If we want to find out what it is about animals which makes them so attractive to each other, we need to look to animals, rather than to evolutionary theory. Consider, for example, the case of the laboratory rat.

## Social attraction in rodents

### *Rats*

Suppose you were to put two laboratory rats together in a large, featureless enclosure and let them run around freely. If you did, as a number of us have done many times over the last five years, you would see the rats at first spending a good deal of time running around the open field, sniffing at the walls and floor and grooming themselves. You would also see them spending a substantial and increasing amount of time in social activity: sniffing each other, huddling next to each other, chasing each other around the field, climbing over and under each other. In fact, if you used a stopwatch to measure how much time rats spend in direct physical contact, you would probably find them soon spending anywhere from 50 to 70 per cent of their time in such activities.

*Gerbils*

Suppose you were to put two gerbils together in a large, featureless enclosure and let them run around freely. If you did, as we have done several times, you would see that gerbils are much more active than rats, skittering and scurrying around and across the open field, trying to burrow into the floor or jump over the wall. You would also see them spending a lot of time in social contact, probably somewhere between 20 and 30 per cent of their time in the open field.

*Rats and gerbils*

Now suppose you were to put a rat and a gerbil together in the open field. How attracted might we expect them to be towards each other? One prediction might be based on the assumption that cross-species pairs might act as the average of the within-species pairs, that is, that the rat and the gerbil would each show the level of sociability characteristic of its species, resulting in an average time in contact of 40 to 45 per cent. Another prediction might assume that the greater novelty and unpredictability of a member of another species might lead to increased interest and social contact in cross-species pairings. Still a third prediction, based on the assumption that 'birds of a feather flock together', might be that within-species pairings would be most sociable.

In fact, the third prediction is most likely correct. In our experiments, when rats and gerbils have been tested together, they have spent an average of only about 15 per cent of their time in contact, substantially lower than the average of the same-species pairings, and significantly lower even than the average time in contact spent by the less affiliative gerbils.

These results are not due to the preferences of either rats or gerbils alone, for we know that if one member of a pair is tethered (and thus unable to initiate social contact), rats spend more time with a tethered rat than with a tethered gerbil, while gerbils spend more time with gerbils than with rats. The results also are not specific to rat–gerbil pairings, for the same pattern obtains when we test rats with hamsters, or hamsters with gerbils. Over a large number of tests, we have found that the average amount of time spent in social contact by cross-species pairs of rodents is less than half that spent by pairs composed of members of the same species. Why?

Although cross-species pairs spend relatively little time in contact, they do not seem actively to avoid one another. In fact, analysis of the average distance animals maintain between each other shows that even cross-species pairs stay significantly closer together than what would be expected by chance if the animals paid no attention to each other. From other data, it seems likely that if animals were completely indifferent to each other, they would spend by chance alone less than 5 per cent of their time in contact. Instead, they spend three times that amount.

We are left, then, with two important facts. First, small rodents are socially attracted to one another, even to members of other species.* They stay closer together than would be expected by chance, and they spend a lot of time in direct physical contact. Second, these animals stay closer to and spend more time in contact with members of their own species than with other rodents. How can we account for these two facts?

**Attraction and evolution**

It would be simple at this point to hark back to our discussion of evolutionary pressures and point to the necessity of conspecific attraction for the continuance of the species. If sexual motivation underlies social attraction, however, we would expect that cross-sex pairs of animals would show more attraction than same sex pairs, or that highly sexed animals would be most gregarious. We have tested these expectations several times and found that sex has little effect on social attraction in rats. Rats are no more attracted to opposite-sex than same-sex partners, and factors such as sexual experience, hormone level or sexual satiation, which have strong effects on sexual behaviour, do not affect sociability. The evolutionary function of an adaptation for a species has little relation to the psychological motivations underlying that adaptation for an individual.

We also suggested earlier that animals may gain a protective advantage from being near others. If such protection forms the basis for an individual's motivation to approach other animals, however, we would expect that animals would be most gregarious in frightening, stressful or hostile environments. These expectations have not been confirmed. Rats are no more affiliative when exposed to flashing lights and buzzers than under normal conditions, and are actually more social in familiar than in strange environments. Once again, the evolutionary function of an adaptation tells us little about the psychological mechanism by which it operates.

**Theories of attraction**

*Innate*

It has often been suggested that the tendency to be attracted to members of one's own species is inbuilt, innate, produced through phylogenetic adaptation and transmitted through genetic inheritance. The European ethologists Lorenz, Tinbergen and Eibl-Eibesfeldt claim that certain animals possess Innate Releasing Mechanisms (IRM) such that specific cues, 'key' stimuli, have the innate capacity to unlock or trigger Fixed Action Patterns (FAP), instinctive social response sequences which occur in virtually identical fashion in all members of the species and which do not seem to be dependent on specific learning experiences. For example, the

* Some aggressive, highly territorial rodents, such as mice, show relatively little attraction even to conspecifics.

young of some cichlid fish, without ever having seen their parents, will approach artificial models coloured like their mothers but will not approach models of a different colour. The form and size of the model have no effect. Many insects and some mammals seem to show automatized social reactions to odours or chemical traces left by their conspecifics, called pheromones.

According to this view, animals do not develop a 'picture' of their conspecifics but rather are programmed to respond to various releasing stimuli emitted by them. Indeed, one criterion for the demonstration of IRMs is that animals can be tricked into responding to simple models that, aside from the key characteristic, bear little resemblance to real conspecifics.

Most of the fixed-action patterns that have been described in animals seem to involve courtship, child care or aggression, and some people believe that comparable phenomena exist at the human level. However, the variety and diversity of human sexual and child-raising practices and the number of ways people have found to express hostility and inflict pain argue against the notion that such behaviours are stereotyped, unmodified by experience.

*Learning*

Another kind of theory which claims that social attraction is based in part on inherited factors suggests that certain kinds of stimulation are inherently pleasurable and thereby sought out, as if nerve endings were somehow wired directly to pleasure centres in the brain. Harlow, for example, believes that many young animals derive 'contact comfort' from touching their mother's skin, and that this contact comfort is an important reward leading to social approach. To explain why monkeys like monkeys while snakes like snakes he jocularly expands his hypothesis to suppose that:

Each animal by God is blessed
With kind of skin it loves the best*

The rewards animals provide for each other, according to this type of theory, are based on genetically transmitted characteristics; contact comfort, warmth, pleasurable odours, mother's milk, etc. Animals learn that by approaching each other, they can obtain these rewards.

*Imprinting*

A third kind of theory, which has received a great deal of experimental attention over the past dozen years, suggests that although some animals may not have built-in tendencies to approach other members of their own species, they do have an innate predisposition, at a certain early age or 'critical period', to respond to and 'imprint' on any moving object in their

* In considering animals that come together in larger groups, Harlow might have formed a sub-hypothesis that, 'Some animals are born endowed with kind of skin to draw a crowd.'

vicinity. An animal which has been imprinted on an object will vigorously follow that object and display a strong attachment to it. The first description of imprinting we have been able to find was written by Sara Josepha Hale in 1830. It starts, 'Mary had a little lamb . . .'. Miss Hale later reported that the incident described in the poem was 'partly true', and indeed, the existence of cossetts, sheep more attracted to their shepherd than to his flock, has long been known by country folk.

In 1935 Lorenz published a classic paper, 'Der Kumpan in der Umwelt des Vogels' (The Companion in the Bird's World), in which he claimed that in some species of birds, a wide variety of animate and inanimate objects can acquire the capacity to evoke behaviours normally directed towards other members of the species. Lorenz suggested that imprinting differs from regular learning in that it occurs only at an early stage in the individual's development, that it is irreversible (i.e. that an animal once imprinted on one object cannot have its affections seduced by another object), and that it is not based on rewards or reinforcements.

Imprinting has been most commonly studied in certain birds such as ducklings and chicks, and although certain aspects of Lorenz's theory have not held up too well (for example, the concept of irreversibility), the phenomenon can be dramatic. Lorenz, for example, reports that a young greylag gosling that happened to come into contact with him before seeing any members of its own species continued to follow him around for the rest of its life, and persisted in importunate, though frustrated, attempts at sexual union.

Although in the laboratory imprinting can result in bizarre attachments and unnatural liaisons, in real life it usually results in normal conspecific attraction, for the first moving object a young, newly hatched bird usually sees is its own mother.

*Exposure*

A fourth kind of theory assumes that mere exposure to any salient stimulus object at any time in life can lead to increased liking and social attachment. These theorists (Scott, Zajonc, Cairns) suggest differing limitations to this assumption, but all agree that familiarity breeds liking, not contempt. The reason, according to this view, that animals prefer members of their own species is that the normal conditions of their life are such that they are most familiar with members of their own species.

We have considered four different theories for why animals are most attracted to conspecifics. They differ in the relative importance given to genetic versus experimental factors. They differ in their conception of the kinds of rewards inherent in social intercourse, the processes which initiate social approach, the conditions which are necessary for the development of social bonds, and the effects of unnatural conditions.

These four kinds of theories differ, but this does not necessarily mean that three of them are incorrect. Different theories may work for different species. For example, imprinting is thought by some to operate only in precocial animals, those with relatively well-developed sensory and motor skills at birth. Imprinting has never been satisfactorily demonstrated for altricial animals, like rats and men, who spend some period of time in helpless dependence after birth. As another example, both familiarity and imprinting theorists have great difficulty in explaining the survival of species like the cowbird or the European cuckoo, whose parents lay their eggs in the nests of others birds, and whose parasitic young grow up exposed only to birds of a different feather.

**Stimulus determinants of attraction**

Each of the four theories may work well for different species, but none of them seems to work well for rats. All of these theories assume that animals somehow come to like, be attracted to, get satisfactions from the static stimulus qualities of a conspecific. That is, rats might like each other better than they like gerbils because each rat has an innate or acquired preference for the appearance, colour, shape, texture, smell of another rat.

*Sight*

Recent research, however, suggests that such static stimulus qualities may not be very important. For example, in one experiment we attempted to assess the importance of visual cues such as colour on social attraction in rats. If visual cues, whether innate or learned, are important sources for social attraction, then changing the visual appearance of a stimulus animal should reduce its attractiveness and eliminating the visual capability of a subject should make it less attracted to others. Half of the stimulus animals were dyed an unnatural colour (a deep shade of charcoal grey) and half retained their normal white fur. Half the subject rats were surgically (and painlessly) blinded while half remained normally sighted. Neither of these manipulations had any effect on social attraction in the open field; dyed rats were just as attractive as normal stimulus rats, while blind rats were not only equally active, but were also just as sociable as sighted rats.

*Smell*

This result should not be too surprising, since it is well known that albino rats have relatively poor vision and do not seem to depend too heavily on their eyes to find their way around. Olfaction is an acute sense in rodents, and has often been suggested as a major modality in the regulation of social interaction. Indeed, rats do spend a good part of their time together sniffing and nosing each other as if they take pleasure in their own unique fragrance. If rats are attracted to other rats because of a learned or innate preference for the ratty smell of another rat, then altering the smell of another rat should make it less attractive. Likewise, altering the smelling capacity of a subject rat should make him less attracted to other rats. In a second experiment, we doused half the stimulus rats with *Fleur de Lis*, a popular floral perfume, and left half with their normal ratty odour. Subject animals were rendered temporarily anosmic by spraying a local anaesthetic, Xylocaine, up their noses before half of the test trials, while retaining their sense of smell intact on the other half of the trials. The Xylocaine spray was effective in blocking the sense of smell, as evidenced by the fact that afterwards rats failed to show their usual strong aversion to ammonia. The spray probably also blocked the sense of touch and the chemical sense in the nose.

Being able to smell the stimulus rat had no effect on the extent to which subject rats were attracted to it: rats were just as attracted to the normal stimulus rat when anosmic as when able to smell. Application of perfume had little gross effect on the behaviour of the stimulus rats: anosmic rats did not differentiate between normal and perfumed stimulus rats. Application of perfume did affect the attractiveness of stimulus rats to subjects who had an intact sense of smell, leading to a significant *increase* in attraction. Clearly, the ratty smell of another rat is not necessary to social attraction, since, if it were, rats whose smell has been chemically altered should be less attractive, not more, than normal-smelling rats.

### *Touch*

A final experiment explored the role of touch in social attraction. Rats spend a lot of time in physical contact, rubbing up against each other, crawling over each other, etc. Indeed, removing the opportunity for physical contact seems markedly to reduce social attraction. This suggests that there may be something especially satisfying about the 'feel' of another rat's fur. In order to test this line of thought, we altered the *quality* of physical contact between animals while still allowing contact to take place. This was done by observing hairy and hairless subject rats tested with hairy or hairless stimulus rats. If a particular type of cutaneous stimulation is necessary to social attraction in rats, then changing the quality of cutaneous stimulation should reduce attraction.

'Hairless' rats were first shaved with an electric animal clipper while under anaesthesia and were then treated with a commercial depilatory (Neet) according to the manufacturer's directions. Neet is remarkably effective on rats, leaving them soft and smooth-skinned, with no unsightly stubble or shadow. The hair on their heads and genital regions was not disturbed. Making these rats bald profoundly changed their visual appearance as well as their tactile quality. Hairless rats, in addition to having a different 'feel' from normal rats, looked radically different – removal of the body hair made them look skinny and undernourished, while the intact facial and genital hair gave them an almost lion-like appearance.

These alterations had little impact on social attraction; hairless rats were not less attractive to or attracted by other rats than were the normal, furry controls. Again, pronounced variations in the static stimulus qualities of the experimental rats had little effect on gregariousness. Rats did spend a lot of time in contact, and 'contact comfort' may have been an important motive for their doing so, but any comfort clearly did not derive from the rat-like feel of the other animal.

In none of these experiments did alterations in either the sensory capacity of subjects or the stimulus characteristics of the tethered rats lead to a decrease in social attraction. Although negative experimental results do not necessarily imply the absence of real differences, they do suggest in the present case that any differences may not be very important. In each of these experiments (as in many others) rats became increasingly gregarious with increasing exposure to and familiarity with the open-field testing situation, as competing tendencies to explore and respond to the unchanging non-social aspects of the environment dropped out. Variations in stimulus qualities, on the other hand, led to non-significant differences or even to increases in social attraction. Familiarity with the environment is, if anything, a more potent factor in rodent sociability than the rat-like character of the stimulus object.

*Stimulus combinations*

As long ago as 1920, Stone investigated the effects of sensory impairment on male sexual behaviour in rats. He found that it still developed despite the absence of sight, smell, hearing or taste. In 1944, after extending Stone's research, Beach concluded that the stimulus to which male rats respond sexually 'is a particular pattern of sensations. It is not an odour, a tactile sensation, nor a visual impression which arouses sexual excitement; but rather a given combination olfactory, tactile, visual and probably other sensations . . .'.

It is possible that the results of the present experiments can best be explained in the same way – rats are attracted not just to the ratty sight, smell or feel of another rat, but to the combination of these stimulations, to their patterning, to their whole *Gestalt*. This conclusion is possible, but certainly not necessary. It may be that such static stimulus qualities are simply not very important, either singly or in combination. It may be, as we shall suggest below, that the *dynamic* qualities of the other animal – its movement, the fact that it responds, the possibility of interacting with it – are the essential features of social stimulation.

These results leave us with somewhat of a paradox – we know that rats like rats more than gerbils, and vice versa, but the obvious things that could differentiate rats from gerbils, such as colour, appearance, texture of fur, odour, seem to have little impact on attraction. If these static stimulus qualities do not mediate attraction, what does?

**Interaction and attraction**

Animals, when they come together, don't just sit and stare at each other; they interact. Each member of a pair, seeing the other, initiates actions towards him. Each, seeing the other's actions towards him, responds. Social interaction, then, involves a chain of actions and reactions. The outcome of a social encounter is not predictable from the behaviour of one animal alone, for each can both initiate and respond. The course of social interaction, unlike an animal's transactions with the non-social environment, is only partially predictable by either animal, and only partially under either's control.

Interaction, then, is a major, if not the defining, characteristic of social behaviour. We suggest that not only must animal social behaviour be described in terms of interaction, but that interaction may, for many animals, be a basic source for satisfaction in social behaviour. We suggest that animals are challenged by and enjoy a moderate level of unpredictability, a partial degree of control. That is, we suggest that animals may be attracted to each other, not for the stimulus qualities of the other animal or for tangible rewards that the other can provide, but for the opportunity to engage in mutually satisfactory interaction.

*Rats and objects*

Consistent with this point of view, we find that rats are not very much attracted to a wide variety of non-social objects which do not have the capacity to interact. For example, they show little interest in miniature cars which might elicit their curiosity, in baby bottles filled with hot water which might provide them warmth, in tennis balls which might provide contact comfort, etc. Rats also show little interest in social objects with which they are prevented from interacting. A caged stimulus rat with which the subject cannot physically interact seems little more attractive than an empty cage. An anaesthetized rat or a rat which has been stuffed by a taxidermist elicits little approach. Only a moving, responsive rat, which allows the opportunity for social interaction, seems attractive.

If the process of interaction is a more potent source of social attraction to rats than the static stimulus qualities of the other animal, we should expect that rats would find attractive other objects which have the capacity to interact, even though they bear little resemblance to another rat. In other words, we suggest that laboratory rats don't care how their partners look, feel or smell, as long as they know how to play. If so, rats should be attracted to partners which can approximate the play, if not the appearance, smell and texture of a rat.

*Rats and a human hand*

To test this line of thought, we decided to introduce rats to a social surrogate, a non-rat object with the ability to interact, a human hand. The human hand is just about rat size, soft, warm and flexible, easily manipulated, and clearly not a rat. If rats are attracted to the opportunity for interaction, they should be attracted to a responsive, interacting human hand.

Half of the rats in this experiment were exposed to a tethered stimulus rat, restricted by a light string harness to one location near the outer wall of the open field, but not prevented from responding to or interacting with the subject rat. The other half of the rats were exposed to a human hand protruding through the wall of the open field, unable to chase the rat round the field but able to respond and interact. The hand simulated as closely as possible the behaviours of rats at play: poking, lifting, rubbing and scratching, tapping and tumbling. The behaviour of the hand was clearly idiosyncratic, purposely designed to be optimally responsive and maximally seductive. In pre-tests, we found a very vigorous hand to be most attractive; rats seem to prefer rough handling to more docile petting and scratching. Hands were washed in a vinegar-water solution between tests to keep odours from previously handled rats from exciting the subjects.

Rats are familiar with each other; they are accustomed to the behaviour as well as the appearance of other rats. To give the hand some of these advantages and to measure their importance, half the rats were given extensive pre-experience with a human hand which pulled their home cage open and stroked, scratched and fondled them.

As in previous studies, rats were quite attracted to the tethered stimulus rats, spending about two-thirds of their time in direct physical contact. They were also substantially attracted to the hand, spending almost 50 per cent of their time interacting with it. Pre-handling had no effect on attraction to the tethered rat; it did increase attraction to the hand, especially during the early days of testing. Attraction to the hand increased with continued exposure so that, after a week of testing, all groups showed equal attraction; the tethered rat eliciting 67 per cent time in contact and the human hand 66 per cent.

Clearly human hands can be attractive to rats. Even rats who are unfamiliar with them grow more attracted after repeated exposure ultimately becoming indistinguishable from pre-handled rats. In addition, attraction to the hand compared favourably to conspecific attraction, both in magnitude and quality. Rats' interactions with the hand were similar to their interactions with other rats. They sniffed, nibbled at, and crawled over and under the hand. They ran around it, poked it and prodded it. It may be premature to classify this as social interaction but, from appearances, the hand was treated as a social object.

### Social deprivation and satiation

If rats are motivated to interact with rats or other responsive objects, we might expect this motive, like other motives, to be satiable. That is, rats which have had a lot of opportunity to interact should be less attracted to other rats than rats which have been socially deprived. Indeed, half a dozen studies have shown this to be true. Rats housed in groups are much less gregarious when later tested in the open field than are rats living in social isolation. Periods of social contact as short as several hours or as long as fifteen months lead to significant decreases in gregariousness. This result argues against simple notions that mere familiarity leads to liking, and adds additional support to our suggestion that rats are motivated to engage in interaction. Finally, we can report that social deprivation, which increases attraction to conspecifics, also increases attraction to a responsive human hand.

The evidence we have reviewed suggests that rats like other rats for what they can do together, not what they look like. Why do rats enjoy interacting together? We suspect that it has something to do with the fact that each rat in a pair stimulates the other to activity and is in turn stimulated. Each finds the other somewhat but not completely unpredictable. Each has a proper level of interest value for the other. Social attraction in rats may have evolved in response to selection for curiosity about and need to affect the environment.

Following this line of thought, we suggest that the reason rats like rats more than gerbils, and vice versa, is that rats and gerbils show different rates of activity, different levels of responsiveness. We suggest that for every animal there is an optimal level of interaction, of unpredictability, of control, which makes a companion maximally attractive. We suggest that this optimal level is related to the level of the animal itself, so that every animal likes other animals of its own level of responsiveness. In short, inspired by Harlow, we suggest that:

Each animal by God created
Is optimally complicated
To make its species mates elated
But never either feared or hated.

### Summary

In this chapter we have concentrated on the determinants of social attraction in animals. We have tried to give some feeling for the central place the study of animal social behaviour has for our understanding of animate evolution. We have claimed that the motives which impel individual animals to affiliate may be very different from the functions that affiliation serves for the species. We have reviewed a number of different theories of why animals affiliate and have observed that different theories may apply to different species. With respect to the laboratory rat, we have suggested that the process of interaction which characterizes social behaviour may also serve as a major motivation for engaging in it.

We have concentrated on why animals come together but have paid little attention to the details of what they do once they do gather. This is itself a fascinating area of study and many investigators have concerned themselves with aggressive and altruistic behaviour in animals, with sexual and maternal behaviour, with dominance hierarchies, clique formations and social organization. We have also focused on one species of animal, the laboratory rat, and paid little attention to the incredible diversity of social behaviours exhibited by other species.

The laboratory rat is in some ways an artificial animal. It has been for many generations removed from the natural environment in which it originally evolved. It has been domesticated; extreme aggressiveness and individual violence have been selected out. The laboratory rat lives in stacks of cages under highly crowded conditions and is dependent on others to bring it food and remove its wastes. It has no sense of the purpose of its existence and little control over the course of its future.

These conditions make it difficult to generalize from the laboratory rat to other species. Other species may affiliate for entirely different reasons and find entirely different satisfactions in doing so. These conditions, however, are strangely reminiscent of the contemporary human situation. And although we have only an intuitive basis for doing so, we suspect that the reasons humans like humans are in many ways similar to the reasons rats like rats.

**Further reading**

ALLEE, W. C., *The Social Life of Animals*, Abelard-Schuman, 1938.

EIBL-EIBESFELDT, I., *Ethology: The Biology of Behavior*, Holt, Rinehart & Winston, 1970. A beautifully illustrated presentation of ethological methods and concepts.

ETKIN, W., *Social Behavior and Organization among Vertebrates*, University of Chicago Press, 1964.

KLOPFER, P. H., *Habitats and Territories*, Basic Books, 1969. Interesting discussion of species differentiation and accommodation to habitats and to each other.

LORENZ, K., *Der Kumpan in der Umwelt des Vogels*, 1935. Appeared in English as *The Companion in the Bird's World*, *Auk*, vol. 54, pp. 245–73. Classic presentation of the imprinting concept.

MOOREHEAD, A., *Darwin and the Beagle*, Harper & Row, 1969; Penguin, 1971. A vivid narrative of Darwin's voyage on the Beagle. Beautifully illustrated.

TINBERGEN, N., *Animal Behavior*, Time-Life Books, 1965. An excellent introduction to the field of animal behaviour.

ZAJONC, R. (ed.), *Animal Social Psychology*, Wiley, 1969. Reprints of classic experiments with valuable introductory remarks.

## References

BEACH, F. A. (1944), 'Experimental studies of sexual behavior in male mammals', *Journal of Clinical Endocrinology*, vol. 4, pp. 126–34.

CAIRNS, R. B. (1966), 'Attachment behavior of mammals', *Psychological Review*, vol. 73, pp. 409–26.

CAPPELL, H., and LATANÉ, B. (1969), 'Effects of alcohol and caffeine on the social and emotional behavior of the rat', *Quarterley Journal of Studies Alcohol*, vol. 30, pp. 345–57.

CROZE, H., and MUNZIG, H. (1971), 'The death of an elephant', *Life*, vol. 70, pp. 60–65.

DARWIN, C. (1859), *On the Origin of Species*, Dent edn, 1947.

DOBZHANSKY, T. (1970), *Genetics of the Evolutionary Process*, Columbia University Press.

ECKMAN, J., MELTZER, J., and LATANÉ, B. (1969), 'Gregariousness in rats as a function of familiarity of environment', *Journal of Personality and Social Psychology*, vol. 11, pp. 107–14.

GRANT, V. (1963), *The Origin of Adaptations*, Columbia University Press.

HARLOW, H. R. (1958), 'The nature of love', *American Psychologist*, vol. 13, pp. 673–85.

LATANÉ, B. (1969), 'Gregariousness and fear in laboratory rats', *Journal of Experimental Social Psychology*, vol. 5, pp. 61–9.

LATANÉ, B., CAPPELL, H., and JOY, V. (1970), 'Social deprivation, housing density and gregariousness in rats', *Journal of Comparative and Physiological Psychology*, vol. 70, pp. 221–7.

LATANÉ, B., FRIEDMAN, L, and THOMAS, J. (1972), 'Affiliation in rats under stress', *Psychonomic Science*, in press.

LATANÉ, B., and GLASS, D. C. (1968), 'Social and non-social attraction in rats', *Journal of Personality and Social Psychology*, vol. 9, pp. 142–6.

LATANÉ, B., JOY, V., MELTZER, J., LUBELL, B., and CAPELL, H. (1972), 'Stimulus determinants of social attraction in rats', *Journal of Comparative and Physiological Psychology*, in press.

LATANÉ, B., NESBITT, P., ECKMAN, J., and RODIN, J. (1972), 'Long- and short-term social deprivation and sociability in rats', *Journal of Comparative and Physiological Psychology*, in press.

LATANÉ, B., POOR, D., and SLOAN, L. (1972), 'Familiarity and attraction to social and non-social objects by rats', *Psychonomic Science*, vol. 26, pp. 171–2.

LATANÉ, B., and WERNER, C. (1971), 'Social and non-social sources of attraction in rats', *Psychonomic Science*, vol. 24, pp. 147–8.

SCOTT, J. P. (1962), 'Critical periods in behavioral development', *Science*, vol. 138, pp. 949–58.

SLOAN, L., and LATANÉ, B. (1971), 'Sex and social attraction in the albino rat', paper presented at the Psychonomic Society, St Louis.
SLUCKIN, W. (1965), *Imprinting and Early Learning*, Aldine.
STONE, C. P. (1922), 'The congenital sexual behavior of the young male albino rat', *Journal of Comparative and Physiological Psychology*, vol. 2, pp. 95–153.
WALTON, D., and LATANÉ, B. (1971), 'Cross and within-species social attraction in rodents', paper presented at Midwestern Psychological Association, Detroit.
WALTON, D., and LATANÉ, B. (1972), 'Visual versus physical social deprivation and affiliation in rats', *Psychonomic Science*, vol. 26, pp. 4–6.
WERNER, C., and LATANÉ, B. (1970), 'Rats are attracted to the human hand', paper presented at the Psychonomic Society, San Antonio.
WILSON, E. O. (1963), 'Pheromones', *Scientific American*, vol. 208, pp. 100–114.
ZAJONC, R. (1970), 'Familiarity breeds content', *Psychology Today*, vol. 3, pp. 32–5.

# Author Index

# Subject Index